Corporate Capitalism and

Corporate Capitalism and Political Philosophy

Suman Gupta

Pluto Press

LONDON • STERLING, VIRGINIA

First published 2002 by Pluto Press
345 Archway Road, London N6 5AA
and 22883 Quicksilver Drive,
Sterling, VA 20166–2012, USA

www.plutobooks.com

British Library Cataloguing in Publication Data
A catalogue record for this book is available from the British Library

Library of Congress Cataloging in Publication Data
Gupta, Suman, 1966–
  Corporate capitalism and political philosophy / Suman Gupta.
     p. cm.
Includes bibliographical references.
    ISBN 0–7453–1755–3 — ISBN 0–7453–1754–5 (pbk.)
    1. Corporations. 2. Capitalism. 3. Community life. 4. Political
science—Philosophy. I. Title.
    HD2731 .G86 2002
    3052.3'5—dc21
                                                          2001004545

ISBN 0 7453 1755 3 hardback
ISBN 0 7453 1754 5 paperback

11   10   09   08   07   06   05   04   03   02
10   9   8   7   6   5   4   3   2   1

Designed and produced for Pluto Press by
Chase Publishing Services, Fortescue, Sidmouth EX10 9QG
Typeset from disk by Stanford DTP Services, Towcester
Printed in the European Union by TJ International, Padstow, England

Contents

To Cheng and Ayan

Acknowledgements

I am grateful to Achim Brosch, Mark Turner, Martin Jenkins and Xiao Cheng for reading sections of this book and making insightful comments, and to Roger van Zwanenberg of Pluto Press for supporting this project and undertaking its publication.

Part I

Philosophical Methods and Capitalist Processes: Means, Definitions, Intentions

1 The Evasiveness of Corporate Capitalism

Nothing evades the approach of political philosophy as deftly, or denies the application of political philosophy as stubbornly, as the condition and practice of corporate capitalism in our time. At this point, at the beginning of this study, I offer this statement intuitively – without the academic frame of validating evidence or authoritative support – but I think it rings true. It is my intention here to bring, insofar as I can, the amorphous unwieldy ever-assimilative area of corporate capitalism in our time (as the millennium turns) *under* the gaze of political philosophy, and render it *subject* to the concerns of political philosophy.

A few preliminary definitions (however tentatively and provisionally offered) and initial resolutions are unavoidable.

So, a tentative definition to set the ball rolling: political philosophy is an attempt at understanding (illuminating, clarifying, elucidating) and conceptualising human communal existence (individuals living together and with an awareness of living together in terms of some notion of collectivity) with a view to conducting this communal existence by certain ostensibly practicable means towards certain apparently determinable ends. The attempt at understanding and conceptualising a given state of human communal existence could itself reveal what the relevant political means and ends should be. But political means and ends need not be based so squarely on analytical or critical grounds. Political means and ends could simply be considered as given, for instance, or could well prove to be relevant only for certain parties and irrelevant for others. These too would come under the purview of political philosophy, at least insofar as the effort of understanding and conceptualising involved in political philosophy would enable an assessment or critique of all available political means and ends, with a view to supporting some and rejecting some or supporting none and finding new ones.

I call this a tentative definition because I would like to reserve the right to modify it and elaborate on it in any way that becomes necessary as this study progresses. As it stands now, without the support of illustration or explanation, it might seem like a bald collection of words – suggestive and coherent in several ways, yet not entirely transparent. I hope to give it more flesh, and substantiate it or elaborate on it in different ways, as this study touches upon specific issues. Even as it stands, however, it is probably coherent enough to indicate why the concerns of political philosophy and the nuances of corporate capitalism in our time meet awkwardly, if at all. Political philosophy begins and ends in its concern (or occasionally lack thereof) for human communal existence. The corporation which is devoted to the maximisation of capital, and the systems and institutions which are designed to allow this corporation more or less free play to do so (roughly what I mean by corporate capitalism), may *need* to take account of the nuances of human communal existence, but do not necessarily derive from or answer to any concern (or even lack thereof) for human communal existence. The means and ends here are no more than those which serve the abstract person of the capitalist corporation (such as a company, for example) itself, or the real persons who invest in some way in the capitalist corporation. There is indubitably a voluntaristic and optimistic energy about political philosophy – 'if we consensually understand and conceptualise we can do what is necessary' usually seems to be the underlying idea. The dynamism of corporate capitalism is of a quite different order. Corporate capitalism essentially presents the heroism and determination which can overcome (by collaborating with or forestalling) apparently uncontrollable or at best only semi-controllable forces – competition, market forces, consumer behaviour, labour constraints, technological constraints, etc. More often than not political philosophy is a celebration of intellectual and moral rationality; whereas generally corporate capitalism exalts the instinct, foresight, intuition, etc. of its participants (entrepreneurs, promoters, investors, managers, and so on). When political philosophy conceives of the happening of politics in the world it is in terms of *rational* action in some universalised sense; when corporate capitalism is involved in the happening of politics it is primarily in terms of *effective* or *efficient* action to serve certain limited and accountable ends – ultimately the maximisation of capital.

Political philosophy and corporate capitalism are both involved in the happening of politics, but there is little other common discursive ground. It is therefore generally true to say that there is no political philosophy *of* corporate capitalism: there is either political philosophy *after* the fact of corporate capitalism (a poor second cousin, trying to do no more than justify what corporate capitalism does and/or achieves in terms which are of no interest to corporate capitalism as such), or more potently there is political philosophy *against* corporate capitalism. But there is something unsatisfying about this situation. Philosophy should be neither partial nor hostile without reason. At least to begin with, philosophy should be neutral.

When I say that I will try to bring corporate capitalism *under* the gaze of political philosophy, make corporate capitalism *subject* to the concerns of political philosophy, I am making a rhetorical gesture. It is a rhetorical gesture that announces at the outset that I am on the side of political philosophy and that I wish to confront corporate capitalism without evasions and without any unnecessary partiality or hostility. I wish to scrutinise (whether I am able to or not is another matter) the condition and practice of corporate capitalism in our time dispassionately and see how these bear upon a philosophical concern with human communal existence and with political ends and means. I particularly attempt this because I suspect that the evasiveness of corporate capitalism to the approach of political philosophy is indicative of something deeper: *that, in fact, the systems and processes of contemporary corporate capitalism are such that they undermine politics, subvert political philosophy, disable the political philosopher and political activist in some essential sense, even while appearing not to.* By confronting corporate capitalism dispassionately and single-mindedly from the side of political philosophy I should be able either to confirm this or discount this.

To scrutinise the condition and practice of corporate capitalism in our time: what could that mean? What is the object to be scrutinised that *is* corporate capitalism, or the frame or area or phenomenon to be observed that *manifests* corporate capitalism? Surely, the political concern with human communal existence – that broad putative *object*, human communal existence – would not in itself provide a frame for the particular attempt to come to grips with corporate capitalism in our time? That object is the object for all political philosophy; the specific political philosophical quest of this study requires a delineation of object (*within* human communal existence) whereby corporate capitalism would be confronted. Human collectivity itself would have to be redescribed or reassessed in a manner which would make it possible to apprehend the working of corporate capitalism in its midst.

This is a problem sociologists are more accustomed to dealing with than are philosophers. When Marx made his first forays into sociology from the realms of philosophy, this was precisely the kind of question he had asked himself. His early critiques of Hegel's *Philosophy of Right*, and his observations on Hegel's *Phenomenology of Spirit* in the *Economic and Philosophical Manuscripts*[1] are within the field of philosophy – these had to deal with the absolute abstractions of individuality, collectivity, history and authority, within a specific mode of philosophical understanding (German idealist). To challenge this effectively though, he had to move away from that mode of philosophical understanding, he had to find a method of redescribing his philosophical object (human communal existence) whereby those absolute abstractions would be dislocated, and the coherence of the philosophical concepts which attend them would be disturbed. Sociology was arguably invented at that point to revitalise philosophy: Marx described the proletariat (in economic terms) as a sub-category within human communal existence in his 'Contribution to the Critique of Hegel's Philosophy of Right: Introduction' and in 'Excerpts from James Mill's *Elements of Political Economy*', thereby allowing class categorisation and class analysis to emerge by the time he wrote (with Engels) *The German Ideology* and *The Communist Manifesto*.[2] That descriptive act, whereby human communal existence became a differently apprehended object, wasn't one that could be characterised in terms of philosophical methods or objectives. That descriptive act, which could be given the form of economic charting out, which could reconceive and rewrite history, is, to my mind, the sociological act whereby philosophy could be dislocated and rejuvenated. Once the sociological description brings the object of philosophical (especially political philosophical) contemplation within view, philosophy can engage with it and progress or regress.

I mention Marx here particularly because he more than anyone else wedded together sociology and political philosophy (especially insofar as they are geared towards political means and ends), and it seems to me that his particular form of sociological description (in terms of social categories) continues to invigorate political philosophy. And when it doesn't, political philosophy still harks back to the very general and abstract conceptualising available from Plato and Aristotle to Rousseau and Hegel and Feuerbach. Of course, modes of sociological description in terms of social categories have become immensely more complex since Marx; and, for that matter, the very general and abstract conceptualising now that is reminiscent of Rousseau, Hegel, Feuerbach, Proudhon, etc. has also renovated itself in interesting and complex ways.

Sociological description by social categories has extended beyond class description to categorisation – by gender, race, culture, sexual orientation, for instance – and these have either shouldered class descriptions in a competitive fashion or negotiated with class descriptions in complex and generally unresolved ways. A considerable section of what passes for 'critical theory' now – postmodernist theory, feminist theory, post-colonial studies, gay studies, cultural studies, etc. – is somewhere in the nexus of political philosophy and sociological description in terms of social categories. These are never too distant from the spirit of a Marxist effort, even if they systematically eschew the specific class analysis and consequent view of materialist dialectics, history and political agenda associated with Marx. That these are not too different from the Marxist spirit is evidenced in the frequent and not incoherent reinsertions of Marxist class analysis within the folds of these areas of critical theory.[3]

The political philosophy that has by and large stayed indifferent to sociological description, and that continues to be reminiscent of the kind of general and abstract conceptualising – often ostensibly addressing a universal human condition or communal existence as a universal phenomenon – also derives from its more or less traditional roots. This is associated with liberal philosophers such as Rawls or Nagel; libertarian philosophers such as Hayek or Nozick or Fukuyama; revisionist socialist philosophers such as Sartre or Miller or Walzer; and some conservative philosophers such as Scruton. When any of these philosophers offer a formulation about political ends and means, this is done in terms of an abstract and potentially universal human community, of abstract and potentially universal human individuals, and of abstract and potentially universal concepts of action and agency and communication and value, etc. The fact that this approach to political philosophy (which is fairly remote from the details and nuances of sociological description, though it often hits upon specific sociologically pertinent observations to validate universalist formulations) can branch off in so many different ideological directions is itself an indication of the multifarious and complex possibilities involved therein.

Modes of sociological description apart from the sort that derive from social categories had come to exist, despite Marx, almost from the outset. In very schematic terms, these could be thought of as the applications of various quanta[4] of sociological description that may be considered to be either more amenable to providing universal terms for the description of all possible sociological phenomena and contexts, or more comprehensive and inclusive in enabling description of sociological phenomena and contexts, than is description in terms of social categories alone. These devolve on the one hand into notions of basic quanta of sociological description (such as 'social things', primarily associated with Durkheim, or 'social action' and agents, primarily associated with Weber); or, on the other hand, into large configurations such as systems, corporations, organisations, discourses, etc. The configurations could either be seen as having a continuous relation with the basic quanta, such that the latter act as the building blocks of the former; or the configurations could determine the characteristics of the basic quanta, such that the former could determine which kind or kinds of quanta become relevant and in what sort of relationships (a view of sociological description which is sometimes associated with thinkers like Parsons, Luhmann, or Foucault, for instance). These modes of sociological description do not indicate a dismissal of description according to social category (such as class); more often than not class, for instance, gets accommodated into descriptions by discourse formations, systems analysis, organisation theory, and so on, or gets constructed in terms of social action or social facts.

These different modes of sociological description that are not concerned essentially with the social category do give rise to considerations which overlap with political philosophy. Thus, for instance, Habermas's synthetic use of different modes of sociological description (including discourse formations, systems analysis and social action analysis) leads him to concerns which are close to (if at all distinguishable from) that of political philosophy. So, his description of the difficulties of legitimation in capitalist economies, and his conviction in the efficacy of communicative action for effective political and social mediation,[5] are clearly with regard to problems and resolutions of political means and ends in the most general sense, and therefore within the remit of political philosophy. Unsurprisingly Habermas often finds himself thrown back to the German idealists.[6] Indeed, it is probably facile to try to distinguish rigidly between the contingencies of sociological description and the concerns of political philosophy; these arise, as they did for Marx, in such close proximity that distinctions are blurred. However, sociologists and political philosophers have often been at pains to distance themselves from each other despite a common interest in political means and ends, and at least two major grounds of distinction are worth mentioning (though I am not convinced that these are particularly material). One, sociologists, starting from Marx and Durkheim, have modelled the modes of sociological description and the projections that become possible from such description on scientific practice: that is, starting from empirical observation, deriving law-like or rule-like formulations from that, and making projections or solving problems by inferences based on these. In general this inheritance of sociology (to do with the dominant ideas of the period wherein it found its disciplinary status) continues to manifest itself, though occasionally sociologists do have qualms about an excessive attachment to scientific practice.[7] Philosophers in Enlightenment Europe (particularly the Anglo-Saxon empiricists and the German idealists) were also keen to cultivate a scientific spirit in philosophy, but more as a taking-into-account and an accommodation of science than as an imitation. Two, by and large sociologists, in keeping with scientific practice, gear their interests in political means and ends to the *problems* which arise from and within their descriptions. Sociology therefore usually presents itself with regard to political concerns in a pragmatic fashion: it starts from a given and documentable state of affairs and offers its projections (particularly when pertinent to political ends and means) in terms of its apprehension of that state of affairs. Political philosophy also, of course, hopes to be pragmatic, but generally it begins from certain first principles of politics and *then* apprehends given states of affairs accordingly.[8] The problem-solving and functional approach to political means and ends has recently been evidenced, for instance, in the work and political influence of Anthony Giddens.[9]

As I have observed already, however, most political philosophy in our time that is cognisant of sociological perspectives draws on some social category as the chosen device for describing communal existence. I suspect this indicates an originative confluence of political philosophy and sociological description in Marxist thinking. The pros and cons of class analysis as the principal mode of sociological description, of course, still preoccupy sociologists, and a vigorous debate about these has been carried on in sociological journals in the nineteen-nineties.[10] Clearly, however, class analysis is rapidly being overtaken (or has it already been overtaken?) by the use of other social categories (gender, sexuality, ethnicity, culture, etc.). On the whole though, class analysis and other modes of socio-logical description in terms of social category, and the kind of political repercussions these have had, have been viewed with scepticism by sociologists (though less so by sociologically-informed political philosophers and their shadows, the so-called 'critical theorists') – and, I think, with good reason. To give a sense of these reasons I quote from a recent article dealing with the issue by Floya Anthias. In this, description by social category leads to what Anthias calls the politics of 'difference' (class-centred, gender-centred, race-centred, culture-centred, etc., a politics where each particular categorical space celebrates and finds pride in its difference):

> The recognition and celebration of difference, in all its guises may lead to political and moral relativism. This can be found in arguments and policies around those multiculturalisms which ratify and celebrate difference. Perhaps multiculturalisms do 'let a hundred flowers blossom' to coin Mao Tse Tung's words, but we need to remember that difference is not politically neutral. Chal-lenging dominant ethnic, gender and class-based cultural constructs, as multiculturalism does, and as the celebration of difference does, is part of the fight against inequality and subor-dination, but on its own isn't enough. In any case, the right to difference can also be turned on its head. If there are differences of culture and differences of need, and each group may legiti-mately make claims to resources in terms of those differences, then the dominant group may also legitimise its greater claims to resources in these terms. Difference may be constructed therefore as an ideological weapon and be part of a strategy of domination or contestation. In addition, epistemological agnosticism [...] may be politically disabling. Once the notion of sisterhood or a racialised divide is rejected, then there may be no obvious basis for a feminist or anti-racist position. However, the negation of collective action debilitates the possibility of understanding social inequalities, as well as movements and processes, as a more than ad hoc coalition of social relations and forms.[11]

Anthias's sentiments here are close to mine, and though I do have a certain faith in the overall efficacy of class analysis and what it has achieved, in a general sense I find myself uncomfortable with the present vogue for using sociological description in terms of social category for the political purpose of simply celebrating difference – and for precisely the reasons outlined here. In fact, I do also accept Anthias's mode of *containing* such categories within an overarching perspective on 'social outcomes' – I might as well quote that here too:

> Gender, ethnos (ethnicity and 'race') and class may be seen as crosscutting and mutually interacting *ontological spaces which entail social relations and social processes (having experiential, inter-subjective, organisational and representative dimensions)* that coalesce and articulate at particular conjectures to produce differentiated and stratified *social outcomes*. Any analysis at the level of social outcomes cannot look at each social division in isolation from the other, therefore. The analogy of a *grid* may be useful which can be overlaid onto individuals. The different grids are experienced con-textually and situationally as sets of simultaneously and mutually effective discursive instances and social practices.[12]

In fact, when I do get down to attempting a political philosophi-cal confrontation with the current condition and practice of corporate capitalism, I do so with a sociological awareness – but not one that is subsumed by description in terms of social categories alone. I do initiate that effort by focusing on one particular *social outcome*. But more of that in its place.

Provisionally though, that might answer the questions with which I had begun this brief overview of the relation between political philosophy and sociology: what is the object to be scrutinised that *is* corporate capitalism, or the frame or area or phenomenon to be observed which *manifests* corporate capitalism? In the first instance, that object would be a few details, a few facts, which would be familiar to us as a social outcome of contemporary corporate capitalism. With that in focus I will proceed to cast that *grid* which Anthias so usefully mentions above.

Before I enumerate the social outcome with which I commence though, it might be useful to delineate some of the characterising features of my grid (mine, not Anthias's – the difference lies in my political philosophical intent).

2 The Political State

In the grid that I simultaneously cast upon and draw out from the specific social outcome – the initiative focal point – that I am yet to state (when I do that my confrontation with corporate capitalism may be considered to have commenced), there are two sorts of formations which appear constantly. Indeed, no approach to corporate capitalism in our time could be undertaken without a reasonably clear grasp of these formations: namely, the political state and the capitalist corporation. It seems to me that the most general connotations of these should be explored first, for no other reason than that these terms are apt to be confusing at times.

Despite the currency of viewing political formations in terms of national and international (or increasingly, 'global') levels, in the following I am concerned essentially with political states and *not* with national formations. A prodigious amount of thinking and writing has been devoted to the two concepts of political state and nationhood; what I have to say here about these constitutes a condensed statement of a position rather than a considered conclusion drawn from existing ideas and literature. I am aware of a certain risk involved in trying to focus on the notion of the political state, and more particularly in trying to define it – warnings of the danger of trying to find an inclusive-enough definition for a *modern* (in the sense of being pertinent to the late twentieth/early twenty-first century) state, or for *a* (in the sense of being autonomous and self-contained) modern state without being cognisant of global factors which impinge upon statehood, are familiar enough.[1] It seems to me however that this needs to be attempted in the first instance, even if, as for all definitions offered so far, in a provisional fashion.

My understanding of the political state is old-fashioned in the sense that it draws on Weber and Durkheim. And yet, I know of very little which may be considered to be 'new' and which has the general efficacy of Durkheim's and Weber's definitions; and in drawing upon them I hope to be neither ahistorical nor anachronistic. It seems to me that in recent sociological and philosophical studies either political states appear as a certain *kind* of state (interventionist, neutral, totalitarian, democratic, military, liberal, etc.), in which case consideration is given to certain political states which assume specific aims and processes for themselves, and these do not therefore present a general definition of the political state *per se*, or that general definitions tend to go back to Durkheim and Weber. Perhaps this has something to do with the fact, as Nisbet observes, that they were pioneering 'sociologists of pluralism' who were concerned with understanding the protean manifestations of authority.[2] So, it is to Durkheim and Weber that I turn to give my general understanding of the political state, taking one pertinent observation from each. Once I have a general working definition of the political state I should be able to assess its particular accommodations with capitalism.

To begin with, the common ground that Durkheim and Weber shared: the political state functions with regard to the conduct of a collective (usually defined in terms of membership and territory), and represents this collective to its own members and to other similarly constituted collectives. It does so either by guiding the conduct of the collective in certain determined directions (fulfilling social and political aims, objectives, goals, etc.); or by providing a framework whereby the conduct of the collective can be regulated (providing organisations, systems, institutional requirements, etc.); or by both. The two ways in which the political state may function with regard to a collective are dealt with trenchantly by R.M. MacIver[3] (roughly between Durkheim and Weber) – MacIver thinks of the guiding state as an 'association', and of the framework-providing state as an 'institution'. These seem to me to be suggestive and useful ways of thinking about the political state, and are implicit in both Durkheim's and Weber's observations on the subject. Further, the association-like and institution-like functions of the political state are usually effected, either conjointly or separately, through the following kinds of action: economic, legislative/judicial or military. What these areas of action may specifically involve, and how these are related to specific ideological bents, are issues that I take up at greater length elsewhere.

Weber's famous and still-relevant perception in trying to define the state in general terms is that the state cannot be defined in terms of its professed *ends*, since 'All the way from provision of subsistence to the patronage of art, there is no conceivable end which *some* political corporation has not at some time pursued.'[4] Therefore, the best way to define the state in a general fashion is to do so in terms of *means* – from which follows Weber's classic definition of the modern state (I do not address the issue of 'modernity' at the moment since the modern state is all that we need to deal with in the context of contemporary corporate capitalism):

> The primary formal characteristics of the modern state are as follows: it possesses an administrative and legal order subject to change by legislation, to which the organized corporate activity of the administrative staff, which is also regulated by legislation, is oriented. This system of order claims binding authority, not only over the members of the state, the citizens, most of whom have obtained membership by birth, but also to a very large extent, over all action taking place in the area of its jurisdiction. It is thus a compulsory association with a territorial basis. Further-more, to-day, the use of force is regarded as legitimate only so far as it is either permitted by the state or prescribed by it. [...] The claim of the modern state to monopolize the use of force is as essential to it as its character of compulsory jurisdiction and continuous organization.[5]

Weber clearly emphasises the institution-like function of the state, and definitively disregards the association-like function: for Weber the state primarily undertakes the maintenance of a framework whereby the conduct of the collective is regulated (at least that is the thrust of Weber's presentation, which is not to do with *ends*). The part of this definition which has attracted more notice is 'the claim of the modern state to monopolize the use of force' – where force was described shortly before the above-quoted passage as 'the common features of the various *means* of exercising authority which are used within the state in enforcing its order, abstracting them from the ends they serve'.[6] The state, in other words, undertakes its institution-like function by *enforcing* its economic, legislative/judicial, military acts; what provides a common denom-inator for all of these acts and characterises the *means* at the disposal of the state is that these depend on the state's ability to use force. All the actions that a state may undertake would always be carried out or implemented with a superior claim to force to that of any other agent within its territory or jurisdiction, perhaps with a sole claim to force.

In deciding to look at the means and not the ends in his definition of the state, Weber clearly overplays the institution-like function of the state and underplays the association-like function. This does not mean that Weber's key generalisation about the means – the monopoly on the use of force – cannot extend to association-like functions of the state. There is every reason to believe that in trying to guide the conduct of a collective along certain determined lines the state would employ the force over which it claims monopoly, just as it would to regulate the conduct of a collective in a certain framework (to impose its order). Though Weber's focus on the *means* entails a corresponding lack of attention to *ends* with regard to the state, this needn't be the case. The state can be defined in terms of *means*, and yet such a definition could be cognisant to a large degree of the fact that states do concern themselves with ends (however varied). The means need not be, as Weber implies, simply an auto-perpetuation and reification of order – or the continuous reapplication of itself – but also the *means to an end*. Anyway, it is with that slight adjustment that I draw upon Weber's perception in my understanding of the political state.

So, the political state is with regard to the collective – demarcated by territory and/or membership – with either an institution-like or an association-like function in MacIver's sense (or both, of course). That statement needs to be made sharper: what precisely do I mean by saying a political state *is with regard to* the collective? There is a relationship here, taken as understood so far, which could be thought of in several ways: the political state *represents* the collective to itself and other collectives, the political state exists at the *behest* of the collective (some method or process of putting the state into place has been undertaken at some stage or at least acknowledged by the collective), the political state *functions* for the good or bad continuance of the collective as a whole (and in a variegated fashion for different parts of it), and so on. All of these (and other) possibilities are useful for coming to terms with the protean forms of the political state; what interests me though in seeking a general understanding of the state is not the particular nuances of these different possibilities, but the common ground that exists therein. Such a common ground, it seems to me, is picked out by Durkheim:

> Let us see how the State can be defined. It is a group of officials *sui generis*, within which representations and acts of volition involving the collectivity are worked out, although they are not the product of collectivity. It is not accurate to say that the State embodies the collective consciousness, for that goes beyond the State at any point. In the main, that consciousness is diffused: there is at all

times a vast number of social sentiments and social states of mind (*états*) of all kinds, of which the State hears only a faint echo. The State is the centre only of a particular kind of consciousness, of one that is limited but higher, clearer and with a more vivid sense of itself. There is nothing so obscure and so indefinite as these collective representations that are spread throughout all societies – myths, religious or moral legends, and so on ...[7]

In other words, whatever the modality or functionality or significance of the relationship of the political state to collective – however close the collective strives to be in the actions of the state (say, through a completely effective democratic process), or however responsive the state tries to be to the aspirations and intentions of the collective (say, through certain measures for 'taking the pulse' of citizens) – there is inevitably an unavoidable *distance* between the political state and the collective it is with regard to. The state cannot, as Durkheim puts it, *embody the collective consciousness*. The state is 'clear' where the collective is 'diffuse', the state is 'limited' where the collective is 'multifaceted'. At any given point the state is a crystallisation (whether for good or bad) from and with regard to the muddy waters of collectivity.

This, incidentally, is precisely the point at which the concepts of state and nation part company most clearly, and the reason why it is the political state and not the nation that I focus on in the following pages. Going back to Weber momentarily, the difference between the concept of nation and that of the political state is marked out in this regard with particular clarity when a definition for the former is contemplated:

If the concept of 'nation' can in any way be defined unambiguously, it certainly cannot be stated in terms of empirical qualities common to those who count as members of the nation. In the sense of those using the term at a given time, the concept undoubtedly means, above all, that *it is proper* to expect from certain groups a specific sentiment of solidarity in the face of other groups. Thus, the concept belongs to the sphere of values. Yet, there is no agreement on how these groups should be delimited or about what concerted action should result from such solidarity.[8]

Whereas the political state exists at an inevitable distance from the collective, though also inevitably with regard to the collective, the nation exists (as a frame of values, as a consciousness) within the collective itself – in terms of solidarity, or self-affirmation of collectivity, or self-presentation of collectivity, especially in juxtaposition against other collectivities. This is a view of the nation that is more or less consistent with later reflections on the subject.[9]

There is another clarification I need to make here with regard to my understanding of the political state. The two qualities of the political state that have been mentioned above – its monopoly of force, its inevitable distance from the collective while being with regard to it – could lead to the idea that the political state is a particular sort of political formation or (to use a more loaded term) corporation, with a specific ideological bent. Or, in other words, these qualities can lead to the belief that insofar as a state is a state and therefore has these qualities it serves particular sorts of ideological interest and exercises certain ideologically biased prerogatives. I might as well clarify immediately that this is *not* my view of the matter.

My view of the matter is that insofar as there is human communal existence, insofar as there is a collective with whatever conception of collectivity, there would be some sort of political state serving association-like and/or institution-like functions, and this state would be characterised by its monopoly on force and its distance from the collective while being with regard to it. These are the common denominators of political states *per se*, irrespective of whether they promote particular ends or impose specific sorts of order. A political state is therefore an inevitability, and that which defines a political state should not be made subject to value judgements (the inevitable is not in itself good or bad, it may seem so in certain contexts – e.g., death is inevitable and is not in itself a bad or good thing, though it may seem so if presented within specific circumstances). Having a monopoly on force, or a certain distance from the collective it is with regard to, are not in themselves good or bad, desirable or undesirable (these are just definitive terms); in specific circumstances, for certain ends and/or orders and/or with regard to certain collectives, these may prove to be desirable or undesirable qualities. But so far as a definition of the political state goes, these just inevitably *are*, there is no inference to be drawn from this immediately. Inferences may become available from these once we start considering *what sort of* state is at issue. The political state, as characterised above, is an inevitability given human communal existence – or simply *is*.

I think this sense of the inevitability of the political state is implicit in Durkheim's and Weber's reflections, but not, for instance, in Marxist thinking. This probably has something to do with the fact that Marxist sociology leads into political philosophy (into the opening up of political means and ends) whereas Durkheim and Weber stop at sociology (the description of what *is* is of overarching interest). At any rate, the Marxist conception of the political state apprehends its monopoly on force and its inevitable distance from the collective, but often equates these definitive terms with morally unacceptable qualities. This means that the political state *per se* becomes an undesirable formation (rather than a necessary one); and as such the political state becomes associated only with undesirable modes of social organisation (capitalist, feudal), and is deemed unnecessary in certain hypothetically describable social organisations.

Marx himself, of course, didn't write in a systematic fashion on the political state; his scattered reflections on the role of the state in political economy have however been widely discussed. Poulantzas's perception that the Marxist conception of the state 'has the particular function of constituting the factor of cohesion between the levels of a social formation'[10] seems to me to have the sort of general efficacy that Durkheim's or Weber's perceptions show. The elaborations that are possible from this, and have been made,[11] move in two predictable directions: that the political state as a formation, by dint of its ability to use force and its distance from the people, has the primary function of exercising domination and control for its own (its constituent members'?) interests in a parasitic fashion; or that the political state is simply an instrument for the much larger class interests which it is set up to protect, and is thereby the repository of aristocratic or bourgeois power. At any rate, this understanding of the state means that its inevitability with regard to *any* collectivity is not recognised: the state is inevitable only if there are efficacious social categories or levels of social formation (especially classes), and the idealist socialist conception of the classless society would therefore necessarily involve the erasure of the political state itself – not just the particular political states that pertain to feudal and capitalist societies, but the very conception of the political state itself. This view is taken to its logical conclusion early, in Engels's reflections on the 'withering away of the state',[12] which in turn is elaborated in terms of revolutionary practice in Lenin's *The State and Revolution*.[13] In the classless society of the future the perceptions of the governed would, it is believed, merge seamlessly into the perception of government; since that is the case, the need for force as well as the necessary distance that define the political state would vanish. For Marxists, therefore, the political state itself, with all its defining terms, becomes the subject of moral disapprobation, and becomes indelibly associated with an undesirable mode of communal or collective existence.

Laudable as that idealism was in its time, it seems to me that the necessary relation drawn by Marxists between the political state *per se* (as defined above), and particular kinds of states seeking particular ends (bourgeois, feudal), is a false relation. The sort of near-biological or evolutionary change that, according to this perspective, would be required to erase the very notion of the political state seems to me to be ephemeral, and, in a paradoxical fashion, this simply underlines the inevitability of the political state in political philosophical conception possible now. Recent history, I feel, supports this position as more realistic in our time (and what other time can we conceive in terms of?). I believe it is more useful to think of the defining terms of the state (playing association-like or institution-like roles in MacIver's sense, a monopoly on force, a necessary distance from the collective it is with regard to) as in themselves value-free, and consider how these may devolve given certain organisational principles and ideological ends.

Before moving on from these initial observations on the political state, a final consideration. What happens when in a specific situation one of the defining criteria for the political state gets arraigned elsewhere, or is somehow appropriated elsewhere? For instance, what is the status of the political state when its monopoly on force is contested by a formation – say, a military junta, a mafia organisation, a business corporation, a revolutionary organisation, a spontaneous mass movement, etc. – in a manner which is effective with regard to the collective (that is, which is not potentially exercisable but actually exercised to that effect)? Or, alternatively, what happens when the distance between state and the collective it is with regard to is somehow eroded, so that the conception of government loses its clarity and becomes as diffuse as the manifold conceptions which exist within the collective itself? (This is a purely theoretical question since I find it difficult actually to visualise such a situation – but, I suppose, it is conceivable.) As I understand this, since, in such situations, the defining terms no longer attach to the formation which ostensibly passes as the political state, its status as political state would itself have to be relegated. If the state's monopoly of force is at stake, then two outcomes are possible. That formation which has wrested this monopoly from the state or has presented effective rivalry would, whether it intends to or not, by the very fact of being effective with regard to the collective in question, merge into the political state or become part of its formation – it coalesces into the functioning and description of the political state. Or alternatively, there would ensue a power struggle to determine where the political state is located. As far as political philosophical conception goes in our time, if the necessary distance between political state and the collectivity it is with regard to is somehow dissolved we would have to consider the cohesiveness of the collectivity itself to be at stake – this may lead to fragmentation and social restructuring, or it may lead to anarchy.

3   The Capitalist Corporation

The other formation that needs to be grasped in a preliminary fashion is, of course, the capitalist corporation. This might seem to be a statement of the obvious: corporate capitalism would naturally pertain to the capitalist corporation, one might feel. Yet, understanding the capitalist corporation in a preliminary fashion and understanding corporate capitalism (the endeavour of this study as a whole) are quite different and distinct things. I suggest eventually that corporate capitalism incorporates a network of interrelations and cross-relations which goes far beyond the parameters of one or some or all capitalist corporations, which encompasses the ends and means exercised by a wide variety of states under the aegis of capitalist ideologies and the different levels of social organisation under the political state, as well as the different levels of organisation between political states, finally encompassing the world. It is because of the extent and scope and complexity of corporate capitalism in our time that I have chosen to assume the method outlined above: to start with an appropriate detail, a specific social outcome, and then throw a grid over it, expand from it, till some sense of the whole extent of corporate capitalism in our time can become visible for philosophical contemplation. So, while it is true to say that corporate capitalism has to do essentially with capitalist corporations, as an ideology its effects and structures extend far outside the ostensible boundaries of capitalist corporations – however generally and inclusively these are conceived.

For a preliminary understanding of the capitalist corporation, an elementary description of capital – and of the capitalist – is worth quoting here, even though it states the glaringly obvious. So, a momentary return to the original apprehension of capital (and the capitalist) in Marx:

> The simple circulation of commodities – selling in order to buy – is a means of carrying out a purpose unconnected with circulation, namely, the appropriation of use-values, the satisfaction of wants. The circulation of money as capital is, on the contrary, an end in itself, for the expansion of value takes place only within

this constantly renewed movement. The circulation of capital has therefore no limits.

As the conscious representative of this movement, the possessor of money becomes a capitalist. His person, or rather his pocket, is the point from which the money starts and to which it returns. The expansion of value, which is the objective basis or mainspring of the circulation M–C–M [money–capital–money], becomes his subjective aim, and it is only in so far as the appropriation of ever more and more wealth in the abstract becomes the sole motive of his operations, that he functions as a capitalist, that is, as capital personified and endowed with consciousness and a will. Use-values must therefore never be looked upon as the real aim of the capitalist; neither must the profit of any single transaction. The restless never-ending process of profit-making alone is what he aims at. This boundless greed after riches, this dispassionate chase after exchange-value, is common to the capitalist and the miser; but while the miser is merely a capitalist gone mad, the capitalist is a rational miser. The never-ending augmentation of exchange-value, which the miser strives after, by seeking to save his money from circulation, is attained by the more acute capitalist, by constantly throwing it afresh into circulation.[1]

The elementary idea of capital (money that is circulated to expand its value and for no other purpose) is clear enough to serve my purpose for the moment, and so is the idea of the capitalist (he who puts his money into circulation, or owns such capital, with the sole end of making its value expand), and that is all I wish to focus on at the moment. This needn't be complicated yet by considering the types of capitalist who might emerge (industrial capitalists, financial capitalists, etc.); and nor need it be obfuscated by delving into Marx's moral sentiments here (that analogy with the miser, the mortal sin of greed). That also means that I do not wish to immediately chart out, as Marx did and as indeed it is customary to do, the *contradictions* of capitalism: these are implicit in the *economic* conception of capital itself (which inevitably involves a field of economic action wherein the validity of the conception can be examined), but can be postponed till I go on to in the next remark. I want, in the first instance, simply to focus on that bare idea of capital, and (for my purposes, more importantly) the capitalist, with a dispassionate eye.

Shorn of any immediate consideration of contradictions, or of moral qualifications, or of economic qualifications, this is simply a statement of process: a capitalist invests his money and keeps it in circulation as capital with the primary purpose of expanding its value. At this moment this is a value-free statement of process char-acterised *only* by the notion of expansion of value (which translates into expansion of capital, increasing ability to reinvest and circulate, expansion of profits), a *continuous* process of expansion of the value of capital. Size matters here: the bottom line is the relation between input value and output value of capital; and *success* for the capitalist, that which enables the capitalist to be a capitalist, is the increase in value from input to output. This is a crude matter of size, in a completely material fashion: as he grows more successful, the capitalist qua capitalist grows too (that is, the capital in question, the functions involved in keeping it in circulation and the activities which revolve around this process grow too), and at some stage in the process this growth of the capitalist means that the individual or individuals who initiate the process are subsumed into the capitalist corporation which then acts as one *large* individual. Hence an initial understanding of the capitalist corporation follows: the capitalist corporation is the capitalist grown large, such that the capital involved, the functions and activities involved in keeping it in cir-culation and keeping it expanding, grow larger and more complex. This is, of course, implicit in Marx's examination of capitalism, as he was perfectly aware:

> The minimum of the sum of value that the individual possessor of money or commodities must command, in order to metamor-phose himself into a capitalist, changes with the different stages of development of capitalist production, and is at given stages different in different spheres of production, according to their special and technical conditions. Certain spheres of production demand, even at the very outset of capitalist production, a minimum of capital that is not as yet found in the hands of single individuals. This gives rise partly to state subsidies to private persons, as in France in the time of Colbert, and as in many German states up to our epoch; partly to the formation of societies with legal monopoly for the exploitation of certain branches of industry and commerce, the forerunners of our modern joint-stock companies.[2]

But Marx did not examine the corporate character of capitalism fully, neither insofar as the political state intervenes into or mediates the process of capitalist production, nor insofar as the capitalist corporation assumes its form as such. In general Marx either dwells on capitalists as individuals (at least conceptually) or as a class, and when the capitalist corporation becomes imminent Marx tends to see this as individualised through kinship (the company as preserve of the capitalist family), and perhaps tending to fragmentation of the single enterprise into different enterprises. At the same time, it is worth reiterating that the corporate nature of advanced capitalism, and therefore the implicit existence of the capitalist corporation in advanced capitalism, can always be inferred to some extent from Marx's formulations – especially, for instance, in his reflections on the tendency towards the concentration of the means of production in capitalism, so that: 'In a given society the limit would be reached only when the entire social capital was united in the hands of either a single capitalist or a single capitalist company.'[3]

That Marx didn't examine the capitalist corporation at any length was, of course, a matter of historical contingency, but there was enough there to allow an initial understanding of the capitalist corporation. A complex examination of corporate capitalism of a certain sort (again, conditional to its historical contingencies) was undertaken in a pioneering fashion by Weber. But I will not go into that here – at the moment I am not aiming for an exegesis of the development of the concept of the capitalist corporation, I am simply trying to provide an initial understanding to facilitate an analysis of a prevailing condition of corporate capitalism (there will be occasion enough to draw on Weber when I get down to that). For the moment, it seems to me that the perceptions sited above will be adequate for my purpose; and that these can be drawn towards a brief, uncomplicated and fairly precise initial definition of the capitalist corporation – such as the one given by Galbraith:

[The corporation's] purpose is to do business as an individual would but with the added ability to assemble and use the capital of several or numerous persons. In consequence, it can undertake tasks beyond the financial reach of any single person. And it protects those who supply capital by limiting their liability to the amount of their original investment, ensuring them a vote in the significant affairs of the enterprise, defining the powers and responsibilities of directors and officers, and giving them access to the courts to redress grievance. Apart from its ability to mobilize capital and its lessened association with the active life of any individual, the corporation is not deemed to differ functionally from the individual proprietorship or partnership. Its purpose, like theirs, is to conduct business on equitable terms with other businesses and make money for their owners.[4]

This is useful in that it defines the capitalist corporation as a sort of excessive or super individual, or as a progression of the growth that starts from the individual capitalist. On the other hand, though this is too detailed to be quoted here, Galbraith pre-empts issues which I would rather approach later, and already complicates the simplicity of an initial definition of the capitalist corporation by bringing in questions of structures, hierarchies, legalities, liabilities, etc. All I want to do by evoking Galbraith here is to give an impression, rather than a clear picture, of what is initially included, though not elucidated, in my definition of the capitalist corporation. Actually, Galbraith didn't even consider the above to be a sufficiently precise statement of the matter, for, as he goes on to say:

> there is no such thing as *a* corporation. Rather there are several kinds of corporations all deriving from a common, highly accommodating legal but very loose framework. Some are subject to the market; others reflect varying degrees of adaptations to the requirements of planning and the needs of the technostructure.[5]

There is a valuable lesson to be learnt by keeping that qualification in mind: the more precise one tries to be about that definition, the more one specifies its nuances and technicalities, the more likely it is that the definition itself will become remote and meaningless. Somewhere along the line the definition itself becomes opaque – the question 'what is being defined?' reverberates as 'who is trying to define it?' (an accommodative legal definition? ... an accommodative political philosophical definition? ...). There is always that evasiveness of capitalism to contend with.

I should emphasise here again that I regard the capitalist corporation (especially in its self-apprehensions, when it tries to present itself as such) as a *concrete embodiment* of several levels of conceptions of size. So capitalist corporations are always the *largest*, *big* or *small*; catering to *quantifiable* clientele (whether seen in *local*, *national*, *international* or *global* terms); to *measurable* degrees of success (in terms of profit, quality of product, status, etc.); incorporating a *numerical quantity* or a *quantifiable quality* of workforce (in terms of skill, training, ability, disposition, etc.); at a *measurable* stage of movement into the future (leading, progressing, growing, expanding); in its *accommodative* or *assimilative* abilities (to meet demands, to cater to tastes, to include a range of criteria for workers, or a range of consumer and investor convenience, etc.). Different conceptions of size, which get concretely embodied in the capitalist corporation, form the core of capitalist discourses at large. An understanding of capitalism, in all its protean manifestations and encompassing scope, is usually seen in abstract to rotate around various conceptions of size; and these proliferations of the capitalist conception of size, the accommodations of different adjectives and metaphors for size in capitalist thinking, has been the subject of numerous theoretical expositions on capitalism. In asserting this I do not wish simply to take account of the theorisation of capitalism in terms of its most determinate and most focused preoccupation with size, that is, with economic *growth* alone, and with all else as a function of that: that has been the consistent focus of critique and justification for advanced capitalism since the nineteen-sixties (trenchantly reflected, say, in Raymond Aron's *Eighteen Lectures*, in Galbraith's *The New Industrial State*, in Mandel's *Late Capitalism*, or in Habermas's *Legitimation Crisis*).[6] I wish to draw attention to the conceptions of size which pertain to every aspect of capitalist discourse and societal existence, which dissociates itself from the economic base and subsumes conception itself within a capitalist ethos, which thereafter includes economic growth rather than derives from it – perhaps, in the first instance, most effectively elucidated in Marcuse's *One-Dimensional Man*. Here advanced capitalism (not exactly the same emphasis as corporate capitalism) – despite its obvious shortcomings – is seen as an all-encompassing totalitarian phenomenon which simply makes coeval discourses seem so obvious and natural that no oppositional space can be found, let alone acted upon – though paradoxically Marcuse also suggests that an awareness of this prevailing situation can itself lead to a 'great refusal', some sort of effort to find alternative oppositional discourses.[7] At a relatively early stage of thinking about advanced capitalism, and along similar lines, but with a more straightforward emphasis on the connotations of size in capitalist discourses, Lefebvre's understanding of capitalism's self-legitimation by simply occupying 'space' is also clearly pertinent here:

what has happened is that capitalism has found itself able to attenuate (if not resolve) its internal contradictions for a century, in the hundred years since the writing of *Capital*, it has succeeded in achieving 'growth'. We cannot calculate at what price, but we do know the means: *by occupying space, by producing a space.*[8]

Examinations of the connotations and proliferations of conceptions of size in advanced capitalism and coherent discourses at large are now legion. Size becomes status, quality, shock absorber, moral value, assimilation and containment, influence, progress, power, social conscience, etc. And as I see it, the capitalist corporation is a concrete manifestation of this preoccupation with size that is at the heart of advanced capitalism and all its discourses.

Finally, there is another crucial distinction I need to make here apropos the capitalist corporation. Even corporations which are not ostensibly capitalist or are not constructed to serve capitalist ends can be *viewed* as capitalist corporations; or, more precisely, can be brought under the logic of capitalist goal-orientations (that is, *viewed* in terms of the imperatives of maximising capital, or of return for investment). So, corporations such as hospitals, educational institutions, government welfare organisations, non-governmental charity organisations, etc., which are not established and need not be conducted for the *primary* purpose of capital expansion, could nevertheless be *viewed* in those terms – or, at least, if not quite in terms of capital expansion perhaps in correlated terms of 'cost-efficiency' or 'cost-effectiveness'. Insofar as this study goes, despite this possibility such corporations are *not* capitalist corporations, unless given such a definition for legal or administrative purposes in a corporate capitalist environment (for instance, brought under the aegis of public sector capitalist corporations). The practice of viewing such corporations in this manner is an integral part of corporate capitalism, and could be viewed as one of its key characteristics, along with corporate capitalism's political and social accommodations (the manner in which political and social entities and systems relate to capitalist corporations). I will have occasion to dwell on this at a more appropriate juncture; for the moment, I hope the above will serve as an initial understanding of capitalist corporations.

4 The Contradictions of Capitalism

I have, in the above, attempted to convey an *initial* understanding of the capitalist corporation as a formation and, in that context, of capitalism as a process in a neutral fashion, that is, without immediately bringing in any moral evaluations or pragmatic considerations of the contradictions or possible crises therein. I have done this on the grounds that the latter cannot be attempted without a fuller understanding of the pragmatic frame within which such processes and formations may operate (say, in terms of real world economics or real world political ends and means that are assumed), and that, after all, is what I am at the moment leading up to rather than beginning from. This might seem to be an unclear and confusing position – especially since I have, in the above, already drawn on perceptions (Marx's and others') which can scarcely be evoked without some understanding of their apprehensions of the pragmatic frames or real world situations within which capitalism is analysed, and therefore their apprehension of the crises or contradictions implicit in capitalism. It seems to me unavoidable that even at this initial stage I will have to be cognisant of the kinds of pragmatic frames and real world situations from which Marxist and other views of capitalism have derived, before disengaging myself from them for a while in the attempt to come to grips with corporate capitalism in our time. At the very least, I will have to demonstrate what sort of presumptions about pragmatic frames and real world situations can lead to certain notions of crises and contradictions in capitalism – if for no other reason than to clarify that these are not presumptions which should immediately be associated with the above neutral understanding of capitalism and the capitalist corporation. So, a brief excursus into certain familiar ideas associated with capitalism seems to me in order here. The excursus draws on economic and political terms that are associated with these ideas, but with the reminder that these are not terms that will necessarily inform this study thereafter: my interest in this area is not primarily with regard, for instance, to economic necessities and systems, but with regard to political ends and means (with political philosophy).

The excursus is offered in two sketchy sections: the first touches upon Marx's position apropos the real-world conditions and considerations attached to the operation of capitalism and the crises/contradictions which become available from that; and the second reflects briefly on modifications of these that are necessary in the context of or with the experience of advanced capitalism, and particularly corporate capitalism.

1 The following could be thought of as the pragmatic frame or real world considerations in terms of which Marx was able to delineate his understanding of capitalism and discern certain contradictions therein. One may think of these as the preconditions to the Marxist *conception* of the real operation of capitalism (not to be mixed up with the historical preconditions of capitalism – the mechanics of manufacture, primitive accumulation, etc. – which Marx spells out within *Capital*).

One, the most fundamental and familiar of Marxist concepts: the concrete and indelible presence of labour as that which determines the value of commodities, where labour is *essentially physical–nervous exertion, with a view to producing usable commodities, mediated by skill and knowledge (of how to use means of production)*. The *visceral* character of the Marxist conception of labour, given famously as a direct contest between humans and nature,[1] which is imbued with every nuance of physical effort, is the absolute centre from which the rest of Marx's analysis of capitalist processes follows. The distinction between use value and exchange value follows in terms of quantity of labour time involved; the discernment of surplus value, which is the *raison d'être* of capitalism for Marx, becomes a matter of exploiting labour beyond that which is necessary for the production of use value; the great social categorisation of working class (those who labour and therefore give value to commodities) and capitalist class (those who do not and consume and use and own surplus value) follows; the division of total capital into constant capital (that which goes into acquiring materials and means of production) and variable capital (that used to purchase labour and therefore primarily responsible for giving value to commodities) arises from that; the clarification that despite appearances it is *only* labour and *no* other kind of effort involved in the circulation of capital which gives value; and so on – these steps in Marx's analysis of capitalism, and the centrality of the visceral concept of labour, are too familiar to need rehearsal. This particular Marxist concept of labour is undoubtedly the foremost precondition of Marxist conception.

Two, the background political/social organisation within which the Marxist understanding of capitalist processes unfolds can be described as essentially liberal in character: the unexamined ethos within which Marxist capitalism follows its ever-expanding route is one in which inconsonant political intervention is minimal and the philosophy of free trade and laissez-faire economics dominates. As far as Marx goes, political and social organisations and institutions which prevail arise out of capitalist processes and change according to the exigencies of capitalist processes – they are determined by capitalists' requirements at given stages of development – and can only be opposed by fissures opened by class conflict, which itself is also the product of (and exacerbated by) the processes of capitalism.

Three, the overall frame in terms of which Marx analyses the totality of capitalist processes – that is, in terms of which he presents the circulation of capital as a whole in *Capital, Vol.2*; and calculates the aggregate productivity and exchanges and conversions of social capital (in all its branches and spheres of production), and derives the social effects of capitalism in all its complexity, in *Capital, Vol.3* – is confined to what he offers as a 'given society'. Though he doesn't clarify what exactly the 'given society' is, it is abundantly clear that it is a limited frame of reference – not immediately a global or world frame – perhaps best understood as a zone of administration (a nation or country where the liberal capitalist-friendly social organisation is uniformly available in legislative and judicial terms and at a suitable stage of capitalist development). It is clear that when Marx reflects on world trade, he is talking of trade across 'given societies'; and that when elucidation of the increasing world-scope of capitalism, through colonialism, is offered this is seen as an economic extension across and between certain kinds of 'given society'.

Four, as Ernest Mandel rightly points out at the beginning of his *Late Capitalism*, by and large Marx's analysis of capitalism is with the presumption of a state of equilibrium[2] in the 'given society' in question. So, he starts with the premise that capitalism *is* in process, and that the capitalist system *is* being successfully productive and accumulative, and sets about trying to unravel how it is so, what is the logic of the process and what it leads up to. This essentially means that he examines each stage of the capitalist process – the extraction of surplus value, the setting of labour time and wages, the hypothetical exchanges between the two departments (producing means of production and producing articles of consumption) of the total production, the distribution of the aggregate social profits, etc. – as being geared towards maintaining a balance, and of being open to certain adjustments if this balance is disturbed (having measures to counteract inevitable and necessary crises). And related to this: Marx also usually starts analysing a specific step in the capitalist process so that this tendency towards maintaining balance is apparent at its simplest formulation, and is shown to be consolidated in more complex formulations. So, Marx habitually establishes the tendency to maintain balance in terms of simple reproduction before moving on to progressive reproduction.

Five, Marx's understanding of capitalism develops in opposition to the prevalent thinking that emerges from within capitalism and enables its process. By this I do not merely wish to indicate that Marx's exposition of capitalism is constantly in terms of opposition to (and of course derivation from) extant theories of political economy (Adam Smith, Mill, Ricardo, Senior, and others) – this he does constantly in *Capital,* and particularly in *Theories of Surplus Value*, with a view to demonstrating that the academic pursuit of political economy has been largely devoted to justifying capitalist processes and enabling their continuance. More fundamentally, Marx's conceptualisation develops as at odds with the thinking from above involved *within* capitalism; i.e., how the capitalist naturally views the process with the objective of fulfilling his ends, what sort of economic calculations go into this, the manner in which he expresses the pure instrumentality of the labourer, and the modes of reducing the understanding of the process to the mathematical figures that concern him (investment, profit, wages). One might say that an essential precondition for the Marxist understanding of capitalism is that it has to struggle against what appears to be the 'natural' discourse of capitalism. Much of Marx's exposition is clarified in terms of what it is against, what cobwebs of the apparently obvious are cleared away. For example, Marx clarifies the status of the wage form by demonstrating that it is essentially designed as a concept to erase 'the division of the working day into necessary labour and surplus labour' – the wage seems to pay off the labourer for all his effort, whereas actually it merely provides more-or-less the equivalent of the labourer's necessities (use value) and extracts the surplus value more-or-less unpaid.[3] Along similar lines, and more importantly, Marx shows how the capitalist's constant pre-occupation with rate of profit (surplus value divided by total capital) is designed to hide the actually relevant rate of surplus value (surplus value divided by variable capital), thereby obfuscating a full understanding of the role of labour, the idea of surplus value, and the problem of why social capital shows a tendency for the rate of profit to drop.[4] Numerous such examples can be cited, but are probably unnecessary here.

Six, behind the struggle against what appears to be the natural discourse of capitalism, there is also a certain effort to overcome the limitations of language itself with regard to what he wishes to explain through it. Stylistically, Marx limits himself to the following: expository prose whereby arguments are developed in logical steps starting from basic definitions and recognisable (hypothetical or actual) situations; allusive discussions where he draws upon ideas and expressions which are familiar to political economists of the time; and simple mathematical formulations which are used almost exclusively for exemplary purposes (these do not go beyond basic algebraic expressions, deal primarily with hypothetical numerical figures to concretise and demonstrate the kinds of exchanges involved in the capitalist process, and are innocent of the kind of mathematical abstraction and sophistication found in modern econometrics). With this equipment in hand, Marx often finds that the complexities of the capitalist processes that he tries to unravel tend to get expressed in paradoxes. So, he begins his exploration of the circulation process of capitalism (M–C–M'), and the consequent discovery of surplus value, with the paradox that the expansion from M to M' has to have 'its origin both in circulation and yet not in circulation'.[5] But even when that paradox is resolved by the explanation of surplus value, the nature of the process of circulation still remains paradoxical, insofar as it is both reproductive (there is unending repetition and reiteration involved) and yet also progressive (accumulation occurs, the size of capital increases, numbers of workers increase, constant capital increases relative to variable capital, capitalism moves on to a further stage, and so on). Where Marx deals with this most succinctly, in the examination of circulation of capital in *Capital, Vol.2*, he in fact invents a mode of signifying this dual-edged cyclical process of reproduction and expansion (which both has an air of mathematical conciseness, and yet exceeds the precision of designation in mathematical signification). The total process, as Marx lays it out, takes the form (given that P is production):

M–C ... P ... C'–M'–C ... P ... C'–M'–C ... P ... and so on,

or, as Marx himself puts it, given that T_C is the total circulation process, there are three formulas for the circuit of capital:

i.   M–C ... P ... C'–M'
ii.   P ... T_C ... P
iii. T_C ... P (C')[6]

This clearly is not to be taken as either a precise mathematical expression in the sense that each subsequent P and C' and C may be different given a purely simple reproductive cycle, and would certainly be different in a progressively reproductive cycle. That is expressed in the differentiation of C and M from C' and M'. And yet in the reiteration of C before P at each stage, and in the constancy of P, the simultaneous sense of cyclical repetition is retained.

Now, given these preconditions for the Marxist conceptualisation of capitalism, and the analysis that occurs within the limits of these preconditions, Marx is able to bring out certain contradictions and possible crises in the process of capitalism. I feel it is important not to lose sight of the fact that the specific sorts of crises and contradictions that Marx brings out apropos capitalism are *dependent on* and *conditional to* these conceptual preconditions. The crises and contradictions in question are of three sorts: the explicitly discussed economic crises/contradictions, the self-evident social contradictions, and the implicitly available moral contradictions of capitalism.

One, economic crises/contradictions. These arise out of the endlessly accumulative nature of capitalism. Sometimes, given the conceptual precondition of capitalism's tendency to maintain equilibrium, such crises actually regulate capitalism's reproductive spiral by letting the steam out of the system, so to say; such crises can be seen as safety valves which enable capitalist processes to continue *through* cycles of crises. This is where such cycles of crises as are anticipated in the latter part of *Capital, Vol.2* may be mentioned; that is, in the course of elucidating the circulation of capital in terms of two 'departments', the first to do with *means of production* and the second with *articles of consumption*.[7] I do not go into these in detail here: briefly, Marx delineates how small-scale crises can arise within the exchanges of the second department, between the processes underlying its two components (necessities and luxuries), and how these crises ultimately have the effect of maintaining the status and control of the capitalist class intact, and keeping the working class in its place.[8]

Sometimes however, the tendency of the state of equilibrium to persist in capitalist processes, such that these are actually facilitated by small-scale crises, cannot be maintained; a crisis may grow so large that the equilibrium can be seriously damaged, perhaps gradually permanently destroyed. This is where the more fundamental economic contradiction of capitalism, the tendency of the rate of profit to fall as capitalism develops (expounded in *Capital, Vol.3*) comes in. The idea is, briefly, that the capitalist class in a given society would be constantly determined to make production grow and surplus value accumulate, and would therefore determinedly ensure that labour power is exploited more efficiently without necessarily increasing the variable capital which goes into buying it. In doing this the capitalist class would be interested only in the net profit – how much return comes in from total investment (hence rate of profit is surplus value divided by total capital) – and would effectively hide the actual relation of labour to production (revealed by rate of surplus value, or surplus value divided by variable capital).[9] In a given society, therefore, this single-minded concentration on profit which obscures the status of labour in capitalist production would result in increased input of fixed capital to buy the technology and instruments and means of labour which would ensure more efficient exploitation of labour. Gradually, as capitalism develops, a larger part of the total capital would consist of constant capital relative to variable capital. However surplus value, and therefore ultimately all profit, derives solely from labour, so that as capitalism develops, even if the rate of surplus value stays constant or increases, the rate of profit (which is calculated against total capital, which increasingly has a relatively larger constant capital component and a relatively smaller variable capital component) would tend to drop – in a given society this would manifest itself as a tendency for the general rate of profit to drop.[10] Marx envisages several ways in which this tendency can be checked – increasing intensity of exploitation, depressing wages below the value of labour power, cheapening the elements of constant capital, relative overpopulation, foreign trade, increase of stock capital[11] – but these can only be methods of postponing the inevitable, since after each of these measures is adopted the process of capitalist expansion would gradually subsume it and the tendency would revive. As Marx sees it, the progressive tendency of the rate of profit to fall is '*just an expression peculiar to the capitalist mode of production* of the progressive development of the social productivity of labour',[12] and this leads him to remark upon the transitory character of capitalist production, and conclude that capital inevitably provides its own limits.[13]

Two, social contradictions. The distinction made here between the moral and social contradictions of capitalism as seen by Marx may in fact seem to go against the grain of Marxist thinking; in Marx's writings certainly the moral and the social are inextricably entwined and are implied in each other. The distinction I have made here therefore demands clarification, which could briefly be given thus: social contradictions are with regard to social organisation (the organisation of a given society which enables it to conduct itself as such) and result in or could result in conflict which would disturb or even destroy that social organisation; moral contradictions are deviations from a given set of norms (however obtained) which pertain to either a given society or to humans in general. Social contradictions *may* but *need not always* arise out of an awareness of moral contradictions; moral contradictions *may* but *need not inevitably* cause social contradictions. In the case of Marx's understanding of capitalism there is a self-evident causal relationship between moral and social contradictions; but these are still most clearly understood separately.

The fundamental social contradiction implicit in capitalism arises from the exacerbation of class conflict in capitalist processes. The conceptual precondition of understanding social organisation in terms of classes as social categories allows for a sharpened perception of the social contradiction of capitalism. According to Marx, capitalist processes do not simply emerge from the relationship of capitalist to worker (capitalist class to working class); increasingly, as capitalism gains momentum and develops, the class relation itself becomes subsidiary to the endlessly reproductive cycle of capitalist production, and capitalist processes subsume and control the class relation:

> Capitalist production, therefore, under its aspect of continuous connected process, of a process of reproduction, produces not only commodities, not only surplus-value, but it also produces and reproduces the capitalist relation; on the one side the capitalist, on the other the wage-labourer.[14]

This ever-increasing conflict between the two classes is largely due to the nature of labour itself (as a conceptual precondition): its visceral physical nature, its proximity to human effort, which when stretched (as it must be as capitalist exploitation in search of surplus value takes its necessary path) could all too easily become physical suffering. The suffering of the working class is only to be contrasted to the consuming excesses of the non-labouring capitalist class. That contrast is compounded by the fact that as capitalism develops, the contrast grows greater. Capitalism increases the numbers of workers; makes sure that some of them are unemployed (in the form of a reserve labour force); reduces wages, increases working hours, introduces machinery, tries to spend as little as possible on the conditions of labour etc. as and when it becomes expedient – the suffering of the worker is always on the verge of getting worse, is always subject to the whim of the next economic crisis. On the other hand, the capitalist classes increasingly accumulate more and more surplus value, and protect their assets through loans, reserve funds, etc. as a class; as capitalism develops, the means of production are more and more concentrated in the hands of the capitalist class; as capitalism develops, the capitalist class takes control of legislative and legal procedure to serve its interests to larger degrees. The polarisation of the working class and the capitalist class is, in Marx's conceptualisation, caught in an endlessly reproductive spiral of getting worse – inevitably at some stage a total destabilisation of the capitalist social organisation would be inevitable. In *Capital* Marx does not go into the precise mechanics of this breaking point (after all he was more concerned with analysing the happening of capitalism in a state of equilibrium), but then he had touched upon that already in *The Communist Manifesto*. The great destabilising wrench would come whenever the working class, through its ever-increasing suffering and its perception of the ever-increasing concentration in the capitalist classes, simply understood the mechanics of capitalism and became aware of the power of its own class-character – would *arise*.

Three, moral contradictions. The norms in terms of which the moral contradictions in capitalist processes (deviations from those norms) are revealed, according to Marx, derive from an understanding of the primal relationship of humans to nature. This primal relationship has, as Marx sees it (and in this he draws on Hegel), historical roots (as drawing upon an entire history of the human attempt to come to grips with and conquer nature for human survival and fulfilment) and is constituted within human nature (humans understand themselves and their place in the world accordingly). So, labour is essentially the direct contest between humans and nature for the production of use value and that remains the essence of labour and the concept of value in terms of which all developments can be gauged; the production of use value is essentially the production of a complete and usable product for the producer's consumption, and the producer therefore develops a dynamic relationship with the process of production as a whole and the complete product in terms of which he understands his success and fulfilment; the act of so producing and consuming and controlling nature manifests itself in people's sense of possession – there is a direct correlation established between labour and production and possession – and it is through this process that humans define their place in the world and therefore themselves. In the stages leading up to capitalism, and especially within capitalist processes, each of these facets of the primal relationship between humans and nature is contradicted. The dislocation of the relationship of labour to the production of use value for the producer's consumption is taken to different kinds of extreme in slave societies and capitalist societies. Marx juxtaposes the dislocation in the slave society (for the slave labourer) and that in capitalist society (for the wage labourer) several times in *Capital*.[15] The extraction of surplus value from the worker's labour so that it becomes the property of the non-labouring capitalist is itself a dislocation of the primal relationship between humans and nature, both insofar as it goes beyond production for use value and insofar as it contradicts the primal understanding of property rights or possession. The primal relationship that the worker develops with the complete process of production and the whole product is drastically contradicted at the early stage of capitalism itself – at the stage of manufacture – and gives rise to the distinctly Hegelian *alienation* of the worker.[16] This only gets exacerbated as capitalism develops, as mechanisation is introduced, as the expendability of the individual worker increases, and so on. Sometimes these moral contradictions become manifest, Marx observes, in the absurdity of legal systems that support capitalism, especially in legal strictures regarding property rights or possession in capitalist society.[17]

What makes these moral contradictions dangerous, and could eventually lead to social contradictions/crises, is that the capitalist (and all those who support the capitalist process – the state, political economists) constantly seeks to hide the effect capitalism has on the primal relationship between humans and nature, constantly seeks to hide the very character of capitalism itself. The entire calculation of surplus value is obscured by the focus on profit; the fact that value derives from labour is obscured deliberately by the mendacious wage form; the money form involved in every conversion of capital itself obfuscates the process of circulation of capital and the various components of capital; and so on – the entire truth of the process of capitalism is hidden by sometimes functional, sometimes deliberately mendacious, sometimes deliberately misconceived tissues of partial truths and falsehoods. The realisation that this is the case could become the backbone of a working-class consciousness, could become the sinews of the social contradictions, and lead to transformation.

That seems to me to cover the Marxist understanding of the contradictions of capitalism. Time to move on to the context of advanced capitalism.

2 The consideration of advanced capitalism, and reflections on contradictions/crises (or lack of these) therein, is probably best approached as framed by and following from revisions, renovations, updatings and corrections of the conceptual preconditions which attach to Marx's formulations. It seems to me that the basic conceptual precondition which underlies all the others listed below is that these appear or are presented with reference to Marx's conceptualisation itself. In that sense, I feel, that it is probably more accurate to think of the area of *advanced* capitalism (an amorphous and diverse conglomeration of ideas related to increasingly diverse and complex considerations of contexts and histories) as *post-Marxist conceptualisations* of capitalism. When I say post-Marxist conceptualisations of capitalism are with reference to the Marxist conceptualisation, I do not gesture simply towards thinking which is developed directly with Marx's formulations in mind, but simply to the fact that it is *all* inevitably with an awareness of these (whether hostile, favourable, or simply different) – and the all too tangible political effects of these. This includes Weber's approach to capitalism through western rationality, which never quite eschews a Marxist understanding of class structures or the Marxist notion of socialist centralisation. This obviously includes reconceptualisations of the current state and future of capitalism available, for example, in the work of Schumpeter (whose *Capitalism, Socialism and Democracy* begins with a compendium of the shortcomings in Marx's

formulations as a sociologist, economist and philosopher); in the entire effort of the Frankfurt School thinkers to update and accommodate Marxism within a sociological overview of capitalism (culminating in Habermas's *Legitimation Crisis* and *Theory of Communicative Action*); in the impressive attempt made by Ernest Mandel, especially in *Late Capitalism*, to draw out the progression of capitalism in the later twentieth century from Marxist economics. I also include among post-Marxist conceptualisations the ideas of those economists and philosophers who are most vehemently opposed to Marxist formulations, and who often try to draw their roots by circumventing Marx and going back to Adam Smith (such as Popper, Hayek, Nozick, Fukuyama, to whose ideas Part III of this study is devoted) – the very act of circumventing Marx is painfully self-conscious. This ubiquitous and inevitable awareness of Marxism itself, I repeat, forms the first conceptual precondition of post-Marxist conceptualisations of capitalism. The other changes in the conceptual preconditions which frame approaches to capitalism are now given pointwise.

One, particularly vital readjustments to the Marxist conceptual preconditions have occurred with regard to the understanding of labour. Indeed, since this formed the centre of Marx's formulation, the qualifications on this have manifold repercussions which are aptly seen as providing the basis of several conceptual preconditions, and that is how I present the matter here. Importantly, the basic understanding of labour as a physical–nervous exertion to control nature (mediated by skill and knowledge), the very visceral *quality* of labour, of the effort involved and the suffering of its over-exploitation, has to some extent been eroded by technological developments. Increasing technological advances towards automatisation, which is implicit in capitalist processes and which Marx had clearly anticipated, have unsurprisingly taken place. This means that some of the purity of labour, some of the sense of effort involved in it, some of the potential suffering that is implicit in it, has been depleted – some of the identifying features of those who labour have been removed – and consequently some of the impetus for political analysis and mobilisation contained in it has been reduced. In Marxist terms this also means, as Mandel has thoroughly discussed in *Late Capitalism*,[18] that the economics of capitalism has shifted from the focus on commodity production to one on the production of means of production. This also means (in a more un-Marxist sense) that the role of knowledge – technological know-how, competence, potential

– has taken a more determinative place in capitalist processes than Marx had allowed.[19] It becomes a more independent (rather than mediatory) factor in the confrontation of humans and nature. It becomes substantively embodied within the reproductive process of capitalism itself. That in turn has several repercussions, which will become manifest as I proceed.

Two, the relationship between labour and value as given by Marx has been reconsidered and largely dispensed with. Several points in this connection should be noted. There are certain problems in the labour theory of value (for example, how should it be applied to the commodity labour itself? what are its mechanics in a state of dise-quilibrium? etc.) which seem to necessitate a different or a more inclusive theory of value. Not least importantly, other modes of cal-culating value would render the capitalist process conceptually more comfortable, and pragmatically more effective. Simplistically speaking, the problem is to find a common denominator for all com-modities that would allow allocation of values on a comparable scale. Labour in abstract (labour as working time) does provide such a common denominator, but if it seems unsatisfactory for any reason it is natural to contemplate others. In fact, the prevailing consensus now has more or less discarded the labour theory of value in favour of (in many ways more inclusive) utility as a common denominator. The shift of calculations of value according to marginal utility (pushing the thrust of valuation away from the productive process in itself into the mechanics of production and consumption) and the law of diminishing marginal utility (the more consumption of a commodity increases, the less the value of the commodity) has held sway, and has largely determined wage-calculation and employment figures, in the twentieth century. It has of course been noted that utility is not an unproblematic factor either, since it cannot really be considered a common denominator – each commodity marks a different sort of utility.[20] If the labour theory of value is adhered to it would follow that increasing automatisation, a necessary aspect of the development of capitalism, would itself eventually disturb the appropriation of surplus values on which capitalist processes rest; and full automatisation would mean the disappearance of surplus values. Hence Mandel's argument that capitalism, even at an advanced stage, will not proceed beyond partial automatisation even if full automatisation becomes possible.[21]

Three, the sociological description in terms of classes that followed so clearly from Marx's understanding of the quality and economic status of labour is also disturbed if that conceptual precondition is altered. In a sense the clarity of class analysis, with the broadly described working class and capitalist class, was problematic even in its inception. There was, for instance, always the somewhat grey area of the place of intellectuals in class analysis – the many refinements which locate intellectuals as a specific stratum (functionaries of the capitalist class) which is essentially bourgeois or petty bourgeois in character could never wholly overcome the potential for unpredictability and change within it. I have examined the complexities of the place of intellectuals in socialist political philosophy in some detail in *Marxism, History, and Intellectuals*.[22] Increasingly, with the depletion of the primarily physical–nervous quality of labour and the gradual emphasis on the role of knowledge within capitalist processes, the problematics of class analysis grow in complexity. On the one hand, intellectuals become more of a proliferating product of capitalist processes (just as labour was in Marxist terms an ever-growing product) and are often seen as possibly constituting a threat in themselves to that process (a point I elaborate soon). On the other hand, the working class has a tendency to appear less polarised in relation to the capitalist class: it tends to get, in Marcuse's terms, more easily *assimilated* within capitalist processes and less concretely *exploited*.[23] Along with these growing ambiguities within class analysis there is also the development of other modes of sociological description and analysis pertinent to understanding capitalist processes (I have touched on this already). Since Weber, sociological analysis in terms primarily of the organisation (and the rationale thereof) of various overlapping layers of very broadly defined corporations (political, social, industrial, financial, etc.), or in terms of systems (ideological, discourse-based, cultural, economic, etc.) has proved fruitful.

Four, the political status of any 'given society' which has to be considered with relation to capitalist processes has changed substantially from that which Marx had in mind (a liberal, standoffish, collaborative political ethos which frames the free development of capitalist production, circulation, competition). If the political status of a given society (nation, community, administrative zone, etc.) is considered to be embodied in the political state, one could maintain now that the political state which collaborates with capitalism – the capitalist political state – has a more *defined* role with regard to the workings of capitalism, to the capitalist organisations and processes. The grounds of collaboration with capitalism, the conditions and expectations in negotiations which are implicit therein, have simply acquired a certain clarity which the liberal state assumed by Marx, allowing for and enabling the free play of capitalism, didn't have. The legal and legislative prerogatives of the capitalist political state; the limits to which it intervenes in wage disputes and labour problems; the degree to which it enables general welfare and necessary services; the initiative it might take to protect certain kinds of enterprises or industrial sectors; the measure to which it controls economic planning over the area of its jurisdiction; the conditions under which and the fora through which it negotiates with other political states (given societies) about international economic policies – all these are clarified to an extent which gives the capitalist political state an apparently more measured and interventionist role in capitalist processes. The contemporary liberal capitalist state is not simply the behind-the-scenes liberal state underlying Marx's conceptualisation of capitalism. I suppose one could say that the capitalist political state has now *come to be* whereas in Marx's time it was still in a formative stage and following the growth of capitalism on its heels.

Five, on the same note and perhaps somewhat more importantly, the contemporary capitalist political state does not *frame* the workings of capitalism in a comparable sense to Marx's conceptualisation. The fact is that the capitalist political state is now less in a position to play an effective interventionist role with regard to capitalist processes than ever before simply because these processes are much larger in scope than they were ever before, extending beyond the control of any single political state. The determination that political states (as embodying 'given societies') were able to exercise in political and economic terms at an international level – in world trade, particularly in and immediately after the phase of colonialism – has ceased to exist. The manner in which industrialised nations were able to exploit less technologically developed nations in the circuit of capital in precisely those terms is rapidly becoming a thing of the past. The entire tendency of capitalism now is towards maintaining an economic system which is less dependent on the political determination of states and more dependent on the quirks of global markets; creating large corporate structures which are not contained within the jurisdiction of any single political state; of homogenising processes of production wherever capitalism extends itself; of unifying markets and transforming market conditions for that end – the entire phenomenon which now passes for 'globalisation'.

Six, a significant conceptual precondition now also pertains to the nature of the media and discourses which are available for conceptual efforts, the tools on which any effort to enunciate a conceptualisation of capitalism must depend. As knowledge itself assumes a more central position in capitalist processes, and becomes subject to these processes and proliferates, the conditions of thinking and indeed the very form of thinking undergo significant changes. An increasing degree of specialisation has occurred in every sphere, and with it an increasing territorialisation of information, a corresponding delimitation of advanced education and research, and the development of specialist discourses – the changing culture of academia has been examined often in recent years.[24] All-encompassing or comprehensive models of sociolinguistic and cultural analyses have increasingly tended to encode their inability to encompass and comprehend – their inevitable self-failure – within their formulations. Recent 'movements' pertinent to cultural studies or critical theory (post-structuralism, deconstructionism, post-colonialism, postmodernism, new historicism) ostensibly extend their scope or reach by formulations which are anti-definitive and pluralistic, and at the same time restrict their effectiveness and applicability in any comprehensive or encompassing sense because of that.[25] While thinkers seem to reach out to ever broader and more inclusive arenas of knowledge (interdisciplinary efforts thrive, sensitivity to different contexts increases, etc.) there appears also an increasing sense of inevitable fragmentation and defeat in the endeavour. The kind of holistic thinking which allowed Marx and his descendants and adversaries to unify economic analysis, social–cultural description, political theory, historical exposition, etc., seems more unapproachable and therefore less pertinent. There has also developed over the last few decades both an increasing proliferation of access to information (especially through technological developments in mass media and communications) and a firmer commodification of knowledge. The superlative mass of accessible informations and points of view is itself an incentive to ultra-specialisation (focusing on the analysis of ever more microscopic levels of information), and a disincentive to holistic/comprehensive/generalistic thinking (either by disregarding such thinking, or by making it increasingly aware of its inherent limitations and failures). The superlative mass of information and perspectives also allows for firmer commodification of knowledge to occur: thus the value of certain kinds of knowledge is set in the marketplace (education, employment, etc.); legal and juridical prerogatives on knowledge (what has to be withheld from or exposed to public view) become more clearly defined; the means of knowledge dissemination itself becomes a field of enterprise (obviously in educational organisation, but as importantly in the manner in which knowledge is marketed to target groups and categorised and contained by enterprises – mass media corporations, internet providers, government agencies, and so on – which control its dissemination). On the whole, while access to information and perspectives increase, and with these the sheer mass of available knowledge increases, the subtle control of knowledge also increases and comprehensive thinking decreases and is often institutionally discouraged. To be pat, individuals seem to get more direct control of what there is to be known, and because of that tend to surrender their ability to assimilate, conceive, organise, synthesise and form opinions to others (information and knowledge providing enterprises, specialists, professionals, etc.). Knowledge has, of course, always been controlled, traditionally by direct control on access; now the control is more covertly exercised *through* the increase in access, and in the process the very forms of knowledge, the perceptions of knowledge itself, have changed significantly.

Seven, despite the difficulties that forms of knowledge pose with regard to approaching capitalism in a holistic fashion, any effort in that direction has to be aware of the claims to general *success* made by capitalists and capitalist states. This is a significantly different ideological ethos in which to consider the matter: for Marx the necessity of considering capitalism was, in the first instance, an analytical effort simply to unravel its processes and then to propose the political–philosophical positions which arise out of that analysis; now it's a matter of taking account of capitalism's emendations on Marx's understanding, capitalism's claims to success and the development of modes of validating this success, capitalism's claims to defeating contending ideologies and corresponding social organisations. Apropos the latter, capitalism now appropriates within its processes, and explains in terms of its structures, the immense technological advances made in the twentieth century. It is generally asserted, and with undeniable justice, that at least the development of technological advances in terms of social applicability, production and distribution owes much to the entrepreneurial drives within capitalism. The consequent and enormous changes in the conditions of life (which take us back to the diminution of the suffering of labour, and the increasing disbelief in Marx's immiserisation thesis) is therefore also claimed by capitalism. The translation of these into economic measures (however contentiously) – such as measures of economic growth (say in terms of GDP and GNP), standard of living, infrastructural investment, poverty, etc. – has been useful in determining, legitimising and persuading people of capitalism's economic success. Capitalist states (political states collaborating with and dependent on the economics of capitalist processes) have managed to associate themselves (I do not go into the mechanics of this at the moment) with democratic processes. Capitalism therefore (and, again, however contentiously) claims the success of supporting the ethical cause of individual freedom and self-determination. The gradual weakening of such consent in the case of more ostensibly centralised socialist states, coupled with the extension of capitalist processes and structures, enables capitalism to declare a victory over contending ideologies.

Eight, and finally, the focus of capitalism for Marx (essentially the individual capitalist or the – usually kinship-based – capitalist firm, and the conglomerate character of these embodied in the capitalist class) has changed to the increasingly larger, autonomous and more complex capitalist corporation. This is the substance of the next part of this study, and the underlying centre of the study as a whole. At any rate, relationships and formulations that seemed obvious to Marx and Marxists initially have necessarily had to be reconsidered. This reconsideration ranges from such basic issues as the meaning of property or the nuances of management to such broad issues as the definition of market and the regulation of trade.

Given these adjustments to the conceptual preconditions of approaching capitalism in the post-Marxist ethos, what happens to the understanding of the contradictions/crises of capitalism? On the whole, holistic approaches to capitalism (not specific factors and phenomena within capitalist processes, but the economic–social–ethical nexus in capitalism as a whole), with a view to discerning whether there exist any fundamental contradictions/unresolvable crises therein, have become unpopular in the last couple of decades of the twentieth century. Earlier sociologically and economically focused perceptions of the changes within capitalism (but still holistic in temper), and endorsements of the achievements of capitalism, are exemplified by Max Weber's and Joseph Schumpeter's works. These are interestingly combined with a continuing belief in the survival of fundamental contradictions in capitalism that would eventually lead to its dismantling. Both clearly regretted that this was the case.

The actual enumeration of such fundamental contradictions in capitalism occurs with greater clarity in Schumpeter's work than in Weber's. In Weber's case apprehensions of contradictions in capitalist social organisation occur in considering details of the rationality underlying capitalist accounting and corporations[26] (I discuss some of the ideas involved here in Part II). A more focused discussion of the contradictions of capitalism, and therefore of the projected end of capitalism, appears famously in Schumpeter's *Capitalism, Socialism and Democracy*. After dispensing with some of the more obvious economic and ethical concerns that occupied thinkers at the time, Schumpeter's bleak forecast for the future of capitalism ultimately rests on his perception of social contradictions. There are broadly three of these. One, that the development of corporatism in capitalism, and the necessary routinisation and automatisation of the entrepreneurial function that occurs in that process, would gradually absorb and render impotent the entrepreneur and the bourgeois class that provide the impetus to progress in capitalist development, and that this would eventually result in the decay of capitalist processes. Since this is closely connected with the condition of corporate capitalism, and is therefore of particular interest here, perhaps closer attention should be given to Schumpeter's words here:

> [I]f capitalist evolution – 'progress' – either ceases or becomes completely automatic, the economic basis of the industrial bourgeoisie will become reduced eventually to wages such as are paid for current administrative work excepting remnants of quasi-rents and monopoloid gains that may be expected to linger on for some time. Since capitalist enterprise, by its very achievements, tends to automatize progress, we conclude that it tends to make itself superfluous – to break to pieces under the pressure of its own success. The perfectly bureaucratized giant industrial unit not only ousts the small or medium-sized firm and 'expropriates' its owners, but in the end it also ousts the entrepreneur and expropriates the bourgeoisie as a class which in the process stands to lose not only its income but also what is infinitely more important, its function.[27]

The growing routinisation and automatisation of the entrepreneur-ial function would, amongst other things, according to Schumpeter, loosen that seminal impetus to entrepreneurism – the substance of property. Consequently the entrepreneurial function would gradually be replaced by a more short-term and uninnovative executive function. This would also mean that in the process, capitalism would itself destroy the institutional structures that had allowed its emergence in the first place, by enabling the dissolution of the small traders, retailers, peasants, gentry, etc. Two, that there already exists a social predisposition to hostility which capitalism wouldn't be able to answer to and would eventually surrender to. There are several reasons for the hostility and capitalism's inability to counter it effectively: that capitalist rationality wouldn't be sufficient because generally social hostility is not in itself rational (social thinking is not intrinsically rationalistic); that such hostility and aggression would be all the more difficult to check because capitalism undermines the framework of sacred (irrational) traditions which could serve that purpose; that there would in a capitalist society always be the have-nots and the deprived who would be able under the circumstances effectively to vent their anger, etc.[28] Three, that this general social hostility would find a particular voice and outlet in a specific product of capitalism, a growing intellectual mass (and in this Schumpeter anticipates thinkers like Alvin Gouldner and Ernest Mandel)[29] and its quite different sort of hostility to capitalism. Since capitalism invests in rationalism – in education, dissemination of knowledge, etc. – there would come to exist a larger number of educated and informed people, with a developed critical bent of mind, without a distinctive class character, who moreover could not always be absorbed into the professions, and who would feel that their talents were being wasted in the given order, and who would be able to rationalise their discontent with capitalism as being of a moral variety.[30] What follows is Schumpeter's forecast of a particular brand of socialism that would probably successfully (and despite his reservations) replace capitalism.

Holistic approaches to advanced capitalism and examinations of the possible contradictions/crises therein have, understandably, appeared from updated Marxist or broadly revisionist socialist per-spectives. Thus Ernest Mandel's updated Marxist economic analysis of contemporary capitalism in *Late Capitalism* sees a steady *intensi-fication* of all contradictions as capitalism focuses its resources on means of production rather than the product in the movement towards increasing (but nevertheless partial) automatisation – the third technological revolution:

> The combined upshot of [the] main economic characteristics of the third technological revolution is a tendency for all the contradictions of the capitalist mode of production to be intensified: the contradiction between the growing socialization of labour and private appropriation; the contradiction between the production of use-values (which rises to the immeasurable) and the realization of exchange values (which continues to be tied to the purchasing power of the population); the contradiction between the process of labour and the process of valorization; the contradiction between the accumulation of capital and its valorization, and so on and so forth.[31]

Mandel's book largely devotes itself to elucidating how these contradictions get exacerbated and yet crises are postponed as the capitalist process reduces the turnover time of fixed capital, accelerates technological innovation, invests more in the service sector, moves towards increased international centralisation, maintains permanent inflation in holding crises at bay by producing money, institutes a permanent arms economy, often follows neo-imperialistic policies – features that are as familiar at the turn of the millennium as they were in the nineteen-sixties. Those initially associated with the Frankfurt School and later bringing some of the revisionist thinking of the Frankfurt School to fruition in examining capitalism, such as Herbert Marcuse and Jürgen Habermas, also find the contradictions of capitalism to be evidenced in its developed stage. For Herbert Marcuse this is primarily an ethical matter: the contradictions lie in the obscenity of surfeit and wasteful super-capitalist cultures in the midst of distributive injustice, marginalisation, and deprivation; and in the insidious totalitarianism of thought control and lack of freedom which advanced capitalism enables while appearing to espouse and institute the very opposite.[32] On the whole, Marcuse found consolation in the late nineteen-fifties and early sixties in anticipating a 'Great Refusal' and a new type of socialist revolution, only to be disappointed in these expectations. In *Legitimation Crisis* Habermas, though cognisant of most of the above-mentioned changes in conceptual preconditions, and orienting the sociological approach to capitalism more in terms of systems theory, goes beyond the characteristic problems of advanced capitalism (which occur in disturbing ecological, anthropological and international balance) to discern several levels of more essential crisis: economic crisis in capitalist economic systems (which is pretty close to Marx's account thereof); political crisis (which can occur if the rationality or legitimacy of political systems come into question); and socio-cultural crisis (which could result from lack of motivation impelled by, for instance, the destruction of traditional support systems).[33] I have already mentioned Henri Lefebvre's conviction that the contradictions of capitalism slip through the ever-expanding scope and territorialisation of advanced capitalism.[34] Also worthy of mention are the reiterations of capitalism's transient nature in the wake of (cycles of) economic crisis in the west in the eighties and nineties[35] – but insofar as these pertain to the fundamental contradictions of capitalism these generally have little to add to the points mentioned above already.

On the whole, it seems to me that the last two decades of the twentieth century have abandoned attempts at holistic conceptualisations of capitalism that attempt to discern whether contradictions exist in capitalism and what shape these take. On the other hand, triumphalist (and occasionally resigned) assertions in favour of capitalism are now legion: these either focus on certain aspects of the capitalist process (its various claims to success) in the context of the 'failure' of contending economic and social organisations, and/or demonstrate how the benefits of capitalism outnumber its possible contradictions, and/or are concerned with problem-solving with regard to perceived contradictions/crises in capitalism within the frame of capitalism (therefore denying that these contradictions may be *fundamental*). This body of writing, especially in recent proliferations, is too ponderous for me to go into here. Besides, I come back to this in some detail, at least insofar as it is relevant to the concerns of political philosophy, in Part III of this study.

However, there is, I believe, a widely prevalent sense of unease with the triumphalism of contemporary capitalism. Almost all the kinds of contradictions/crises anticipated by the above-mentioned thinkers have surfaced in a regular fashion. The advanced capitalist nations have seen an almost continuous cycle of economic crises since the Second World War despite the consolidation of generally upwardly mobile economic growth. New incumbents in global markets and capitalist economies have achieved impressive results, but largely at the cost also of increasing inequality and poverty. United Nations Development Program (UNDP) reports of 1998 indicate that the gap between rich and poor has increased however the statistics are read, and that compared to a couple of decades back some of the poorest countries are significantly worse off. Even the 1999/2000 Development Report from the World Bank notes that globalisation has led to increased inequality and that one cannot depend on trickle down to effect any significant change in this. UNDP and World Bank statistics also indicate that the countries that have been most successful in combating poverty while achieving economic growth in the last three decades (China, Malaysia, Indonesia, Vietnam) have been those that have tried to ensure general equity and controlled redistributive processes – or retained provision for doing so – in a manner which is inconsistent with a high degree of liberalisation of economies. At the same time, in advanced capitalist countries in Europe, America and Australasia, at least one issue which has attracted media attention consistently over the last two decades is the astronomical pay-packets of higher level executives in corporations and the unimaginable gains which some entrepreneurs have shown (a lot more on this in Part II). Advanced capitalist countries have also, concurrently (unsurprisingly) with the gradual diminution of the 'socialist threat', increasingly grown more thrifty in welfare expenditure: a perpetual crisis seems to afflict the provision of health expenditure, old-age support, unemployment benefits, policing expenditure, educational resourcing, etc. in a large number of post-industrialised contexts. Also connected with the diminution of the 'socialist threat' has been the re-emergence of fairly old-fashioned labour problems, albeit controlled by a depletion of effective union representation and privileges (carefully engineered over the last three decades) – disputes regarding working hours, wages, conditions of service, etc. Increased routinisation of management practices in corporations has consistently raised, and continues to raise, ethical questions; increased insecurity of employment and atomisation of work experience and increased expenditure in accounting and corporate policing are matters of ethical concern which are only likely to be exacerbated in the future. Some headway is now being made regarding the adverse effects of corporate capitalism on the environment, but these are very far from being resolved. Greater autonomy of the processes of corporate capitalism and greater concentration of resources therein and the consequent loosening of state control have arguably also meant that the scope for political corruption has increased: at any rate, incidences of political corruption related to corporate activities and finances are constantly available in the media. The neo-imperialist policies and interventions of advanced capitalist countries – motivated usually by economic considerations hidden behind paternalistic rhetoric – has been the cause of widespread unease in too many instances since the war to need enumeration here. Vocal ideologues like Noam Chomsky, Edward Said, Fredric Jameson, and others, continue to draw attention to these in a trenchant fashion. The manner in which these policies and interventions are sieved through such international organisations as the United Nations, the World Bank, the World Trade Organisation and NATO has been a matter for protest all too frequently in recent years (doubts about NATO intervention in Serbia and protests during the WTO conference in Seattle – setting a trend for such protest since, most recently in Genoa – are the notes on which the last year of the twentieth century appropriately ended).

This bare compendium of reasons for unease in the contemporary ethos of globalised corporate capitalism can be carried on, but the point, I think, has been made. Despite the triumphalism of capitalism now, and the difficulties posed in considering capitalism in a comprehensive fashion due to the conceptual preconditions enumerated above, there is probably reason for doubting that the contradictions of capitalism have disappeared or are doing so.

5 Intentional Systems

After that excursus in sections 1 and 2 of the previous chapter, the point that I can make apropos contradictions of capitalism at this initial stage is probably entirely obvious, but nevertheless useful in that it allows for a clarification of the scope of political philosophy. The obvious point is easily made: given that the political state is defined with a focus on *means* (as having a monopoly on force, as embodying a crystallisation of the collective consciousness it is with regard to), and that the capitalist corporation is defined with a focus on *ends* (enabling an endlessly reproductive process of expanding capital, essentially by expanding the scope and intensity of that process), it is conceivable – though not immediately necessary – that contradictions would arise between the political state and the capitalist corporation. The means-orientation of the political state may (or may be made to) cohere with the ends-orientation of the capitalist corporation, but equally it may not. It may not precisely because ultimately the political state (with its definitive means-orientation) is with regard to the people–land–resources it represents, and the capitalist corporation (with its definitive ends-orientation) has no such necessary allegiance. In other words, the political state is always potentially at odds with the capitalist corporation because it is *political* (the promised clarification of the scope of political philosophy is imminent). Briefly, that means that different kinds of *intentionality* are implied in the two definitions which may happen to complement each other but which do not coincide.

The idea that there are different intentions embedded in the political state and the capitalist corporation is, I think, obvious from a common-sense point of view: however the precise relationship between these different intentions (possible complementarity but without coincidence) needs more rigorous elucidation, especially since this is inextricably entwined with the understanding of political philosophy which underlies this study. In fact within this observation, or rather within the nuances of different intentionalities, lies a particular feature of political philosophy that informs this study generally and provides its impetus. The feature in question is with regard to the concept of *political will* – but it would be premature to go into that straightaway. More immediately, a rigorous elucidation of the different intentionalities in question will necessarily have to begin with the connotations of the term *intentionality* here.

The relevant connotations of the term intentionality that I have in mind here can be usefully drawn from the now familiar reflections on that term in the analytical philosophy of mind and language. In drawing on these I do not wish to associate intentionality with any philosophical consideration of psychology: neither in the manner of Searle (who sees intentionality as certain kinds of mental states)[1] and nor in the manner of Dennett (who understands 'folk psychology' as our evolved attempts to predict each other's behaviour by approaching each other as *intentional systems*).[2] The emphasis on psychology revolves too much around the placement of the individual vis-à-vis the world or other individuals, whereas this study is concerned with the collective entity embodied in the capitalist corporation or political state. Nor, for that matter, do I intend to make these references an excuse for discussing the (usually) liberal politics that is explicitly associated with such analytical philosophers.[3] It is primarily Dennett's notion of *intentional systems*, however, which I feel may be useful here. This is given as:

> the concept of a system whose behavior can be – at least sometimes – explained and predicted by relying on ascriptions to the system of beliefs and desires (and hopes, fears, intentions, hunches...). I will call such systems *intentional systems*, and such explanations intentional explanations and predictions, in virtue of the intentionality of the idioms of belief and desire (and hope, fear, intention, hunch ...).[4]

This notion can, despite Dennett, be dissociated from the psychologistic (and, for that matter, the evolutionism connected with that) because it is conceived in the first instance as being indifferent to (though relevant to) the specific constitution of the human mind: Dennett sees intentional systems in an instrumentalist fashion which, for instance, can be as much mechanical as human (the analogy of the computer appears constantly); which does not have to express a conscious will or volition:

> the definition of intentional systems I have given does not say that intentional systems *really* have beliefs and desires, but that one can explain and predict their behavior by *ascribing* beliefs and

desires to them, and whether one calls what one ascribes to the computer beliefs or belief-analogues or information-complexes or intentional whatnots makes no difference to the nature of the calculation one makes on the basis of the ascriptions;[5]

and which is untrammelled by ethical or metaphysical presumptions: 'The concept of an intentional system is a relatively uncluttered and unmetaphysical notion, abstracted as it is from questions of the composition, constitution, consciousness, morality, or divinity of the entities falling under it.'[6]

This indifference to the specific constitution of the human mind allows for a relocation of the notion of intentional systems to the collective entities in question here. In such a relocation the following points (which generally rely on Dennett's notion) can be made.

a. There are three factors involved in the consideration of intentional systems in Dennett's sense. One, the *manifest form* of the given intentional system (that which *can be seen* to embody certain beliefs, desires etc.); two, the *agency* which ascribes and explains–predicts (that which *sees* beliefs, desires etc. embodied in the given intentional system and explains–predicts on that basis); and three, the *projection* of the behaviour of the given intentional system in specific circumstances if and when these arise (that which is *expected* of that which *can be seen* by that which *sees*). Strictly speaking, intentionality cannot be specifically located in, or even predominantly in, any one of these factors: intention cannot be discerned unless it is with regard to an intentional system; intention cannot be discerned unless there is an agency to discern it; and intention cannot be said to have been discerned unless some projection with regard to the intentional system is made by the agency. Intentionality lies at the nexus of these three factors.

b. With regard to the capitalist corporation the division between explaining–predicting agency and the manifest form of the given intentional system which Dennett carefully maintains need not be retained. It makes sense to consider the capitalist corporation as an intentional system only insofar as agency is *contained* within its manifest form. This is because within such corporate structures there are inevitably mechanisms which allow self-ascriptions of beliefs, desires, etc.; agency-dictating spokespersons are appointed and contained within such entities (as chief executives and high-level managers, advisers or consultants, publicity departments, think-tanks, and so on) to enable such ascription and explanations–

predictions therefrom; and such corporate entities usually present themselves and operate in terms of self-projections. (The strictures which Dennett lays down for having special stories for the failure of such projections[7] continue to apply within such a framework.) Essentially, it makes sense to consider the capitalist corporation as an intentional system where the explaining–predicting agency is contained within itself because the end towards which the capitalist corporation is directed (the very reason for its existence) is predetermined – the end is maximising capital in circulation, maximising profits. The capitalist corporation is there to reach that end, and it appoints explaining–predicting agencies within itself to enable assessments and analyses of its success or failure in reaching that end, and perhaps to encourage movement in the direction of that end. The containment of agency within the manifest form of capitalist corporations as intentional systems is consistent with its ends-orientation.

c. In approaching the political state in a similar manner the distinction between explaining–predicting agency and manifest form of intentional system does need to be maintained. The political state is in fact primarily a *particular kind* of explaining–predicting agency which applies itself to the *people–land–resources within the area of its jurisdiction* (the italicised phrase is the intentional system in this case). And the projections that the political state may offer as a result of its application is with regard to the people–land–resources within the area of its jurisdiction – with regard to *that* as the intentional system. It is in this sense that Durkheim's understanding of the distance of the political state from the people–land–resources it is with regard to may be understood: the clarity which the political state presents on behalf of and with regard to the people–land–resources under its jurisdiction is a function of its role of being an explaining–predicting agency. The clarity of the political state (as opposed to the inevitable diffuseness of perception of the people–land–resources itself) is because it explains–predicts that intentional system, and embodies its role as such in an institution-like or association-like manner (to go back to MacIver's terms). The political state's explaining–predicting agency role derives from its apprehension of the constitution of the people–land–resources under its jurisdiction (its attribution of beliefs and desires which apparently pertain to that), and intentional projections for the people–land–resources are made by the political state as a result. The intentional ends are therefore something that the political state cannot wholly predetermine (it cannot determine its own intentions as a capitalist corporation does, it determines what comes out of its understanding of the larger intentional system which it represents). That may well be an aspect of Weber's perception that the political state cannot be *defined* in terms of the ends it espouses.

d. Here's an observation which is pertinent to both the capitalist corporation and the political state, especially the latter: Dennett's understanding of the explaining–predicting agency is more or less as a passive factor (it explains and predicts the behaviour of the intentional system, it doesn't necessarily impinge upon that behaviour), whereas the role of the agency in the intentional systems which are pertinent to the capitalist corporation (itself) and the political state (the people–land–resources under its jurisdiction) is necessarily an active one. The agency which is contained in the manifest form of the capitalist corporation not only explains and predicts its own behaviour with a view to achieving its predetermined end, it *acts upon* its self-explanations and self-predictions to *direct itself* towards that predetermined end. This means that the agency within the capitalist corporation can effect suitable changes and modifications within its own constitution, can impinge upon its own behaviour, can moderate itself according to its projections. One may think of the capitalist corporation as some sort of collective *organic entity*: self-contained, self-determining, self-projecting, self-modifying. The intentional system pertinent to the political state as explanative-predictive agency is not an organic entity; there is no such indelible identity between political state (agency) and people–land–resources (given intentional system). To imagine there is such an identity, that there is such an organicity at work politically, could lead to the fascist blunder.[8] However, the political state definitively has an active role as agency with regard to the people–land–resources as intentional system in a more crucial sense than is the case for the capitalist corporation. Not only does the political state perform as explaining–predicting agency regarding the given constitution of the intentional system, i.e. people–land–resources, and makes projections on that basis, the political state also *acts* on its agency-like perceptions to ensure or alter the path of the intentional system towards or away from the projected outcome. The reasons why the political state may do so would depend on what ends it may consider to be desirable or otherwise (and there are so many possible options here that none, Weber had decided, could be considered to be definitive of the political state); the means by which the political state acts in such a way is embodied in its establishment and being, its legislative and judicial function (so, Weber had rightly felt, this is where the political state becomes amenable to definition, in terms of the means at its disposal, its monopoly on force). The political state is a particular kind of active explaining–predicting agency which is with regard to and acts on behalf of and with effect on an intentional system (the people–land–resources under its jurisdiction) which is separate from it.

e. The active principle exhibited by the capitalist corporation which contains the explaining–predicting agency within itself – the active principle which is implicit in the capitalist corporation's organic behaviour with a predetermined ends-orientation – could be thought of as *capitalist drive*. The active principle which enables the political state as explaining–predicting agency to act upon (be effective on, to direct) the intentional system – the people–land–resources – it is with regard to (or which it explains, tries to predict) could be thought of as *political will*. The political will of the political state is more than simply a monopoly on force: *it is an intentional use of the power it has by dint of such a monopoly, for whatever ends it wishes to achieve and in terms of whatever understanding it has as an explaining–predicting agency, with regard to and with effect upon the people–land–resources under its jurisdiction (or the intentional system).* The distinction between these two active principles is self-evident, but worth emphasising anyway. The capitalist drive is that intentional movement which the capitalist corporation exhibits with regard to itself. The political will is that intentional movement which the political state exhibits with regard to and on behalf of and with effect on the people–land–resources under its jurisdiction. The capitalist drive is self-contained; the political will has a larger embrace. Before entering into the possible relationships and contradictions between capitalist drive and political will – between capitalist corporation and political state – it might however be prudent to expand the scope of these active principles to a necessary extent.

f. The political will is not exclusively the preserve of the political state; and nor is the capitalist drive entirely confined (though more so than the political will) to the capitalist corporation. This is obvious. The political state is undoubtedly best placed to exercise a political will over its sphere of influence (the intentional system it is with regard to), but conceivably oppositional and/or supersedent and/or competing political wills can be expressed and perhaps even exercised both from within and from outside that sphere of influence. So, for example, a non-governmental organisation (like an independent watchdog of some sort, or some media organisation, or voluntary social-service formation), or perhaps a political party or alignment which is not within the institutional or associational structures of the political state and aspires to that status, could express oppositional and/or contending political will from within the sphere of influence. On the other hand, international trade or human rights or development organisations, or other stronger (in terms of weapons, or international influence, or wealth, or whatever) political states, could also exercise a political will that may oppose and/or supersede that of a political state. Individuals within or without the polity may express a political will – however limited the effect may be of this – by choosing to cooperate with extant political processes or refusing to, by expressing an opinion with regard to political issues and by trying to disseminate it. But in this study I am concerned primarily with the collective entities.

g. The capitalist drive is evidently more self-contained since it operates with the coincidence of agency and intentional system (both embodied in the capitalist corporation), but clearly this too is not to be understood as entirely so. In saying this I don't mean that the capitalist corporation is necessarily constrained by extrinsic factors – the state of markets, the degree to which different political states and international regulatory bodies control or foster capitalism, the competition faced from other corporations, and so on – the capitalist drive is, of course, always conditional on these, is understood as being so, cannot be understood as otherwise. These extrinsic constraints, in some sense, *define* the discreteness of a capitalist corporation's drive, underline the self-containedness of that, put it into relief and make it apprehensible. The role of these extrinsic factors is therefore *within* the accommodation and construction of the capitalist corporation – that is not the thing I am gesturing towards. What concerns me is that the capitalist drive of a capitalist corporation (or many capitalist corporations) can have political effects outside itself as an intentional system. Insofar as those who own membership of a capitalist corporation are also incorporated in some polity, insofar as productivity of the capitalist corporation would impinge upon the area outside itself (in terms of GNP and GDP, in terms of employment statistics, environmental issues, service issues, educational prerogatives, welfare provision, etc.), a significant political effect is inevitable with the capitalist drive, and the latter would be of interest to those in a position to exert a political will. So, though the capitalist drive is self-contained in a larger sense, and predetermined, and as such accommodative with regard to whatever extrinsic constraints are there, it is not a matter of indifference to the political will and nor can it afford to be indifferent to the political will.

h. Nevertheless, the capitalist drive is not of itself coincidental with political will or vice versa; the explaining–predicting agencies and the intentional systems concerned in these active principles, their intentional impetus, are significantly different. So though neither can be indifferent to the other, they cannot really act as one. Their relationship would have to be negotiated – either as collaborative or as not. There is always a potential for conflict in this relationship – there always simmers the possibility of contradiction in capitalism in this sense – and that really is all that I wanted to point out at this early point of the present discussion.

The above, admittedly self-evident, theoretical qualifications enable a useful point to be made about the scope of political philosophy. Let me go back to my tentative definition of political philosophy at the beginning:

> political philosophy is an attempt at understanding (illuminating, clarifying, elucidating) and conceptualising human communal existence (individuals living together and with an awareness of living together in terms of some notion of collectivity) with a view to conducting this communal existence by certain ostensibly practicable means towards certain apparently determinable ends.

If this is juxtaposed with the particular explaining–predicting-agency-like function of the political state with regard to the people–land–resources under its jurisdiction as an intentional system, a certain clarification of the scope of political philosophy follows. Both the function of the political state and the doing of political philosophy are broadly with regard to the same 'object': understanding human communal existence with a view to conducting this wherever is not too distant from explaining–predicting people–land–resources in an intentional fashion. Ends are not predetermined in either (they have to be determined). In fact, the link is self-evident: the political state *exercises* a political will towards whatever is conceived as a justifiable end with regard to and on behalf of the 'object'; political philosophy *contemplates* what justifiable ends might be and where political will should emanate from and how it should be exercised with regard to the 'object'. In some sense political philosophy underlies the (any) political state – or rather political philosophy underlies any exercise of political will. This is closely connected with the status of any political state, but the scope of political philosophy extends to whatever agency expresses or acts upon a political will. The collective existence that political philosophy concerns itself with may well be that which the political state is concerned with, but it may also be different (some other form of collective identification, perhaps in terms of nationhood, perhaps global, perhaps class or ethnic or gendered collective identification). But political philosophy is ultimately concerned with the possibilities and nuances of political will from wherever. As far as the following discussion goes, political philosophy here is primarily concerned with the contemplation of the political will as this attaches to certain putative political state formations.

The prolonged excursus into the issue of the contradictions of capitalism is now done – and effectively leaves us, I hope, with a *tabula rasa* of some sort with some structural possibilities for the political philosophical contemplation of corporate capitalism in our time.

With the above initial definitions and methodological observations in place it is now possible to take these political philosophical reflections on contemporary corporate capitalism further. The above has drawn a tentative framework from within which corporate capitalism can be approached from the perspective of political philosophy, and has also given some indication of the limitations of such a framework. Briefly, I attempt the following in the proceeding parts:

One, I endeavour to do that which I had considered at the beginning of this part: start from a particular social effect and expand out of that microscopic level to throw a grid over the macrocosmos of corporate capitalism, but with a constant awareness of the possibilities of political philosophy, of the determination to make corporate capitalism (against its grain) subject to political philosophy. In a pre-emptive fashion I may also state here that the social effect which would, I hope, enable a broad political philosophical grid to be thrown over corporate capitalism is *the phenomenon of and discourses surrounding the rise of corporate managerialism*. This might seem like an unlikely point for a political philosophical effort to start from, and a rather trivial vantage point from which to initiate such an encompassing effort. That may be so: but this is a phenomenon which is at the heart of corporate capitalist organisation and is both most likely to allow insights into it as well as most likely to divert attention away from it; it could enlighten an understanding of corporate capitalist processes as easily as it could obfuscate such understanding; and, if nothing else, this phenomenon and appraisals thereof have acquired rich symbolic resonances which are worth exploring. At any rate, it is a familiar entry point that can be exploited without immediately entering a field of theoretical presumptions and abstractions.

Two, after trying to get a political philosophical grip on the condition of contemporary corporate capitalism, I present an analysis of such political philosophical texts as are seen to champion the cause of contemporary corporate capitalism most exultantly. This will entail primarily an examination of a range of philosophical works starting with Popper and Mannheim, and leading up to Hayek, Nozick, and Fukuyama. I argue that in these thinkers and their like, one discerns the construction of an edifice of ideas which is actually anti-political in character.

Part II

Reasons, Causes and Practices in Contemporary Corporate Capitalism

6 Classical Sociology and Managerialism

It is my intention, I have said at the beginning, to make contemporary corporate capitalism subject to the gaze of political philosophy. To that end this part tries to throw a grid over, and thereby trace a picture of, contemporary corporate capitalism. Once such a grid is cast and such a picture begins to emerge the relevance to political ends and means may begin to be considered. In the understanding of a state of affairs which is the grid and the picture, and in the clarifications regarding political means and ends that might follow, the desire to bring contemporary corporate capitalism under the gaze of political philosophy may perhaps be fulfilled. To facilitate the casting of the grid, the tracing of the picture, I need a suitable foothold: a particular social outcome from which the grid could be cast, the tracing of the picture can begin, and then proceed to expand and gradually comprehend the conceptual field of contemporary corporate capitalism. The rise of managerialism in corporate capitalism is that foothold.

Any consideration of the rise of managerialism in the context of contemporary corporate capitalism must, of course, start with an attempt at understanding the function and role of management/managers in capitalist corporations.

In brief, to begin with I argue the following below: *though managers/management appear to hold an indispensable position and are largely understood to have an integral role in corporate capitalist processes – that is, in processes of production and product-dissemination, and the circuit of capital generally – their role and position are not such as they appear to be and are generally understood to be. Managers/management are actually* dissociated *from and have a* negative *presence within such processes. This dissociativeness and negativity may manifest itself in different ways, but the core of the phenomenon is that managers/management are not indispensable or integral to capitalist processes. However, the apparent status of managers/management is carefully maintained because it does serve a very useful purpose (rather than role) within contemporary corporate capitalist* organisation *(though not within the* processes *involved) – to some extent the following is devoted to discerning what this purpose is.*

Before I go on to expand on this thesis there are certain clarifications that I need to make. First of all, I would like it to be understood that what I have to say pertains essentially to the capitalist corporation (of whatever shape and scale and form) and not to public sector organisations, especially those directly answerable to political states, which collaborate in corporate capitalism. This is despite the conflations and superficial overlappings that seem to occur in sociologists', economists' and management-experts' perceptions of capitalist corporations and public sector (including state) organisations. Such perceptions appear to go back to the roots of classical sociology – so that one finds in Durkheim's understanding of the harmonies of labour division (despite the anomic possibilities), for instance, something that cuts across every level of social organisation in a similar fashion, and for that matter every level of biological organisation as well; or one finds in Weber's rationalistic explanations of all corporations (loosely any socially active collectivity) a certain terminological similarity which blurs distinctions. The conflation of the managerial functions and roles which pertain to capitalist corporations and public sector organisations and even the political state itself are now constantly available in popular management guidebooks, newspaper and media features, and economic texts. The political state is often described as a capitalist corporation itself with large capital investments, a workforce and an executive stratum, often acting as trading partner or competitor with regional sectors within its jurisdiction, other political states, and certain capitalist corporations; political states often describe themselves in that fashion too, strive to reflect capitalist corporation-like behaviours, follow capitalist corporation-like accounting procedures, and appoint 'spin-doctors' and 'publicity departments'; the functions which were traditionally understood as being the prerogative of the political state now all too often pass into the hands of capitalist corporations of different sorts; and so on. However, from the perspective of political philosophy such obfuscations and superficial overlappings are unacceptable.

This is simply because, given the rigours of assessing political means and ends, the capitalist corporation and public/state organisations are indelibly differentiated by their different means and ends orientations, in precisely the ways that have been outlined above in considering the differences between capitalist corporations and political states in terms of intentional systems. The ends-orientation of the capitalist corporation (maximising profits) is always a given: and the capitalist corporation therefore acts as its own intentional system interpreter, and acts on itself as an intentional system to fulfil its intended ends. The political state's ends-orientation is open, though the means at its disposal are clear: it therefore acts as the interpreter (a crystallisation) for the people–land–resources it is with regard to as an intentional system, and acts on that intentional system to fulfil what it perceives as the pertinent intentional ends. The capitalist corporation is answerable to nothing but itself; the political state is inevitably answerable to the people–land–resources it is with regard to. Whatever the similarities might be between the economic roles played by certain political states and certain capitalist corporations, whatever the analogous features that might exist between the executive levels of public/state organisation and capitalist corporation, whatever the apparent merging of public and private spheres may suggest, and whatever the systemic correlatives might be, the indelible fact of definitive difference between these formations in terms of intentionality is supersedent. I will revisit this necessary and indelible distinction – not to be erased by any conflation – at suitable points below; for the moment, let it be understood that my observations about the function and role of management/managers are essentially with regard to capitalist corporations.

Second, I should also make it clear here that the following addresses management/managers in a very general sense and without making sufficient distinctions between different types of management or different levels of managers, or without analysing the different kinds of corporation or corporate sectors that these are relevant to. In a sense I am not addressing the function and role of management/managers in any concrete and practical sense at all, rather I am trying to discern these as concepts or ideas that are able to be accommodated or appropriated in a wide range of concrete and practical contexts. In attempting this I am not in fact doing anything that is inconsistent with management discourses that appear in the guise of being 'real-world' and practical; indeed, arguably the management discourses which have proliferated with the rise of contemporary managerialism are often designedly dissociated from the specifics of the types and levels of management involved and of the kinds and sectors of corporations involved – that, in fact, is one of the manifestations of *dissociation* which defines the concept of management as negativity. This is a point that I dwell on at greater length later. However, to some extent this must be self-evident to all who have any interest in this matter: the routinisation of management practice which allows upper level managers to hop across the most diverse enterprises in the most diverse contexts, which allows management consultancy firms to proliferate as a burgeoning and relatively new service industry catering to (any and every) very different corporations, which makes possible popular management textbooks and guidebooks (such as those written by Peter Drucker or Tom Peters) consisting entirely of *ad hoc* prescriptions and aphorisms to be produced and consumed with ever greater frequency, testifies to that dissociation.

And third, what I have to say about managers/management applies only insofar as this involves the activity of management in itself. Many of those involved in management and designated as managers (lower and middle-level managers in corporations) actually devote themselves to management only to a limited extent, and have to be able to combine this in a necessary fashion with technical skills and specific functions which are in fact absolutely integral to capitalist processes, and seminal to the circuit of capital. What I have to say below applies to those who do not have to combine their managerial functions with anything else, who are able to exercise their managerial prerogatives as such and not do much more, who deal with management as such or deal *purely* with management. In general this applies mainly to upper-level managers (directors, CEOs, board members, some division managers in large corporations, etc.). In some instances, the following also applies to middle-level managers *insofar* as they are involved in management as such.

Broadly, the classical sociological formulations of Marx, Durkheim, and Weber were concerned with the transitions involved within a social-historical process from a (necessarily somewhat hypothetical) inchoate simple individual-social condition through to the complex capitalist individual-social condition of their times. A specific consideration of managerialism does not appear for obvious historical reasons till the work of Weber; but the dissociative character of management/managers is foreshadowed in the formulations of Marx and Durkheim in influential ways. At any rate, a precise understanding of various connotations of the dissociative character of management/managers in corporate capitalism is enabled by an understanding of the concept of sociological dissociation itself in the work of Marx and Durkheim. I start therefore with the former.

In the Marxist teleology the initial simple and primitive individual-social condition – the idealised starting point of human civilisation[1] – is a sort of 'natural' existence wherein there is no mismatch between individual interest and communal interest in economic terms, between labour value and the value of produce (since production is only according to use value), between intellectual endeavour and physical–nervous effort (these are unified in the production of use value), between labour and possession (what is produced through labour is possessed by he who labours). Each subsequent step towards increasing degrees of social complexity – primarily through the division of labour, and the consequent stratification of classes, and the formation of class interests and class conflicts – is given as a dissociative step, which breaks up the natural wholeness and balance of the initial simple individual-social condition. In the Marxist teleology each such dissociation is a distortion away from the natural fairness of that simple initial condition where there was no mismatch between labour expended, the value of the produce, and the right of possession. So the first level of complexity wherein the break between intellectual labour and physical labour occurs[2] leads directly to feudal social formations and labour exploitation: now those who do physical labour would have to produce for themselves as well as for those who don't do physical labour, and the latter would necessarily organise society to ensure that this happens, and if possible happens to their advantage. The dissociative distortion involved is highlighted in the feudal serf or slave labour exploitation that almost universally comes about, where the mismatch between labour and possession is absolute (the labourer doesn't even possess himself). The next significant level of complexity (wherein the seeds of capitalism lie) appears at the stage of manufacture,[3] where the process of physical labour is itself broken down into specialised units (and the now specialised labourers are given a wage for their exertions), which in turn enables the intensification of labour and the production of surplus values which are appropriated by a new manufacturing class. Two degrees of dissociation occur here: the dissociation between the labourer and the production-process/product (labour gets fragmented); and the dissociation between labour and possession (the manufacturer appropriates the surplus value and pays the labourer a wage instead).

Both these dissociative steps are also given as distortions from the initial simple condition: the former dissociation causes the alienation of the worker and a kind of industrial pathology; the latter enters a spiral of ever-increasing inequality and exploitation and injustice, which can only get exacerbated as the simpler reproductive processes of manufacture are sucked into the more efficient and intense reproductive processes of industrial capitalism. Further, from the Marxist perspective, each stage of dissociation from an initial simple condition is *measurable* as degrees of distortion in economic terms. The hypothetical initial simple condition had a certain natural equity in it. In the capitalist process the degree of dissociative distortion is marked by the degree of economic mismatch between the value of the goods that are produced by the labour of the worker and the wages that workers get in return: the degree of dissociative distortion is precisely marked by the amount of surplus value that the capitalist appropriates in the process without actually producing any value. All this depends, of course, on the centrality of the labour theory of value in Marxist economics.

I have summarised these already familiar points of the Marxist perspective mainly to accommodate and locate a concept of dissociation through it. It also helps bring out such foreshadowing of management/managers, in terms of dissociation, as is available in Marx's formulations. Before I go on to do so, it is worth noting that the Marxist view of dissociation as distortion from an initial simple condition is largely an ethical matter which needn't attach to the idea of dissociation from other perspectives (Weber's, for instance, which I come to soon).

In the Marxist perspective, a foreshadowing of management/ managers is available in the latter's *association* with the functions of capitalists. It is not therefore management/managers *per se* who are seen in dissociative terms, but they may be thought of as colluding in and exacerbating the dissociative function and role which defines the capitalist for Marx. I have outlined the dissociative character of capitalist processes/the capitalist class/capitalist society already: in the context of the nineteenth-century industrial capitalism that Marx was interested in, management/managers could be thought of as no more than functionaries of capitalists, serving capitalist interests (hence the *association*), and thereby facilitating and indeed exacerbating the distortive dissociativeness of capitalists. This means, in fact, that management/managers do not have a distinctive presence separate from capitalists in Marx's view, but a certain space may be inferred for them in Marx's formulations insofar as they are thought of as performing the functions of capitalists without actually being capitalists or owning capital (in the Marxist framework managers may be, in other words, thought of as capitalists by proxy). The particular dissociative edge which is peculiar to the foreshadowed management/managers in the Marxist perspective is contained in the difference between being a capitalist and being a capitalist by proxy. The *association* (as opposed to *identity*) itself marks a significant distance; association is little more than exaggerated dissociation.

It is possible to infer a foreshadowed presence of the manager in the Marxist framework precisely because Marx doesn't only define the capitalist as one who owns capital and enables capitalist circulation with a view to appropriating surplus value, but also understands the capitalist as one who therefore necessarily undertakes certain functions in productive–distributive–reproductive processes (the circuit of capital), albeit without thereby giving any value to the product. The separation of the capitalist into investor in and valueless contributor to the circuit of capital, means that the capitalist's role can be delegated at least insofar as the latter is concerned. The possibility of delegation – which Marx doesn't dwell on but which is easily available to be inferred – allows the shadowy features of management/managers to emerge. That is the nature of the managers'/management's *association* with capitalists (working as the delegate of the capitalist, being the capitalist by proxy, being the almost selfless functionary who serves the capitalist's interests ...) in the Marxist perspective. In fact, this associative relationship between management/managers and capitalists which can be inferred from Marx's formulations was accepted by early sociologists generally (by Durkheim and Weber too), and given flesh by such social-historical accounts of the early appearance of management/managers as are available, for instance, in Sidney Pollard's or Graeme Salaman's works.[4]

To grasp the manner in which management/managers exacerbate the dissociative distortions of capitalists, all one has to do is go into the details of the valueless contribution that the latter make to the circuit of capital. This Marx deals with at some length in considering the time of circulation as differentiated from the time of production or labour-time, and the costs of circulation in Part I of *Capital, Vol.2*. The time of circulation is understood by Marx as the different sorts of interruptions which necessarily occur in the continuity of the production process: interruptions, for instance, which occur by the time taken up in exchanges (buying and selling), in book-keeping, in storing at various stages of production, in transportation, etc. Marx thinks of these interruptions as necessary in 'advanc[ing] the product, form[ing] a part of its life, a process through which it must pass'.[5] From the management point of view one might significantly add to these interruptions the time taken in coordinating and controlling different forms and divisions of labour (the modern term would be something like 'personnel or human resource management', as opposed to 'financial management', 'sales management', 'publicity management' and other department managements which are entailed in the interruptions that are listed above). Marx's understanding of these interruptions that form the time of circulation of capital, and the costs thereof, can be given in a two-fold fashion. One, that none of this time nor the labour that is represented by this time actually contributes to the value of the product – nor goes towards the creation of surplus value – which is solely dependent on labour time: 'The general law is that *all costs of circulation which arise only from changes in the form of commodities do not add to their value.*'[6] Two, that as the industry grows, and the scale of activities involved in the circuit of capital therefore grows, delegation and managerial specialisation would occur, but that that would make no difference to the general law. Marx's view of this can be gauged from the following specific comment on the increasing scale of buying and selling (this is actually a general observation for all such activities, and is replicated by him for each such activity that he considers):

> To the capitalist who has others working for him, buying and selling becomes a primary function. Since he appropriates the product of many on a large social scale, he must sell it on the same scale and then reconvert it from money into elements of production. Now as before neither the time of purchase nor the sale creates any value. The function of merchant's capital gives rise to an illusion. But without going into this at any length here this much is plain from the start: if by a division of labour a function, unproductive in itself though a necessary element of reproduction, is transformed from an incidental occupation of many into the exclusive occupation of a few, into their special business, the nature of that function itself is not changed. *One* merchant (here considered a mere agent attending to the change

of form of commodities, a mere buyer and seller) may by his operations shorten the time of purchase and sale for *many* producers. In such case he should be regarded as a machine which reduces useless expenditure of energy or helps to set production time free.[7]

It seems to me that the continuity from Marx's understanding of the merchant (a mere agent attending to the change of form of commodities) to the more complex machinery of sales and publicity management of later capitalist corporations is self-evident. It also seems to me that the dissociative possibilities of such specialised managerial functions is hinted at here in the perception that 'the incidental occupation of many' is turned into 'the exclusive occupation of a few'. And, clearly, the purely instrumental understanding of such functionaries ('he should be regarded as a machine') underlines the kind of associative relationship between managers and capitalists that can be inferred from Marx's formulations.

It is also clear here why such specialist instrumentalist management-like roles would exacerbate the dissociative distortion of capitalist processes from a Marxist point of view. Inevitably, the saving of circulation time (which may be translated into freeing up more productive time) would lead to an intensification of the productive process, the greater exploitation of labour, the greater extortion of surplus value, and therefore greater imbalances between the capitalist class as a whole (including the managerial functionaries) and the working class.

That, I believe, gives a sufficient account of the dissociative and distortive role of management/managers from a Marxist perspective, and also introduces sufficiently the classical Marxist sociological understanding of dissociation. Another point of interest here is the manner in which this perspective could lead to possible later conflations of capitalist and particularly managerial functions and the role of the political state in industrial society. This has to do with the Marxist conception of the role of the state *within* the revolutionary agenda. The Marxist understanding of the given liberal political state as colluding with capitalist processes has been delineated in the previous part; it was observed there that though Marx had only incidental remarks to offer on this (though enough to infer his reservations about the function of the state) it was Engels and Lenin who had, in the first instance, drawn the implications out clearly. The observations of the former about the function of the state, not just in capitalist society, but within the teleological conception of the unfolding of social processes leading up to revolution and eventual socialism itself, are of interest here. In *Anti-Dühring* Engels declares:

> The modern state, no matter what its form, is essentially a capitalist machine, the state of the capitalists, the ideal personification of the total national capital. The more it proceeds to the taking over of the productive forces, the more does it naturally become the national capitalist, the more citizens does it exploit. The workers remain wage-workers – proletarians.[8]

And he goes on to say:

> As soon as there is no longer any social class to be held in subjection; as soon as class rule, and the individual struggle for existence based upon our present anarchy in production, with the collisions and excesses arising from these, are removed, nothing more remains to be repressed, and a special repressive force, a state, is no longer necessary. The first act by virtue of which the state really constitutes itself the representative of the whole of society – the taking possession of the means of production in the name of society – this is, at the same time, its last independent act as a state. State interference in social relations becomes, in one domain after another, superfluous, and then withers away of itself; the government of persons is replaced by the administration of things, and by the conduct of process of production.[9]

In other words, Engels envisages the state as gradually taking over productive processes first within capitalist society itself, and second in a post-revolutionary situation. The first takeover, according to Engels, would occur as productive processes grow larger and larger in scope and intensity so that these would exceed the control of individual or even specific collectives of capitalists (he actually disregards the possibility of independent large corporations here) and thereby pass into the control of the capitalist state itself. The dissociative specialised controlling functions that managers increasingly play as capitalist processes grow – and which could logically lead to the rise of managerialism eventually – are thereby diverted in the Engelsian conception towards state control (it is at any rate primarily a matter of control). This, it seems to me, sets the stage for the conflation of managerialism with state-like governance and prepares the way for the creation of conflationary discourses, if not for the realisation of Engels's prophecy. Interestingly, in the revolutionary situation too Engels envisages a similar takeover of productive processes by the state, but in this case this act itself leads to the projected dissolution of the state, since in a classless society there would be no need for control and therefore no effective function for the manager state. The idea that the state will wither away clearly derives from the notion that dissociative capitalist control – exerted as a specialist form through managerialism – would cease to be necessary once the class conflict between capitalists and workers is removed. In a sense, this simply underlines again the dissociative conception of management/managers as providing a valueless function in capitalist productive processes.

The weaknesses and idealistic misconceptions involved in Engels's inferences from Marx are self-evident – I don't need to dwell on them here. The point, though, is that these ideas enable a conflationary terminology to develop with regard to managerial functions and state functions. These conflationary terms are seen to recur in Durkheim's and Weber's works.

Finally, on the Marxist conception of management/managers, the objections that can be raised are also, I feel, self-evident. Chief amongst these is undoubtedly the argument that the *measure of dissociativeness* of the capitalist and his managerial functionaries from the productive processes that Marx provides, that which actually enables the functions of capitalists and functionaries within the productive process to be viewed as valueless – in terms of the labour theory of value – can be and largely has now been eschewed. If a utility view of value is assumed, this understanding of dissociativeness can be dispensed with. Given the utility view of value, the contributions of capitalists, managers, and workers become united into a more cohesive corporative value-contribution, and the specific values attached to various layers within corporations come to be determined by other factors (market forces, responsibilities, education, etc.) – something I go into at greater length later. However, any disregard for the Marxist measures of dissociativeness does not necessarily detract from the Marxist understanding of dissociativeness from an initial simple social condition.

It is well known that Durkheim's reflections in *The Division of Labour in Society* seem to undermine the Marxist understanding of dissociativeness from an initial simple social condition (though Durkheim's ideas are directed more straightforwardly towards Herbert Spencer). This fact renders the inferences that can be made from his reflections about the position of managers/management, especially in the consideration of social anomie in capitalist societies, all the more interesting – mainly because it provides a quite different dissociative thesis from the Marxist one. Durkheim's main asseveration is that division of labour should not be viewed as a series of dissociations from an initial simple condition, but as an organic, harmonising and necessary (evolutionarily) development in complex and developed societies, which should be seen as essentially differently constituted from simple societies. Actually, it is arguable that Durkheim's arguments in this area do not actually undermine the Marxist position at all, since they come from a quite different direction. Where the Marxist position derives from a materialistic analysis of the nature of labour (and his view of dissociativeness attaches primarily to that), Durkheim draws his inferences from certain generalisations about judicial systems and developments therein. The disparities and overlappings that are available in Marx's and Durkheim's methodologies and lead to such contradictory positions about a similar area is a tempting academic enterprise which I won't go into here;[10] it seems quite possible that closer comparative examination would show that Marx and Durkheim were talking about quite different social phenomena in addressing division of labour, despite obvious superficial similarities. At any rate, Durkheim's analysis of more cohesive simple societies depends on an examination of the predominantly *restrictive* judicial dictates which prevail in them, and of more complex societies with division of labour, on the increasingly *restitutive* judicial systems which appear in them. The predominantly repressive judicial systems indicate for Durkheim simple societies that are bound by *mechanical solidarity*:

> What justifies this term [mechanical solidarity] is that the link which thus unites the individual to society is wholly analogous to that which attaches a thing to a person. The individual conscience, considered in this light, is a simple dependent upon the collective type and follows all of its movements, as the possessed object follows those of its owner. In societies where this type of solidarity is highly developed, the individual does not appear [...]. Individuality is something which the society possesses.

Thus, in these social types, personal rights are not yet distinguished from real rights;[11]

whereas complex societies with division of labour are bound by *organic solidarity* (and enforced by *contractual solidarity*, which I don't go into here):

Whereas [mechanical solidarity] implies that individuals resemble one another, [organic solidarity] presumes their difference. The first is possible only in so far as the individual personality is absorbed into the collective personality; the second is possible only if each one has a sphere of action which is peculiar to him; that is a personality. It is necessary, then, that the collective conscience leave open a small part of the individual conscience in order that special functions may be established there, functions which it cannot regulate. The more this region is extended, the stronger is the cohesion which results from this solidarity [...]. Society becomes more capable of collective movement, at the same time that each of its elements has more freedom of movement. The solidarity resembles that which we observe among higher animals. Each organ, in effect, has its special physiognomy, its autonomy.[12]

At a slightly later stage, the moral conviction with which Durkheim ultimately asserts his notion of division of labour as an organic harmonising social condition becomes clearer, when he argues that '[i]t is the need of happiness which would urge the individual to specialise more and more'[13] (an argument from which his famous thesis on suicide germinates).

The moralism embedded in Durkheim's ostensibly scientific sociological argument, constantly appealing, as it seems to do, to empirical evidence in the laboratory of society, is a matter of some importance. An obvious observation that follows from the above argument about essentially different simple and complex social conditions is that it presents a certain automatism in the development of social systems. The idea seems to be that social systems are reflections of certain existing states of affairs, and respond to changes within these states of affairs, which come to exist automatically or spontaneously – *automatically* in the sense that they do not exist and change as a result of human agencies and determinations. Human agency and determination are conditional on and contained within the automatic states of affairs and changes that simply occur, that just come about through some grand natural process. Thus judicial systems are merely attempts by different societies to come to terms with (rather than determine out of necessity or interest in the Marxist sense) their state of development. Individuals do not reach collective decisions and determine their social processes; social processes unfold in an automatic biological fashion and individuals find status and eventually happiness by fitting in. Fitting in with the given state of social affairs, in short, is the path to happiness and moral fulfilment – it answers the larger natural automatic movement of society from simpler states to complex organic structures. Durkheim's sociological morality follows from this, and is in sharp contrast with Marx's: in brief, Durkheim's morality leads to quiescence (the need to fit in with a given state of affairs which has come to exist in consonance with natural processes) while the Marxist morality leads to revolutionary conceptions (the need to question and change a given state of affairs which has come to exist logically enough, but by human determination, and has distorted an irretrievable natural condition).

Durkheim's view of anomie – especially the anomie of capitalist society, which consists in the conflict between capitalists and workers – needs to be understood in terms of the larger moral commitments involved. Marco Orrù's study of the history and meanings of anomie brings out rather neatly the morality implicit in Durkheim's view of anomie by comparing it with Jean-Marie Guyau's (which, Orrù suggests, was probably taken by Durkheim from *L'Irréligion de l'avenir*, 1887):

> Guyau builds his concept of anomie on the immanantistic tradition, which argues that the moral codes governing human behaviour are not transcendental, but are situational and embedded in individual relationships. Durkheim on the contrary claims that moral codes constrain individual relationships and are external to them. In both cases the concept of anomie is linked to the author's philosophical interpretation of morality. Guyau is straightforward in this regard, but Durkheim, pulling the cover of science over his work, is less open about the historical antecedents and philosophical implications of his ethical theory.[14]

Durkheim's view of anomie in capitalist society therefore is not with regard to the capitalist system itself. The capitalist system in itself is for Durkheim a kind of embodiment of organic and contractual solidarities, where divided labour can be harmonised to the fullest extent. It reveals anomic tendencies in the form of class conflict and labour dissatisfaction only as a distortion from itself (comparable, in some sense, to that other modern anomie that is mentioned, the professionalisation or specialisation of criminal and anti-social activity)[15] – a pathological form. The cure for the disease, Durkheim predictably concludes, lies in *strengthening* the capitalist system itself; by developing better defined regulatory systems, contractual provisions, judicial prerogatives, leadership criteria, etc., which would enable the capitalist system to fulfil its organic potential. Or, in other words, by clarifying an area of regulation and control which in contemporary terms would easily be identified with managerial roles and functions.

Just as the anomie of capitalist society is, for Durkheim, a kind of moral disorder which distorts its implicit goodness, the managerial provision which would enable its correction is also essentially moral in character. It should immediately be noted that this moral managerial *pharmakon* is therefore not seen as answerable to anything that definitively makes capitalism understandable as capitalism (the maximisation of profits, the use of labour, the relation to markets, etc.). These are unimportant because, for Durkheim, that is the way this complex society has come spontaneously and automatically to be, has naturally evolved to be, and is therefore almost biologically inevitable and morally acceptable. It is to this larger sense of accommodating to the given order of things, of ensuring that the best be made of an already good state of affairs, of ensuring quiescence and predetermined or automatically determined moral rectitude, that the managerial function that strengthens the capitalist system is answerable. This view encapsulates Durkheim's dissociative sociological understanding of management/managers: *for Durkheim managerial functions and roles which are with relation to the capitalist system are actually dissociated from that which allows that system to be understood as such, and associated with a larger anomalous moral conception.* Logically enough, this also allows for Durkheim's peculiar brand of conflationary discourse that bring managerial functions and roles and state governance together: both become equally answerable to that moral order in a similar way.

So Durkheim suggests that to a large extent the anomie of capitalist society can be resolved by clarifying the juridical (regulatory and contractual) framework pertinent to it:

> Today, there are no longer any rules which fix the number of economic enterprises, and, in each branch of industry, production is not exactly regulated on a level with consumption. We do not wish to draw any practical conclusion from this fact; we are not contending that restrictive legislation is necessary; we do not here have to weigh its advantages and disadvantages. What is certain is that this lack of regulation does not permit a regular harmony of functions. The economists claim, it is true, that this harmony is self-established when necessary, thanks to rises or declines in prices which, according to needs, stimulate or slacken production. But, in every case, this is established only after ruptures of equilibrium and more or less prolonged disturbances. Moreover, these disturbances are naturally as much more frequent as functions are more specialised, for the more complex an organisation is, the more is the need of extensive regulation felt.[16]

The existence of such a juridical framework is obviously the legislative prerogative of the state, and Durkheim (following Comte) naturally sees the state as playing a significant role in controlling such social anomie as might arise in a capitalist society.[17] He acknowledges that the state cannot be the exclusive agent responsible for maintaining harmony, and that this must to some degree be a matter of general social consensus:

> The government cannot, at every instant, regulate the conditions of the different economic markets, fixing the prices of their commodities and services, or keeping production within the bounds of consumptionary needs, etc. [...] What gives unity to organised societies, however, as to all organisms, is the spontaneous consensus of parts.[18]

However, given Durkheim's view of the distance of the state from the collectivity, while expressing the collectivity in a crystallised fashion (as discussed in the previous part), it is up to the state to determine whether such consensus exists, and to act upon it. So the state becomes the main agent for ensuring that the given moral order of division of labour acquires the stability and harmony which it implicitly reaches towards. It is clear that the state's responsibility is to the reification of the harmony that is implicitly available, rather than to the maximisation of capitalist productivity in its own systemic terms.

For Durkheim, managerial functions and roles have broadly the same commitment as the state's (to ensure a larger social harmony), and work in a complementary fashion. The former are concerned more directly with a different level of anomie in capitalist society; not the primary one of the conflict between capitalists and workers but the distinct one (at least Durkheim, unlike Marx, sees this as distinct) of the alienation of the worker:

> It often happens in a commercial, industrial, or other enterprise that functions are distributed in such a way that they do not offer sufficient material for individual activity. There is evidently a deplorable loss of effort in that, but we need not trouble ourselves with the economic aspects of the situation. [...] It is well known that in a business where each employee is not sufficiently occupied movements are badly adjusted to one another, operations are carried on without any unity; in short solidarity breaks down, incoherence and disorder make their appearance. [...] Thus, there are cases where the division of labour, pushed very far, produces a very imperfect integration. [...] For the evil to disappear, it is not enough that there be regulative action, but this must be employed in a certain way. We are well aware of the way in which it should be used. The first care of an intelligent, scientific chief will be to suppress useless tasks, to distribute work in such a way that each one will be sufficiently occupied, and, consequently to increase the functional activity of each worker. Thus, order will be achieved at the same time that work is more economically managed.[19]

Durkheim's remedy for the alienation of the worker is to have effective management which would make the worker work in a more integrated fashion (or crudely, to work more and more productively). Management would provide 'intelligent, scientific' leadership to that end (terms that have occupied management discourses continuously since). Workers are viewed simply as specialised organs within division of labour, without any determinative point of view, giving free time to whom would only exacerbate disturbances. Most importantly, the reason why management would undertake this responsibility is not economic (Durkheim pointedly leaves 'economic aspects of the situation' aside) but the larger moral commitment to maintaining the harmony which should come with division of labour – so as to complement the state's efforts in the same direction by providing suitable regulatory frameworks.

In short, Durkheim effectively conflates the role of the state with managers/management, and dissociates the functions and roles of managers/management from the capitalist process itself.

Whereas the sphere of managers/management is implicit and somewhat incidental in the formulations of Marx and Durkheim, in Weber's work it is necessarily explicit and rather more central; and the different kinds of (almost contrary) dissociativeness that can be inferred in the former seem to come to some sort of synthesis in the latter. I suppose Durkheim's sense of harmony in division of labour does underlie the overarching rationalities that Weber is able to discern in (especially capitalist) social and economic organisation, and yet the slippages that Weber is also able to perceive within the overarching rationalities (again especially capitalist) are also reminiscent of Marx's sense of distortion and alienation in division of labour. From the interstices of rationalities, at any rate, emerges Weber's peculiar view of management, and a rather distinct – indeed a comprehensive – understanding of its dissociativeness from the processes of capitalist production and circulation.

Weber is understandably a standard reference point in books by and for managers, and in academic books on management studies and the sociology of management. Interestingly, such books focus almost exclusively on those aspects of Weber's work which in fact hide his dissociative understanding of managers/management;[20] mainly, therefore, they dwell on his notions about leadership and bureaucracy, especially the latter. Both these allow for formulations about the conduct and functioning of organisations which, though not indifferent to the nature of the organisations they are with regard to, are more or less irrespective of those organisations. So, for instance, when Weber formulates what he considers to be the three kinds of legitimate authority[21] – the rational, the traditional, the charismatic – this formulation in itself seems to have a non-contextual and general validity; it is only when Weber accommodates these formulations to specific kinds of social organisations at specific periods of development that they seem to become contextually definite and complex. Similarly, when Weber lays down the broad characteristics of modern bureaucracy[22] these also seem to have a general and non-contextual (except for the characterisation as 'modern') air, though in fact in elaboration within specific organisational structures this general understanding devolves into definite and different forms. What I am getting at, in brief, is that Durkheim's terms generally have a dual edge to them: on the one hand they seem to work in a very general and accommodative fashion (the broad concept of authority, bureaucracy, etc.), and on the other hand a certain number of definite and concrete forms shoulder each other uneasily within each of these terms (specific different forms of authority, specific different kinds of bureaucracy, etc.).

This dual-edgedness of Weber's terminology allows concepts like authority and bureaucracy to be used in a loose and fluid fashion, and it seems to me that this is exploited fully in management texts and discourses. By that I mean that Weber's terms are often appropriated in management texts and discourses to emphasise the general non-contextual accommodative air – to allow management to be conflated with other discourses – to render the view of managers/management a bit hazy and somehow larger than it actually is. This enables, in fact, precisely the kind of conflations that Marx and Durkheim had left open: managerial bureaucracy and managerial authority get invested with a general efficacy irrespective of the kind of organisation they might be with regard to. The activities of management/managers in capitalist corporations and the activities of the state (indeed of different kinds of states) in the modern world seem to be part of the same phenomenon, appear to be systemically similar and operate similarly to roughly similar ends. In this conflationary build-up the distinctions that Weber did in fact carefully make get pushed into the background, as does Weber's understanding of the dissociativeness of managers/management in the capitalist corporation. In fact, even in his observations on modern bureaucracy Weber's distinction between bureaucracy of state and of capitalist corporation is worth noting (though this is presented in a rather glib and offhand fashion, and more or less forgotten as he goes on to describe bureaucracy in a more undiscriminating and general fashion again):

> In the sphere of the state [the] three elements [which describe jurisdictional areas] constitute a bureaucratic *agency*, in the sphere of the private economy they constitute a bureaucratic *enterprise*.

> Bureaucracy, thus understood, is fully developed in political and ecclesiastical communities only in the modern state, and in the private economy only in the most advanced institutions of capitalism.[23]

The distinction between bureaucratic *agency* (state) and bureaucratic *enterprise* (capitalist institution) marks, it seems to me, precisely the sort of difference between state and capitalist corporation in terms of intentional systems discussed previously. The agency certainly represents the interests of something other than itself or larger than itself, while the enterprise has mainly its own interests at heart. This is a distinction that Weber makes lucidly enough: the *description* of bureaucratic structure that might cut across both these spheres (and which Weber decides to unravel in his reflections on bureaucracy) does not detract from the *functional* differences between bureaucracies pertinent to different spheres (even if similarly structured). A focus on the descriptive aspect, though, may allow the latter to be overlooked: especially since, within the reflections on bureaucracy, Weber didn't focus on the functional differences. The reason he didn't do so was because by that stage of his reflections these functional differences and their implications were already clear; the issue of functional differences had been sorted out already in his consideration of the conditions of rationality that are involved. It seems to me therefore that in considering Weber's view of managers/management the reflections on bureaucracy shouldn't be overdetermined (nor on authority, for that matter); pertinent observations – including those about the dissociative status of managers/management – are available in the consideration of conditions of rationality in social organisation. It is to this that I therefore turn.

The distinction between formal rationality and substantive rationality in economic action sets the criteria that allow the later distinction between bureaucratic agency and bureaucratic enterprise to be rendered self-evident.

> The term 'formal rationality of economic action' will be used to designate the extent of quantitative calculation or accounting which is technically possible and which is actually applied. The 'substantive rationality', on the other hand, is the degree to which the provisioning of given groups of persons (no matter how delimited) with goods is shaped by economically oriented social action under some criterion (past, present, or potential) of

ultimate values (*wertende Postulate*), regardless of the nature of these ends.[24]

In the comments on these definitions Weber adds the following:

2. A system of economic activity will be called 'formally' rational according to the degree in which the provision for needs, which is essential in every rational economy, is capable of being expressed in numerical, calculable terms, and is so expressed. In the first instance, it is quite independent of the technical form these calculations take, particularly where estimates are expressed in money or in kind. The concept is thus unambiguous, at least in the sense that expression in money terms yields the highest degree of formal calculability. [...]

3. The concept of 'substantive rationality,' on the other hand, is full of ambiguities. It conveys only one element common to all 'substantive' analyses: namely, that they do not restrict themselves to note the purely formal and (relatively) unambiguous fact that action is based on 'goal-oriented' rational calculation with the technically most adequate available methods, but apply certain criteria of ultimate ends, whether they be ethical, political, utilitarian, hedonistic, feudal (*ständisch*), egalitarian, or whatever, and measure the results of the economic action, however formally 'rational' in the sense of correct calculation they may be, against the scales of 'value rationality' or '*substantive* goal rationality'.[25]

These definitions are confusing if they are taken (as they are apparently presented) to be context-free and general; in fact the definitions – and especially the distinctions between the two kinds of economic rationality – cannot be clear unless one has a pre-emptive understanding of capitalist processes. Briefly, Weber points towards the differences between economic activity which is indifferent to ideology and that which is ideology-led. It is difficult to see how any kind of economic activity can be ideology-free except as a purely descriptive act with regard to an existing state of affairs – a descriptive act without any ambition of changing that state of affairs in any particular or calculable direction. The determination of any direction would exceed the descriptive prerogative of the economic act and would necessarily become available to ideological, or substantive, considerations. Weber's understanding of formal rationality is, in fact, largely a matter of a system in which the provision of needs 'is capable of being *expressed* in numerical, calculable *terms*, and is so *expressed*', is involved with '*expression* in money [or kind] *terms*'; this is plainly a mode of expression which depends on a certain terminology. But in that sense the 'formal rationality of economic action' is hardly contributory to *action* in itself; it is no more than a rigorous but passive expression that precedes, and can be used in determining, action in terms of some substantive reasoning. Weber seems to recognise this implication of his definitions too, in that substantial rationality is seen to 'apply certain criteria of ultimate ends' and is used after the formally rational calculations are noted. But this recognition is immediately obscured by the insistence on 'ultimate ends' (why must substantive rationality be slave to 'ultimate ends' instead of 'immediate ends' or 'pragmatic ends' or 'conditional ends'?), and by asserting that the results of formally rational economic action are measured '*against* the scale' of substantive rationality (the notable opposition that Weber sees between formal and substantive rationality here suggests that two different kinds of economic action are involved, but how is that possible if formal rationality is no more than rigorous description?). Weber's definitions, in fact, go off in two different directions: formal rationality could be that passive element which, when complemented by substantive rationality, produces the possibility of certain economic actions; or formal rationality and substantive rationality could be the bases of different sorts of (often contradictory) economic action. The first of these directions seems to provide a clearer understanding of Weber's definitions in themselves (quoted above), but it is abundantly clear that Weber himself favours the second. His reasons for doing so become clear when one realises that these definitions are in fact given (somewhat mendaciously) with certain preconceptions regarding capitalism in mind; that these definitions make more sense when read retrospectively, after going into Weber's view of capital accounting. By doing this one gets some insights into his conceptual framework (perhaps against the grain of his own presentation thereof), and from that emerges the dissociativeness of his concept of managers/management.

Weber's formulations about sociological categories of economic action is driven by the recognition that capitalism *makes a claim* to working in terms of higher degrees of formal rationality, and therefore to being more strictly rational than other modes of economic organisation and functioning. It is clear from the manner in which Weber presents formal rationality as an independent basis of economic action that he is inclined to accept that claim. For Weber, at the heart of capitalist processes (profit making processes) is capital accounting, defined as follows:

> Capital accounting is the valuation and verification of opportunities for profit and of the success of profit-making activity by means of a valuation of the total assets (goods and money) of the enterprise at the beginning of a profit-making venture, and of the comparison of this with a similar valuation of assets still present and newly acquired, at the end of the process; in the case of a profit-making organisation operating continuously, the same is done for an accounting period.[26]

Capital accounting is, of course, not a capitalist process in itself: it involves none of the activity whereby the circulation of capital and the translation into means of production and products and the generation of profits occurs. Capitalist accounting is that which allows capitalist processes to be expressed in formally rational terms, which gives a rationale to that process even while carefully excluding all substantive factors which are necessarily involved therein; capital accounting, in other words, is that medium through which capitalism *makes its claim* to being strictly rational, while at the same time conveniently sidestepping or deliberately overlooking substantive considerations. But capital accounting does no more than make a claim, and Weber's definition doesn't suggest that it does (though he also certainly thinks the claim is a good one); and it is certainly not a claim that he himself makes. On the contrary, even while noting the claim and examining its implications in detail, and even while admiring the whole system that emerges thereby, he is careful to look behind the claim, to try to find the substantive conditions which underlie the ostensible and apparently encompassing formal rationality.

> The extraordinary importance of the highest possible degree of calculability as the basis for efficient capital accounting will be noted time and again throughout the discussion of the sociological conditions of economic activity. It is far from the case that only economic factors are important to it. On the contrary, it will be shown that the most varied sorts of external and subjective barriers account for the fact that capital accounting has arisen as a basic form of economic calculation only in the Western World.[27]

Charting the substantive and extra-economic (in a formally rational sense) conditions in the rise of capitalism had been the substance of *The Protestant Ethic and the Spirit of Capitalism*,[28] and is arguably the main concern (that which makes his work sociological) of *Economy and Society* too. In the latter, those extra-economic substantive conditions that lie carefully concealed or wilfully suppressed behind the rigours of formal rationality are carefully brought out while the power of formal rationality is acknowledged. The understanding that 'Capital accounting in its formally most rational shape [...] presupposes the *battle of man with man*',[29] itself, it seems to me, airs the substantiveness implicit in that presupposition. The observation that the preoccupation with profit that drives formal rationality is determinedly separate from the sphere of private affairs[30] (indubitably a matter of substantive interest) inevitably leaves one wondering how the chief beneficiaries of such profit once reinvestment is done – whoever they might be – occur in formally rational calculations. Weber devotes a whole section to listing the substantive conditions of formal rationality in a market economy: the most interesting observation here is that formally rational accounting reaches its zenith when there are substantive conditions which allow a 'thorough market freedom' and are associated with 'shop discipline' or 'a system of domination'.[31] That is another way of saying that formally rational capital accounting is effectively that which impels the establishment of these substantive conditions as much as deriving from their possibility, and it does these without acknowledging any substantive ambition.

In short, what Weber's formulations about the different levels of rationality in capital accounting show (possibly despite himself) is the following: *while capitalism seems to be primarily concerned with formally rational calculation geared toward profit without regard for substantive values and reasons, and while this discourse (because that is what it essentially is, a mode of expression) is persuasive and powerful, there is no denying that substantive considerations in fact surround efforts at formal rationalism. Formal rationalism in fact dissociates and overdetermines economic calculability at the expense of substantive considerations in presenting capitalist processes (and thereby forms a claim of superior or pure rationalism by capitalism), whereas capitalist processes are actually complex social–economic matters in which substantive values and reasons and formally rational expression are mutually dependent and linked. Becoming subject to the indications and suggestions of formally rational understandings of capitalist processes – becoming a functionary of the ostensibly formally rational discourse of capitalist processes without acknowledging substantive values – would effectively dissociate one from the total complexity (the reality) of the social–economic process. But such a dissociation itself allows a certain position of control over those processes, because such a functionary would always be supported by the persuasiveness and apparent self-containedness of formal rationality, by its unambiguous rational assertion.*

Those last two sentences do not strictly belong there – I am beginning to anticipate myself – but the point is that Weber's view of managers/management derives from the above.

It is in the course of making these observations about formally rational capital accounting and unravelling the substantive conditions that are presupposed therein that Weber enters his consideration of the role of workers (labour) and managers/management. These are, for Weber, more or less mutually defined: 'Human services for economic purposes may be distinguished as (a) "managerial", or (b) oriented to the instructions of a managerial agency.'[32] In fact, Weber does not actually define managerial functions since (as he goes on to demonstrate) these have varied connotations depending on the mode of organisation that prevails. Provisionally though, Weber may be thought of as presenting managerial functions as those which pertain to the issuing of instructions for workers with a view to providing accounts for the relevant budgetary unit, so as to fulfil the accounting needs according to whatever mode of rationality (formal or substantive) is considered desirable for that budgetary unit. This gives managerial functions a rather wide range, and the precise nature of what such functions consist in would depend on which agent in the economic process appropriates managerial functions.[33] The fact that organisational rationales determine managerial functions; the fluidity of management whereby it has to be understood according to who appropriates it (worker, owner, commune or guild, family); the fact that management seems to have no intrinsic place in economic processes but appears according to whose interests it is exercised in – all these already indicate some of the dissociativeness of Weber's conception of management/managers. What becomes clear as Weber goes further into the nuances of capital accounting is that this is where management/managers become most dissociatively and abrasively visible. When managerial functions become conditional on profit-making capitalist organisations, then managerial functions become primarily a matter of formally rational accounting. In becoming the pure functionaries of formally rational accounting, management/managers commit themselves to denying the substantive conditions which necessarily underlie such organisation; they become therefore potentially subject to substantive irrationality. The kinds of substantive irrationality that capitalist management/managers necessarily give way to to maintain formal rationality becomes a measure of their dissociativeness within capitalist economic processes – potentially from both workers and owners. So, on the one hand, the dissociativeness of management/ managers is seen in the substantive irrationality of expropriating workers from the means of production and making them subject to the domination of entrepreneurs to meet the demands of formal rationality: 'The fact that the maximum of *formal* rationality in capital accounting is possible only where the workers are subjected to the domination of entrepreneurs, is a [...] specific element of *substantive* irrationality in the modern economic order.'[34] And, on the other hand, the dissociativeness of management/managers is seen in the potential for serving 'outside interests' at the expense of owner interests that could also arise from the single-minded devotion to formal capital accounting. This is particularly likely to occur where there comes to exist a

separation of managerial functions from appropriated ownership, especially through the limitations of the functions of owners to the appointment of management and through shared free (that is, alienable) appropriation of the enterprise as expressed in shares of the nominal capital (stocks, mining shares). This state, that is related to the purely personal form of appropriation through various types of intermediate forms, is rational in the *formal* sense that it permits [...] the selection for managerial posts of the persons best qualified from the point of view of profitability. But in practice it may mean a number of things, such as: That control over the managerial position may come, through appropriation, into the hands of 'outside interests' representing the resources of a budgetary unit, or mere wealth [...], and seeking above all a high rate of income; or that control over the managerial position comes, through temporary stock acquisitions, into the hands of speculative 'outside interests' seeking gains only through the resale of their shares; or that disposition over the managerial position comes into the hands of outside business interests, by virtue of power over markets or over credit, such as banks or 'financiers,' which may pursue their own business interests, often foreign to the organization as such.

[...]

The fact that such 'outside' interests can affect the mode of control over managerial positions, even and especially when the highest degree of *formal* rationality in their selection is attained, constitutes a further element of *substantive* irrationality specific to the modern economic order.[35]

On the whole it is accurate to say that Weber's perceptions of substantive weaknesses in capitalist economic organisation arise largely through the dissociative position that management/managers occupy as functionaries of formal rationality in capital accounting.

7 Management Discourses

I have laid out the classical sociological positions apropos managerialism in some detail for the following reasons:

a. to demonstrate that there is a certain likeness in perceptions of the dissociative function of management/managers in quite different, even contradictory, sociological traditions – whether in accordance with an association with capitalist interests and a contribution to the circulation of capital in Marxist terms, or in the moral teleology of Durkheim's view of societal evolution, or in the rational systems-oriented approach of Weber, the peculiar dissociativeness of management/managers inevitably keeps coming up;

b. because the sociological approach provides a sort of macroscopic view of the rise of managerialism, and the specific role of management/managers, which is relevant to a political philosophical apprehension of the matter;

c. more specifically, because this sort of macroscopic view allows a clearer understanding of the increasingly unwieldy area of corporate capitalist management discourses which now hold sway (where management discourses, for my present purposes, are such as are produced by managers for managers and in the interest of managers) – I intend to turn to these briefly now;

d. and because, to grasp the workings of contemporary corporate capitalism (especially in terms of the social phenomenon of the rise of managerialism) it is necessary to chart the departures from and connections to such classical sociological positions.

Corporate capitalist management discourses, as I have called them above, are concerned primarily with the pragmatics of management practice: in specific corporate sectors (industrial, services, information technology and communications, etc.), or with relation to specific sorts of managerial functions (accounting, personnel, publicity, departmental or enterprise-wide, lower or middle or upper or boardroom, etc.), or with regard to certain broad categories of corporations (private or public, large or medium or small, buoyant or crisis-ridden, multinational or regional, etc.), or with regard to specific corporate zones (usually according to demography or nationality – thus, Japanese management received a prodigious amount of attention in the eighties), or with regard to specific management styles (authoritarian or devolutionary, top-down or consultative, traditional or innovative, etc.), or according to issues that determine management styles and practices (leadership qualities, educational requirements, corporate and organisational structures and psychology, remuneration, etc.). Management discourses are therefore primarily concerned with the microscopic or, at any rate, the pragmatic, and are generally ostensibly uninterested in macroscopic views that do not necessarily impinge upon this. Another way of looking at that might be to think of management discourses as conditional on the kind of intentional system that they *must* serve, that is, the capitalist corporation with a predetermined ends-orientation of profit making. Management discourses have to enable the ends-orientation of the capitalist corporation. Macroscopic views of managerialism on the other hand are usually sociological (concerned with the broad descriptive act) or political (roughly falling in with the intentional system that the state is with regard to) – these are clarifications which derive from Part I.

The point about the different approaches of microscopic management discourses and the macroscopic view that encapsulates managerialism is made neatly by John Kaler in an article on 'Positioning Business Ethics in Relation to Management and Political Philosophy'. The anomalous area of business ethics seems to impinge with equal effect on management discourses and sociological and philosophical concerns, except that, as Kaler rightly observes, it is approached quite differently and often at cross-purposes in each.[1] The differences arise precisely due to the kind of predetermined ends-orientation of management discourses and the lack thereof in sociological discourses or the different intentionalities in political discourses. What is interesting about Kaler's article is his demonstration that the apparent differences between these are not as material as they might appear to be, that in fact the microscopic managerial view and the macroscopic political view overlap and impinge on each other in significant ways.[2] I do not go into the details of Kaler's argument at the moment, and merely assert that to some extent I am guided by some such expectation. It certainly seems to me that a political philosophical perspective cannot disregard corporate capitalist management discourses because in fact a systematic examination of some of these does throw up an implicit political philosophical position, and these discourses are arguably designed to convey (somewhat insidiously) or sell such a position. It is because I hope to demonstrate how this occurs and to what effect that I do not undertake a specific argument along Kaler's line.

The kind of management discourses that I address below are in fact those which are not too microscopic or single-mindedly pragmatic in approach; the kind which, while paying full attention to the microscopic issues and pragmatic needs of management/managers, attempt to convey a sense of managerialism at large, as a matter of greater social and cultural efficacy than might be immediately evident. This is usually done in the interests of managers, for it undoubtedly serves managers well to be thought of as supremely important in every respect. It serves the managerial body as a whole well as this self-proclaimed importance gets reflected in the widely held belief that management is something that is not contained in specific capitalist sectors but cuts across all sectors of capitalist corporations – best exemplified, it seems to me, in the enormous growth of management consultancies which are not sector-specific or sector-defined – and indeed every element of capitalist society at large. The kinds of management discourse with an implicit political philosophy that I have in mind have clearly carved out a substantial niche in the book market, regularly becoming bestsellers and establishing the reputations of management 'gurus' (that term of common usage is itself indicative of the kind of almost oracular and broad worldly – perhaps even unworldly – wisdom that proponents of managerialism credit themselves with). Without running through management book production and sales statistics, the place that management discourses have come to hold in the book market, and the perception of management 'gurus' that is widely entertained and promoted, can be gauged by contemplating such revealing facts as that the former CEO of General Electric, Jack Welch, has recently secured a $7.1 million deal to write his autobiography.[3] At any rate, to get back to the point, examples of the kind of management discourse that I am interested in are not difficult to find, and consequently the references on the basis of which I make the following observations are necessarily selective.

Given my interest in the implicit political philosophy of contemporary capitalist management discourses (and comparative lack of interest in the details and numerous branches of microscopic and pragmatic concerns therein), the following is divided into two large subsections. The first deals with classical management discourses

(Taylor and Fayol) and their implicit political philosophy, and the second with the implicit political philosophy of contemporary management discourses (roughly after the nineteen-fifties). To show the connections and differences between the implicit political philosophies (rather than between the nuances of managerial applications) is my purpose here, against the backdrop of classical sociological views drawn above.

Fredrick Taylor's work on scientific management and Henri Fayol's work on the managerial function are usually regarded as inaugurating two somewhat different approaches to the theory and practice of modern management, which were enthusiastically promoted by their followers (for example, Frank and Lilian Gilbreth or Henry Gantt for Taylor, Lyndall Urwick or E.F.L. Brech for Fayol). Their perspectives were fixed on the activities and prerogatives of managers/management in a fashion which is of interest to this study – as opposed to the other influential classical force in management theory and practice, Elton Mayo and his Hawthorne Studies, which focused on workers and their relationship to industrial organisations. The 'human relations' aspect of modern and contemporary management, while inevitably of great interest from a political philosophical perspective, is outside the remit of this attempt to get a grip on managers/management *per se* in corporate capitalism.

The differences between Taylor's and Fayol's works lead to significant variations in their applications in management practice; from the perspective of political philosophy though, what underlies their different pragmatic and microscopic perspectives are similar macroscopic imperatives. That at any rate is my immediate thesis here: both Taylor and Fayol were driven instinctively or in an informed manner to carve a space for management that would apparently dispel its dissociative character (whether in terms of instrumentality as in Marx, or social morality as in Durkheim, or rational order as in Weber); that would make it appear to be more intimately *associated* with capitalist processes, drawing it within those processes. At the same time though, while extracting a space inside capitalist processes, neither Taylor nor Fayol were prepared to give up the distinct advantages of the dissociative character of managers/management: they had no desire to make management in itself an area of work which could be exploited as wage work can, and, more importantly, they did not intend to appear to be in competition with those who actually govern the capitalist process by investing in it and regulating it, who have a stake in specific sectors or aspects of those processes. Indeed, managers/management as such have to collude wholly with the latter, but without, if possible, thereby becoming purely instrumental in capitalist processes. In other words, Taylor's and Fayol's works were designed to wrest for managers/ management a substantial hold in capitalist processes (thereby apparently dispelling its dissociative character), while at the same time obscuring the precise character of this hold (thereby retaining, if anything more effectively, their dissociativeness). Managers have to be the absolutely necessary servants of capitalist masters; they have to be like the capitalist masters to all other servants; they have to avoid competing with their capitalist masters; they have to avoid getting mixed up with their fellow servants; they have to be both master and servant, and neither master nor servant – but they have to be indispensable – and all at the same time. The attainment of this collection of cancellations, of an indispensable negativity, is what Taylor and Fayol attempted to initiate, and what the rise of managerialism in contemporary capitalism has perfected for reasons I shall come to in due course.

For both Taylor and Fayol therefore two processes go into this endeavour: (a) constructing modes of defining management/ managers or formulating managerial roles such that these find a space in capitalist processes while retaining a carefully constructed distance from both capitalists and workers; and (b) presenting arguments to persuade their readers (primarily those involved in the capitalist process other than workers – statesmen, capitalists, managers and would-be managers) that such roles are supremely important and beneficial. In this the two projects are very similar indeed; it is in the details of their means of fulfilling these ends that they are interestingly different.

It is well known that Taylor employed the double-edged ploy of making out that managers are associated with workers in dividing up and assuming some of their responsibilities (almost with an altruistic air), while at the same time fixing workers into an instru-mental position (draining work of all intellectual content) and assessing them – fixing an objectifying utility-gauging gaze on them – effectively dissociating managers from workers. This is done in a scientific spirit: the idea is that managers share in work by taking over the science involved in work (or rendering the worker's part in it devoid of that science), in the process putting the worker in the position of the experimental guinea pig. The curious balance of sharing with the worker (creating an association) while simultaneously distancing the worker is evident in such statements as the following:

> The writer asserts as a general principle [...] that in almost all of the mechanical arts the science which underlies each act of each workman is so great and amounts to so much that the workman who is best suited to actually doing the work is incapable of fully understanding this science, without the guidance and help of those who are working with him or over him, either through lack of education or through insufficient mental capacity. In order that the work may be done in accordance with scientific laws, it is necessary that there shall be a far more equal division of the responsibility between the management and the workers than exists under any of the ordinary types of management. Those in the management whose duty it is to develop this science should also guide and help the workmen in working under it, and should assume a much larger responsibility for results than under usual conditions is assumed by the management.[4]

Or again:

> [Managers] cooperate heartily with the men so as to insure all of the work is being done in accordance with the principles of science which has been developed. [...] The management take over all the work for which they are better fitted than the workmen, while in the past almost all the work and the greater part of the responsibility were thrown upon the men.[5]

In striking this balance of an associative relationship with workers (ostensibly sharing the worker's 'work') which asserts itself by dissociating itself from workers (or dissociating responsibility and intellectual input from mechanical acts, taking over the former and leaving only the latter in the hands of workers) Taylor achieves that useful dissociative position for managers: not a threat to the capitalists since managers are sharing the workers' responsibilities after all, and yet not to be mixed up with workers since the managers' and the workers' actual inputs in the productive process have no overlap whatever. Having achieved this Taylor has two more things to do: one, to emphasise the actual distance between managers and workers (in case there is any confusion on this point, which managers must most strenuously avoid) as clearly as possible, and two, to emphasise the importance of this new-found managerial status without giving capitalists the jitters. The first objective is met easily enough by turning the managerial 'science' into a matter of measuring and observing the pure instrumentality of the worker such that management itself doesn't have to participate in this instrumentality (the essence of motion-time measurements and adjustments which Taylor recommends),[6] and by denouncing patronisingly the laziness and penchant for 'soldiering' of workers.[7] The unthreatening (for capitalists) importance of managers is maintained by some Taylorian rhetoric – promises of maintaining their interests by being good servants, by 'assum[ing] new *burdens*, new *duties*, and *responsibilities* never dreamed of in the past' [emphasis added].[8]

Fayol works, I have maintained, essentially to the same ends though with different methods. His strategy is not to find a space for managers/management is terms of the components of capitalist processes – the specific agents therein and their discrete functions – but in terms of a holistic view of what he calls the 'body corporate' across which different functions are distributed with different strengths at specific points but not in a discrete or contained fashion for different agents. So, Fayol identifies what he considers to be the six essential activities of industrial undertakings, and managerial activity is one of these (the others are technical, commercial, financial, security and accounting). He then goes on (that often-quoted passage from *General and Industrial Management*) to offer a definition of management, which consists of five functions ('to forecast and plan, to organise, to command, to co-ordinate, and to control'),[9] and discussion of these forms the substance of the book. Fayol therefore, unlike Taylor, doesn't draw a space for management/managers out of the space allocated to workers or productive work – he inserts management/managerial responsibility into every level of the body corporate, though to different degrees:

> Management, thus understood, is neither an exclusive privilege nor a particular responsibility of the head or senior members of the business; it is an activity spread, like all other activities, between head and members of the body corporate. The managerial function is quite distinct from the other five essential functions.[10]

So, everyone affiliated to the body corporate from worker to general manager has to perform more or less all the essential activities, with

Table 7.1 Requisite Abilities

Class of Employee	management %	technical %	commercial %	financial %	security %	accounting %	total evaluation
Large Establishments							
Workman	5	85	–	–	5	5	100 (a)
Foreman	15	60	5	–	10	10	100 (b)
Superintendent	25	45	5	–	10	15	100 (c)
Head of Section	30	30	5	5	10	20	100 (d)
Head of Technical Dept.	35	30	10	5	10	10	100 (e)
Manager	40	15	15	10	10	10	100 (f)
Several Establishments							
General Manager	50	10	10	10	10	10	100 (g)
State Enterprise							
Minister	50	10	10	10	10	10	100 (h)
Head of State	60	8	8	8	8	8	100 (i)

This is Table 1 of 'Relative Importance of Requisite Abilities of Personnel in Industrial Concerns' given by Henri Fayol in *General and Industrial Management*, trans. Constance Storrs (London: Sir Isaac Pitman & Sons, 1916/1949), p.8.

increasing degrees of managerial functions as one goes up the hierarchy. In an interesting Table of 'Relative Importance of Requisite Abilities of Personnel in Industrial Concerns'[11] (reproduced here as Table 7.1) managerial abilities range from 5 per cent for workers to 50 per cent for general managers, and technical ability ranges from 85 per cent for workers to 10 per cent for general managers. Or, put otherwise, for Fayol managers are people who do a higher percentage of an essential activity that everyone has to undertake to some extent. In effect, through a slightly different path, Fayol does basically the same thing as Taylor – only more effectively, in that he appears to do it in a more democratic and even-handed manner. He manages to associate management with the *whole* of capitalist processes and thereby give it an indispensable status; he manages to empty productive work of its intellectual content (almost, at any rate – those percentages are indicative – and with the gentler ploy of replacing mechanistic movement reductions by the hazier 'technical ability'); and he manages to portray the manager as doing *more* of whatever the worker and other people down the hierarchy do not do (thus simultaneously dissociating management clearly from the bottom of the hierarchy, from productive work).

So far, Fayol's methods and ends are uncomplicated and logical; what complicates things is that Fayol must also, like Taylor, make sure that the space carved out for management/managers does not in any way seem to threaten that of the true masters, the capitalists. Now one might think that those engaged more or less exclusively in management as Fayol defines it (planning, command, control, etc.) must be indistinguishable from capitalists. Fayol however is careful to dissociate management from capitalists too, and he does this by making a puzzling distinction between governance and management immediately following on the above quotation:

> [Management] should not be confused with government. To govern is to conduct the undertaking towards its objective by seeking to derive optimum advantage from all possible resources and to assure the smooth working of the six essential functions. Management is merely one of the six functions whose smooth working government has to ensure, but it has such a large place in the part played by higher managers that sometimes this part seems exclusively managerial.[12]

It seems to me to be impossible to unravel the distinction between government and management. The little play on words involved in dubbing management a 'function' cannot quite throw the wool over our eyes: this is clearly no more than a rhetorical gesture, a meaningless way of owning allegiance and pledging subservience to capitalists, of tactfully dissociating managers from capitalists. Predictably Fayol doesn't return to this distinction or attempt to clarify the nuances of government further. The meaninglessness of this distinction at any rate becomes clear if we return to that table which I have mentioned before. This actually stretches beyond the general manager to include the 'state enterprise' (clearly, the state itself, government personified) wherein the minister is allowed a managerial ability which is identical to that of a general manager, and the Head of State is allowed just a tiny bit more (60 per cent managerial ability). There is nothing to distinguish the government functionary from the corporate manager, or the 'state enterprise' from the corporate enterprise (an obfuscation that, as we have seen, goes back to classical sociology, and is really quite useful in establishing the status of management/managers), or to distinguish management from government here.

In brief, the theorisations of Taylor and Fayol are geared towards establishing an indispensable space for management/managers in the capitalist process (and I am still speaking of managerialism *per se*, as a kind of independent or pure space), which is nevertheless a dissociated space – a space that asserts itself through a series of cancellations and removals – a negative space which now appears to be of general rather than sector-specific significance in corporate capitalism at large – *a negative space which obscures the relationships which constitute capitalist organisation and its ideological import*. It is a useful space for corporate capitalism as it stands now, but not in quite the way it announces its usefulness and importance. Before I go on to clarify what I mean by that, I need to go through a few further steps in the dissociative negotiations and self-locations of managerialism that will bring me closer to the underlying rationale of contemporary corporate capitalist organisation.

Taylor and Fayol were symptoms of an initial effort of managerialism to advance itself and establish itself: there is a definitive air about their studies, a certain tentativeness at times and a definite over-zealousness at others, a distinct notion of working out and persuading their audience of ideas, that is characteristic of an initial position. To a large extent, it appears to me, contemporary capitalism can be identified as such when this initial effort is done and the place of managerialism is more or less accepted and established in the terms which it set for itself. By the time, at any rate, that Peter Drucker's *The Practice of Management* (1955) appears the objectives of managerialism which Taylor and Fayol were working towards is clearly established; so much so that there is nothing but confidence in Drucker's claims on behalf of management/managers:

> We no longer talk of 'capital' and 'labour'; we talk of 'management' and 'labour'. The 'responsibilities of capital' have disappeared from our vocabulary together with the 'rights of capital'; instead we hear of the 'responsibilities of management', and (a singularly hapless phrase) of the 'prerogatives of management'.[13]

This is supported by a suitably ambitious definition of management: '[management is] the organ of society specifically charged with making resources productive, that is, with the responsibility of organised economic advance, therefore reflects the *basic spirit of the modern age*' (my emphasis);[14] and a bit later:

> Management is the specific organ of the business enterprise. [...] The enterprise can decide, act and behave only as its managers do – by itself the enterprise has no effective existence. And conversely any business enterprise, no matter what its legal structure, must have a management to be alive and functioning.[15]

There is no beating around the bush here. Management has replaced capital (and without being at all equivocal about it, in some significant way managers have replaced capitalists), management reflects (actually a modest way of saying 'determines') societal and economic prerogatives in the broadest sense (the basic spirit of the modern age), and at the centre of all societal and economic prerogatives is of course that which management and managers are primarily with regard to – the business enterprise, the capitalist corporation (there is no need here even to mention the political state, which has to be understood as some sort of subsidiary object of management). Taylor's and Fayol's project has reached a surprisingly expeditious closure, and with it I feel the shape of contemporary corporate capitalism begins to emerge with ever greater clarity.

But the process of the rise of managerialism doesn't conclude there – far from it – this is merely the first step. Managers/management hereafter use and explore the leverage of dissociativeness, the advantages of negativity, in increasingly more ingenious ways. I will come to what precisely these advantages are, to what ends leverage is directed, in due course; first, a few observations about the nature of this dissociativeness in its next stage of development (still ongoing, as I understand it).

Peter Drucker's claim for managers/management is no eccentric one: the sense in his writings that management has become established is confirmed by the prodigious growth of management studies as academic and vocational disciplines, of management discourses and productions; by the degree to which management-speak enters into everyday and professional and media discourses; by the sheer volume of space which management issues and concerns have occupied in economic and social and political and cultural spheres, in subsequent decades (since the fifties). So vast and multifarious is the growth of managerialism in contemporary corporate capitalism that one is inevitably left a bit breathless when one contemplates undertaking a systematic and comprehensive examination of the area. My aim at the moment is however determined by my philosophical perspective – this discussion is necessarily focused (I probably don't need to repeat this again) on the more or less abstract idea of managers/management in itself, the pure notion of managers/management in contemporary corporate capitalism – and the demonstration of the thesis regarding the dissociativeness and negativity of management/managers that I have pre-emptively presented already. For this I do not really need a comprehensive and excessively protracted demonstration; this can be done with reference to a suitably representative and familiar and broad-based set of ideas and expressions. It seems to me that the writings of Tom Peters in the nineteen-eighties are admirably suited to my purposes: I confine myself therefore to some observations about the popular management manuals *In Search of Excellence* (with Robert H. Waterman), 1982; *A Passion for Excellence* (with Nancy Austin), 1985; and *Thriving on Chaos*, 1987. These are addressed by a management 'guru' to other managers and are therefore sufficiently attentive to the details of management practice; they possess an excellent underlying understanding of management in the most general and abstract form as well; they present views which chime in with academically and pragmatically oriented microcosmic views which are currently being (almost exclusively) discussed and disseminated; they are therefore representative of the place of managers/ management in contemporary corporate capitalism; they are usefully contextualised in the crucial period of the nineteen-eighties in the United States (a context I don't intend to go into at the moment); and they are bestsellers (and so can't be more familiar).

Tom Peters's and his co-writers' style of expression is deliberately distant from that which is associated with the rigours of political philosophy – or any kind of theoretical analysis really. It consists of a series of unsubstantiated aphorisms (prescriptions, Peters calls them) which are presented with verve, and depend on the author's authority and confidence to be persuasive. The prescriptive approach is inherited from other 'gurus' like Peter Drucker and Charles Handy. These prescriptions are usually given with a chatty self-evident sort of air which is reminiscent of certain sorts of religious and traditional dogmatic wisdoms (deliberately anti-rational), though the prescriptions are ostensibly offered with exactly the opposite intent (selling 'radical' innovation and change against tradition and dogma). The style of expression in these books – as indeed in most management manuals that I have consulted – therefore works with an obvious paradox: it is meant to serve up the wisdom which demands change without really explaining why change should be necessary. Necessarily what Tom Peters and company say appears to be often self-contradictory and confused, but that is made out to be all right since order and clarity are precisely what they are fighting against. Tom Peters and company do pretend to explain why the change and innovation they dogmatically recommend is necessary: surveys and statistics are pulled up, personal experiences and anecdotes are ranged before the reader. But this effort is complicated by the fact that a modicum of rational construction and inference is required to make sense of it and to give the consequent assertions the kind of general efficacy they demand. This contradicts the anti-rational emphasis of the texts. It seems to be assumed that while rational constructions and inferences may be, indeed need to be, employed in understanding a retrospective situation, they shouldn't be employed in making prospective projections. This is yet another paradox that is implicit in the style of expression here. In fact, such is the fog of self-contradictory and incoherent platitudinising these texts present that they are practically impervious to philosophical investigation, an achievement on which Tom Peters and company may congratulate themselves. In fact they do often congratulate themselves on this score: they *assert* that their prescriptions work in practice and do not need to be theorised, and when they do find themselves straying towards mildly theoretical areas they do so apologetically (and with the conviction that any theorising is beyond the manager's interests or capacities, and should stay so).[16] Working in practice generally means that profits can be shown to have been made when managers have followed such prescriptions in certain corporations. Only certain rationalistic processes can unravel whether such assertions of working in practice are believable, whether the profits can in fact be credited to these prescriptions, whether the singular experiences can be generalised with as much confidence as is evidenced in these texts, and so on – but since rationalism is eschewed, there isn't much choice for the reader in this matter.

In brief, therefore, the texts mentioned above, despite presenting certain advantages, seem to be singularly resistant to philosophical analysis. It is political philosophy that is nevertheless my concern here, and for this I continue to maintain that these are especially revealing texts. To demonstrate this it is unnecessary to go into the arguments (or the lack of arguments) that the texts present. Reading them with a political philosophical intent is already a dislocation of the intended readership (explicitly, other managers or would-be managers). A few observations about the general tenor of these texts and their prescriptive apparatus will serve to make my point.

a. The traditional approach of economic- and sociological-rationalism-oriented management that Tom Peters and company are determined to displace insofar as the practice of managers/management is concerned leads to the championing of a somewhat wishy-washy notion of intuitive management, the unaccountable and valorously unreasonable management by trial and error:

Pathfinding is essentially an aesthetic, intuitive process, a design process. There is an infinity of alternatives that can be posed for a design problem, whether we are talking about architectural design or the guiding values of business. From that infinity there are plenty of bad ideas, and here the rational approach is helpful in sorting out the chaff. One is usually left with a large remaining set of good design ideas, however, and no amount of analysis will choose among them, for the final decision is essentially one of taste.[17]

This emphasis on the anti-rational matter of 'taste', of 'aesthetic' choice, means that managerial decisions/processes/choices are not ultimately accountable and qualifiable and justifiable – for who is to adjudicate what is good or bad taste? The management that depends on instinct and on tastes cannot be a management that can be held responsible for anything that it does. A certain necessary degree of arbitrariness enters into the understanding of managerial impera- tives. Underlying that is the affiliated notion that management is not an acquired skill or ability, is not really learned or taught; a penchant for management is essentially something that certain people are born with. The good manager is one who simply *is* such. This is clearly an operating principle in the world of business recruit- ment: a quick look at advertisements for vacancies for trainee managers in any business periodical or broadsheet reveals that a certain *kind of personality* is sought ('a good communicator', 'an outgoing personality', 'ambitious', 'dedicated', 'leadership qualities', etc. are phrases that repeatedly crop up). And underlying that is the old conviction that in some sense managers can't be taught, no one can really be educated to become a capable manager, an idea that Fayol had reflected on in passing,[18] and which, despite enormous investments in management courses and studies and programmes, lingers unabated in management circles.[19] Managers, goes the theory, are basically people who are such and prove their innate qualities as being such in the field of corporate activity.

Or, to put the matter briefly, management cannot really be *understood* or *explained* or *learned/taught* or *accounted for*, and managers/management cannot really be held *accountable* or *respon- sible* for their actions (choices are predetermined by given personalities, by given instincts and tastes), and managers/ management can only be considered in a somewhat mystical un- enunciable fashion. Mysticism runs hand-in-hand with this contemporary version of managerial thinking (unsurprisingly there are lots of 'gurus' around).

b. Tom Peters and company's understanding of the almost autonomous and practically self-determining nature of corporations (and of corporate capitalism at large) neatly complements the given personalities of managers and the mystical conduct of management. This is underlined by a return of something like late nineteenth- century *fin de siècle* evolutionary discourses – to be more precise, a boom in evolutionary jargons which far exceeds the grand preten- sions even of social Darwinism. Corporations evolve through their own practically autonomous determinations in practically unpredictable directions, corporations are like organisms which evolve through a network of causal factors to do with environment and other organisms, over which the evolving organism itself doesn't have much control (biological analogies are as popular now as they had been at the turn of the nineteenth century). Corporations follow some sort of life process of survival or extinction, as do markets and economies. Managers/management, the argument goes, have to live with this: these ultimately self-determining evolutionary processes can be augmented or taken advantage of, and this is what managers/management are for, but at the end of the day there is only so much managers/management can do in the face of such enormous uncontrollable forces. Managers/management cannot really hope to determine such processes; they can use their instincts and tastes to make the best of them, to make sure by some mystical managerial insight that companies stay in with (become adaptive to) these self-determining processes.

> Indeed, we believe that the truly adaptive organization evolves in a very Darwinian way. The company is trying lots of things, experimenting, making the right sort of mistakes; that is to say, it is fostering its own mutations. The adoptive corporation has learned quickly to kill off the dumb mutations and invest heavily in the ones that work. Our guess is that some of the most creative directions taken by the adaptive organizations are not planned with much precision.[20]

In other words, Tom Peters and company recommend an 'evolutionary, somewhat untidy theory of management'.[21] This untidy evolutionary view of management has of course gone beyond Tom Peters's simplistic grasp of the matter in the eighties. Management theory in evolutionary terms has entered much more sophisticated levels of discussion in systems theory, and complexity theory, and coevolutionary theory.[22]

But all that makes little difference from the political philosophical perspective of managerialism that I am trying to develop here. I have more to say in the next part about the prevailing place of evolutionism in corporate capitalism from a political philosophical perspective. For the moment what all that amounts to is another level of devolution of responsibility and accountability from managers/management – another degree of dissociativeness in the indissoluble and ever-more-significant space of managerialism in contemporary corporate capitalism – another measure of the emptiness, the negativity, of that space.

c. Since managerial activity is not conditional on (or, for that matter, subject to) rational analysis, and since the corporation, and more broadly corporate capitalist systems, it is with regard to are largely self-determining in an evolutionary manner anyway, the whole business of effective management (or management that can be thought of as contributing to the obvious ends towards which a capitalist corporation is necessarily directed) becomes a more intractable affair. There is now no way to justify any particular attitude to management over any other, any particular managerial decision over any other, any specific kind of managerial practice over any other kind, so long as this doesn't go back to 'traditional' convictions in rational management. It is easy enough to see what sort of managerial roles may be involved in specific sector management (which does require a certain grasp of the immediate technologies, environments and people, and of the economic considerations pertinent to those) – that is usually the place of the middle or lower-level manager, who cannot be distinguished from most workers anyway in the contemporary corporation. The idea of work now is obviously not labour in the Marxist sense of physical–nervous exertion; I have touched on this in the first part of this study. There is a more emphatic intellectual content to practically all work now (which will undoubtedly increase with increased automatisation, and the increased focus on modes of production rather than production itself) and the distinction between the skilled worker and the lower or even middle-level manager is hazy. Unskilled labour is only a very small part of corporate capitalism and will undoubtedly become smaller. But as regards the upper levels of management (to come back to the point), where managerial activities are undertaken in some pure sense, it is difficult to discern what exactly the role of managers/management is. This is where the sense of self-importance is most concentrated, but this is where the air of an empty dissociated negativity, of irrational arbitrariness, is most dense. One might be inclined to feel sceptical about the place of managers/management in this pure sense in capitalist processes.

This sort of scepticism, of course, Tom Peters and company are most eager to guard against. The prescriptive style of writing itself is designed to stand against such scepticism: it carries with it all the authority that the doctor who knows best may exert over the patient who has faith in him. More importantly, such scepticism is deflected by the recommendation that managerial control and power be constantly manifested even if the ends for which it is manifested are arbitrary and intractable. Managers/management should always *appear* to be doing something: should always make their place clear by creating change (necessarily arbitrary since it is a hit-and-miss matter of striking the right evolutionary direction) – words like 'innovation', 'incentives', 'initiatives', 'radical', 'revolutionary', etc. proliferate constantly and acquire new connotations in management-speak. This evidence of managerial activity is attended by some notion of intensification – it is not just activity, it is intense hectic conjoint activity which will reveal the power and position of managers/management; another clump of management jargon ('motivation', 'drive', 'synergy', etc.) is devoted entirely to this. In brief, this could be thought of as the managerial philosophy of routinising change, ostensibly to try to 'get in touch' with evolutionary processes, but more obviously simply to cover up its own dissociativeness and negativity. These arguments are best summarised in the words of Tom Peters and Nancy Austin:

> We proposed the following [...]: it *is* a messy world. We hope to demonstrate that. *If* it is a messy world, the *only* way to proceed is by *constant experimentation*: 'Don't just stand there, *do* something.' *If* constant experimentation is the *only* antidote to a messy world, then we need experimenters – or champions (skinks).[23]

What this means for Tom Peters is laid out in his five main prescriptions for managers in *Thriving on Chaos*:

> Five areas of management constitute the essence of proactive performance in our chaotic world: (1) an obsession with responsiveness to customers, (2) constant innovation in all areas of the firm, (3) partnership – the wholesome participation of and gain sharing with all people connected with the organization, (4) leadership that loves change (instead of fighting it) and instils and shares an inspiring vision, and (5) control by means of simple support systems arrived at measuring the 'right stuff' for today's environment.[24]

The explicit routinisation of change for the sake of change and the commitment to demonstrating managerial presence by intensification ('wholesome participation', sharing an 'inspiring vision', 'measuring the "right stuff"') are all pithily – prescriptively – set out there.

d. Managers/management in itself, as a pure area (most closely associated with upper level management), an area of negativity, of emptiness, which by dint of constant pronouncements to the contrary and certain vague theoretical assertions has succeeded in making itself appear to be the single most important element in corporate capitalism. This had been discerned by classical sociologists; it had been envisaged and initiated in practice by the pioneers of management theory and practice; and this has been realised now. In fact, it has been so successfully realised and ensconced that apart from the necessary lip service that has to be paid to maintain the contradictions and efficacy of this position, managers are sometimes prepared to be quite honest about it. Tom Peters and Nancy Austin are (unintentionally?) honest about this in a peculiarly self-congratulatory fashion when they write the revealing chapter 'Attention, Symbols, Drama, Vision – and Love' in *A Passion for Excellence*. Here we have some detailed prescriptions for the people who could really read this book with profit: the 'leaders' of corporations, upper-level managers who are so high up the hierarchy that management in its purest, most unadulterated, form is all they have to deal with, particularly CEOs of certain sorts (of a company established enough that he/she does not have to be too earthily entrepreneurial) – and, of course, the starry-eyed aspiring managers (the larger readership, no doubt) looking for the philosopher's stone (in the absence of acquirable skills or education) from the recognised managerial 'guru'. These final prescriptions are worthy of quotation:

> Attention is symbolic behavior [...]. As a result of our 'symbolic' attention – symbolic of our concerns and our priority – others become engaged. (And let us pointedly remember, symbols – paying attention – are all the manager, who doesn't drive a forklift, has);[25]

note here that insistent *our* (this is a manager talking to other managers) and *others* (presumably those who are not managers or at any rate those who don't know this prescription); note also that this is '*all* the manager has'; and then onward:

> Attention and symbols and drama are about signaling, of course – about the creation of a 'language of attention.' Language is fun-

damental. [...] The conscious use of certain words is a vital form of paying attention. And we all get the opportunity to choose our vocabulary.[26]

So attention is not really paying attention *to* anything, it is simply a matter of appearing to be attentive; corporate drama has little bearing on a phenomenal world, it is little more than a mimetic Aristotelian spectacle, the outer level of unreality in Plato's simile of the cave; and language doesn't communicate, but triggers reactions. The obsession with a kind of shamanistic approach to language in contemporary corporate capitalism, so that language is used in certain dogmatic and formulaic ways to *initiate* affects rather than *express* positions, to control by the repetitiousness of some sort of religious chanting rather than to open up possibilities of interchange, to constrain with all the power of a religious dictate rather than to enable rational agreement and disagreement, is an interesting area which only a competent sociolinguist can wholly unravel. Deborah Cameron's *It's Good to Talk* (2000) seems to me to be a revealing exploration of this matter, though she takes the evidence in question (I think incorrectly) to be indicative of the irrationality of capitalism.[27] I feel there are rational motives behind all this emptiness, but these are not to be revealed at this level of investigation. At any rate, I think no further commentary is needed on Tom Peters and company to demonstrate that their view of managers/management (a representative one in our time) is one that brings managerialism to a pinnacle of dissociation and negativity from capitalist processes as such. Predictably, Tom Peters and Nancy Austin end this revealing chapter with the mindless mysticism which must sustain managerialism of this nature: it all culminates in the manager's/management's 'vision' – with all religious connotations of 'soul-searching' and its not being 'amenable to straightforward analysis'[28] left intact – and the 'vision', it seems, leads to love and 'love translates into joy'.[29]

This self-echoing shell of emptiness, this dissociativeness, is covertly and carefully maintained for a reason, is maintained with *effect*. The questions that naturally arise here are: what reason? with what effect?

I do not intend to return to the issue of sociological perspectives of managerialism, or attempt to take up again and update the classical sociological precepts regarding managers/management. To attempt to do so here would be repetitive and tedious since this could easily be performed by the reader for any particular sociologist or sociological position in the light of the above views. Briefly though, I might as well note that I find that sociological perspectives that have bothered to address managerialism particularly have done so in a manner which simply takes the manager's/management's point of view at face value. For instance, since proponents of managerialism in the above senses have routinely declared their self-confidence, appointed themselves 'gurus' and 'wise men', and thought of themselves as people with 'wide-ranging minds', since they have emphatically declared their own indispensability, sociologists since Schumpeter have tended to draw managers of all sorts into the class or social stratum of intellectuals who arguably play an increasingly significant role in corporate capitalist processes. If anything marks the kind of managerialism discussed above it is its vehement anti-intellectualism. This however is not something that I intend to go into here, since I have dealt with the issue of intellectuals in political philosophy at some length elsewhere.[30] A sociological discussion that does come to mind as being related to the above observations appears among P.D. Anthony's still-relevant and succinct thoughts about managerial preoccupation with the ideology of work and managerial work itself in *The Ideology of Work* (1977). Of the latter he has the following to say:

> We know little about managerial work because the managers, until very recently, have concentrated their attention upon their subordinates and [...] managers' interests seem to have largely defined the curiosities of social scientists. [...] All we do know is that managers seem to have behaved as though they found their work the most rewarding and important thing in their lives. This would seem to suggest the extraordinary success of an ideological appeal directed at establishing the importance of work to the manager, if not to his subordinate.[31]

This is not especially illuminating but it does sum the situation up admirably: managerial *work* we don't know much about, managers claim an extraordinary satisfaction in their work, and sociologists now tend to accept the managerial view of things insofar as sociologists interest themselves in managerialism.

8 The Macro Issues Behind Executive Pay

The dissociativeness and negativity of managers/management in contemporary corporate capitalism are far from being new discoveries, though the depths of that negativeness, the echo of that emptiness, remain to be fully plumbed and analysed. That managers/management wrest and utilise discourses in peculiarly self-serving and (if looked at closely) untenable and decontextualised ways has been noted – I have already mentioned Cameron's *Its Good to Talk*, and I should add to that Frank's books,[1] among others. But there remains that crucial question: what lies behind the dissociated and negative surface of managerialism, what is the rationale which holds that surface together and makes managers/management appear to be the principal elements of contemporary corporate capitalism?

The following observations are a tentative attempt to come to grips with that underlying rationale. In the first part of this study I decided to follow a method of trying to unravel the general political philosophical ideas in contemporary corporate capitalism by examining a specific social outcome and then expanding from there to the larger social landscape, by starting from a specific point and throwing an analytical (not simply descriptive) grid onto the whole from there (instead of, as is more usual, starting from certain given first principles of political philosophy). This I have already undertaken in beginning this part with an examination of managerialism without enumerating any philosophical first principles. In taking this discussion forward to answer tentatively the above question I will continue to follow the same method; only, I would like to thread the argument around a social sub-issue that is related to the broad issue of contemporary corporate capitalist managerialism, but is of a somewhat narrower scope. I thread this argument in fact around the much discussed micro-issue of executive pay, and especially of the role of stock options in this.

The 'micro-ness' of the issue of executive pay has, of course, been routinely emphasised by management 'gurus' of all sorts. In Peter F. Drucker's essay 'Overpaid Executives: The Greed Effect' (1983), for example, it is pointed out that in the scale of corporate economics the place of excessive executive pay is minuscule, and that the prodigious amount of discussion this issue has attracted is more a psychological matter than anything else.[2] Even on that count, though, the issue seems to me to be far from negligible. The fact that it has captured the public imagination, has become the matter of continuous media coverage since the early nineteen-eighties, and has consequently been one that successive governments in corporate capitalist contexts have been and are being compelled to confront (even if only to evade), shows that this is a matter of no small cultural and social significance. Besides it is not true that the significance of the issue is confined to the sphere of social psychology and cultural symbology. Since governments have had to express an ostensible interest in this, the issue has become a legislative and judicial matter, and provides an interesting inroad into the nature of legislature and jurisprudence in contemporary corporate capitalism. A prodigious amount of discussion about the economic implications of this (especially in terms of shareholder interests and agency theory), and about the systemic prerogatives underlying it (the pressures of markets, the alleged divorce between control and ownership, the concept of stakeholding in corporations, the nuances of responsibility and performance in business, etc.), means that the issue of executive pay is now an area which is uniquely placed for the kind of expansive methodology I am interested in. The sheer scope of this discussion, which occurs across very different social, cultural and political contexts under the broad aegis of corporate capitalism – and the fact that at least in the popular imagination excessive executive pay is symbolically linked to the larger inequities of 'globalisation' and 'modernisation' – present opportunities for generalisation which are invaluable from a political philosophical perspective. Indeed, it is no accident that when John Kaler (whose essay I have cited already) tries to demonstrate the link between micro and macro issues, he chooses to do this by focusing on the example of executive pay:

> For example, take the apparently very micro issue of what is perceived to be excessive executive pay. It very obviously leads on to questions about executive accountability and, with that, to questions of corporate governance. Questions of corporate governance concern not just how, but also to whom and for what corporate executives are accountable. Consequently, they are questions inseparable from the issue of corporate social responsi-

bility in that they can only be answered on the basis of presuppositions about what those responsibilities are; most notably, as reflected in differing approaches of the stockholder and shareholder viewpoints [...]. Settling the issue of the social responsibilities of businesses of any kind, be they corporate or non-corporate, is, in its turn, inseparable from determining the social role of businesses. That is to say, their function within society given the responsibilities assigned to them [...]. The questioning need not actually be developed in this way of course. [...] The point is that, logically speaking, this micro question eventually entails some decidedly macro issues.[3]

Kaler's presentation of this example accords so well, from a methodological view, with my approach to this matter that I feel that that longish quotation is justified here.

So, I move on to my observations on this issue, with the larger question stated above in view, and without further ado.

It is probably best to start off with certain general observations on the usual manner in which executive pay is organised in capitalist corporations, and on the underlying thinking behind this organisation. This is of course, like so much else, a specialised and particularly foggy area, and I assume that the reader is not a specialist in it.

The Chief Executive Officer (CEO) and upper-level executives of a company are now usually remunerated in three ways: with a base salary (including perks), with short-term incentives (for example, a share in the proceeds of some sort of specifically financed initiative, or a bonus for some particular target-set activity), with long-term incentives (for example, long-term performance grants, grants of stocks or cash which are conditional to continued employment, grants of stock or stock options which are conditional on the appreciation of the company's stock). It is generally estimated that 80 per cent or more of a CEO's salary is likely to be performance-related rather than set; and that anything between 50 per cent and 80 per cent of a CEO's or upper-level executive's total remuneration over a period of time (say, a financial year) is likely to be accounted for in terms of stock options (which I come to soon). The first and obvious thing to be noted here is that the great emphasis on 'performance-related' pay – or, since that term seems to me to be inaccurate, let's call it conditional pay – suggests that upper-level executive pay is not for fulfilling an obligation (the minimal obligation is accounted for by the basic pay) which can be predetermined, but for doing things which can only be recompensed in retrospect. A simplistic analogy may be that upper-level executives are paid more as a potter may be paid (retrospectively) by a customer for turning out a particularly fine pot than as a plumber may be paid (prospectively) at a predetermined amount for fixing a leaking tap. Payment in retrospect is not determined by confidence in the skills of the person who is paid, while payment in prospect (like a salary) has to be determined thus. This fits in well with the negativity and dissociativeness of managers/management. *CEOs and upper-level executives are, of course, managers in a more-or-less pure sense (let's say, that is 80 per cent of what they do) and the indeterminable emptiness of what they do is acknowledged by a commensurate conditional pay (80 per cent of the remuneration is determined by their doing something, but there is no strict predetermination of what this something is).* Actually that is not strictly accurate either: insofar as that 80 per cent is conditional on their meeting certain predetermined targets, there is predetermination involved here. So let me modify that previous statement: *the indeterminable emptiness and dissociativeness of upper-level management is marked by the degree (80 per cent) to which there is a lack of confidence in its ability to fulfil such targets as can be set before they are actually fulfilled.*

In fact, one way of identifying the degree to which managerial responsibility is allocated at all levels – not as a matter of nomenclature but as a matter of being involved in managerialism *per se* – may well be the degree to which remuneration is made conditional.

Those at any rate are the immediate inferences, which will undoubtedly change as I proceed.

The reasons why the term 'performance-related' pay appears to me to be misplaced are the well-known vagaries regarding what performance in this case is with regard to. Before going into what performance may be with regard to let me dispense with what the *obligations* are which the basic salaries of upper-level managers may be thought of as compensating. In brief, and somewhat idealistically speaking: *the obligations the upper-level executives of a company have to fulfil in return for their basic pay are those that ensure that the minimum interests of all stakeholders in that company are served, insofar as these stakeholders contribute to the processes which define that company as such.*

The stakeholders so understood obviously include all the share-holders (principal or otherwise) who have invested in the company; all the employees (or personnel or workers or whatever the fashion-able term may be) who are compensated (usually prospectively) for fulfilling certain obligations (in practice all managers from top to bottom who draw any basic salary on the understanding of fulfilling minimum obligations are therefore also employees); all the consumers (or clients or customers or whatever the appropriate term might be) whom the company caters for. The picture of stakehold-ing may be considerably more complex than I am suggesting here because each of these (shareholders, employees, consumers, etc.) may themselves be companies linking up with other companies in similar ways – but let's leave aside that consideration for the moment. The *minimum* interests of these stakeholders are those that are contrac-tually arranged and therefore come under the aegis of the law (naturally the law marks compulsion or *obligation*). Insofar as upper-level executives ensure the functioning of the company such that the *minimum* interests of stakeholders, which are contractually set out, are served, they could be thought of as earning their basic pay.

The area to which a term like 'performance-related' pay *might* apply is that which is *not* covered by obligations (those that are, at least in principle, enforced by law). This may relate to the perfor-mance of duties/responsibilities/activities which are other than those that are contractually determined, or the performance of duties/responsibilities/activities which are contractually determined, but at levels (qualitatively or quantitatively) which cannot be con-tractually set out – so long, of course, as these excessive or extra performances can be thought of as contributing to some or all of the stakeholders' interests. This naturally cannot come under the aegis of the law, and typically no company law makes provision for more than the minimum interests of stakeholders (I offer this as a general statement, open to testing, and when I wish to refer to specific laws pertaining to a corporate capitalist context in the future I will site British Company Law as a representative instance). Some general definition of a commitment to go beyond minimum stakeholding interests may be made by an association of companies, or an associ-ation of certain kinds of stakeholders or perhaps an independent ombudsman in something like a 'Code of Good Practice'.

In the fact that upper-level executive pay is largely conditional on this sort of excessive or extra performance (which 'performance-related' pay gestures towards, but inappropriately – a point I am yet to clarify) we have another aspect of the recognition of the disso-ciativeness of managers/management. Insofar as upper-level managers are paid for services, they may be thought of (as I have stated above) as employees in a traditional sense. But the pay structure and the thinking underlying the pay structure makes the difference. The employee who might voluntarily or through encour-agement do something extra is usually *promised* reward after evidence of this is available (by extension of service, by a bonus, or by a promotion, etc.); to a large extent the upper-level manager's pay structure is sustained exclusively by the hope or expectation of such excessive or extra performances and the *right* to be paid for it once evidence of this is available. This underlines the dissociation of the upper-level manager from the ordinary employee: the *right* of recompense in terms of hope or expectation, as opposed to the *promise* of reward in terms of possible achievement, is a mark of the greater stability of the upper-level manager's position (though the opposite is often made out to be the case). The underlying idea is that at that managerial level where incentive pay dominates the total income the manager has acquired a stability and status beyond which he need not go (one can only hope and expect). This stability and status is implicitly not available to the employee.

I think this is a crucial distinction that is often not recognised and is apt to be misunderstood.

It is because there is a combination of hope and expectation and at the same time a right involved, and because this is an area which is open to confusion, that that which is thought of as 'performance-related' pay for upper-level managers is in fact not '*performance*-related' at all – it is often no more than conditional pay. It is an area which has proved to be notoriously open to manipula-tion, which defeats the notion of excessive or extra performance (qualitatively or quantitatively).

The question arises: 'What exactly are the excessive or extra managerial performances and how are these to be measured so as to be compensated in a manner which is proportional to the degree of such performances through conditional pay?' This has proved to be a difficult question to answer, and there are in fact no certain answers. Clearly, such extra or excessive managerial performance cannot be gauged and compensated in themselves (this cannot be a matter of measuring overtime or specific end products): what can *probably* be measured are the effects or outcomes of such performance. Given that the capitalist corporation must be predeterminedly and definitively ends-oriented, the measure of effects and outcomes can only be broadly in terms of the company's profits and liquidity. So, it has become customary now for upper-level managers to be given conditional pay in a manner that is bound to measures of profit-making (mainly appreciation in stock value). But this is fraught with some remarkable problems, which I will come to once I have clarified the most popular mode of conditional pay which adheres to this thinking and which has come to be the mainstay of executive pay since the nineteen-eighties – executive stock options.

Here's a text book definition of options: 'Options are contracts to buy or sell a particular stock for a fixed price at or before a specified date in the future'[4] (investors pay a certain amount for an option). And of the two main kinds of options:

> A *call* option is a right (but not an obligation) to buy a given number of shares of the underlying stock at a given price (striking price) on or before a specific date (expiration date).
> A *put* option is the right (but not an obligation) to sell a given number of shares of the underlying stock at a specified price on or before a specific date.[5]

An investor in options makes a profit if at the expiration date the share price has appreciated to more than the sum of the striking price and the price paid for the option. Normally profits made by options trading are subject to capital gains tax. Since options listings started in 1973, trading in options has grown phenomenally, and its volume now exceeds the total volume of trading in stocks on most stock exchanges. That is all, I think, that is needed as preliminary information.

And here's a text book description of executive stock options:

> Executive share schemes normally take the form of share options. Essentially the rules of these schemes provide for executives to be given an option to buy shares at a future date for their market price at the time the option was granted. Provided that the share price appreciates, the individual makes a profit when the option is exercised and the shares sold.[6]

Executive share options may either be subject to income tax or to capital gains tax. The immediate point to be noted here is that such options are *given* to upper-level managers in exchange for their long-term commitment to the company, or in exchange for a smaller basic salary, and so on – but not as a financial exchange (in this respect executive share schemes generally differ from employee share schemes where employees do actually pay, however that payment may be exacted). In financial terms generally this is a no-loss affair for managers: if stock value depreciates the manager simply doesn't exercise the option, if it appreciates the manager can make money without having to spend anything. The advantages of compensation by executive stock options are generally deemed to be the following:

(a) the possession of stock options gives the upper-level manager a clear target to work towards (and the only one that matters in capitalist corporations) – increasing share value (the implicit assumption here is that the manager can be personally responsible for meeting such a target);

(b) the possession of stock options also gives the manager a sense of ownership, and therefore a commitment to ensuring the overall health of the corporation beyond the minimum obligations, as well as a particular commitment to protecting shareholder interests (the issue of ownership has repercussions which I will come to soon);

(c) since executive stock options are usually long term (usually ten years) and conditional on continuous employment, they can be used by the corporation to retain upper-level managers;

(d) corporations which are not immediately solvent, but which have potential, can recruit the sort of managers they want by using stock options instead of immediately having to dole out salaries at the market rate.

The advantages of stock options are enumerated in (often confused) detail in such influential documents in this area as the Greenbury report.[7]

The precise impact of stock options and other share schemes on upper-level executive salaries can be gauged by looking at Table 8.1, taken from the 1999 'Forbes Super 100' list of top CEOs[8] (I only give the top five), which also gives a sense of the kind of figures and salary increases (in US dollars) that may be involved at the top of the corporate executive pyramid.

After this digression let's return to that question and the difficulties with it: 'What exactly are the excessive or extra managerial performances and how are these to be measured so as to be

Table 8.1 Top CEOs

Rank Pay 1998	Super 100	Company	Chief Executive	Age	Salary $	Stock gains (thousands)	Total Compensation 1998	1994–1998
1	35	Walt Disney	Michael D. Eisner	57	5,764	569,823	589,101	631,014
2	20	Intel	Craig R. Barrett	59	2,244	114,232	116,840	NA
3	1	General Electric	John F. Welch Jr	63	10,000	46,540	68,285	164,134
4	14	Morgan Stanley DW	Phillip J. Purcell	55	8,888	40,051	48,962	108,064
5	5	IBM	Louis V. Gerstner Jr	57	9,375	32,802	42,381	86,418

compensated in a manner which is proportional to the degree of such performances through conditional pay?' It is impossible to give an unambiguous answer to this question.[9] If we stick with the matter of stock options as providing conditional pay to recompense such performances for upper-level executives, it becomes amply clear (and is well known now) that gains made by upper-level executives exercising their executive options have little or no relation to their excessive or extra performances. To begin with, even if there is evidence that share value appreciates through the efforts of the corporation, it is a very debatable point indeed whether the upper-level managers and their decisions and performances can be held solely (or even largely) responsible for such efforts and whether such responsibility is commensurate with the gains in conditional pay they are apt to make. The common tactic of trying to prove that certain managerial decisions make differences to a corporation's productivity and profitability[10] is misplaced in the presumed narrowness of matching managerial decision to outcome without regard for any complete survey of the total allocations and networks of responsibilities and efforts which must exist in any corporation. To hold singular managerial decisions as responsible for such outcomes in itself presumes a direct relationship between these at the expense of every other level of corporate effort and contribution to the outcome. Now the only sensible way in which this equation can be made – and is sometimes made in legal and management terms[11] – is in some symbolic sense: for example, that upper-level management assumes a symbolic responsibility for the whole corporation and therefore enjoys the privilege of taking credit for the performance of the whole corporation. But that symbolic status cannot be paid for the corporation's performance: one cannot be paid for *being what one is* as if one is actually *doing something* to earn that pay conditionally. Between being something and doing something there is an enormous gap and to reward anyone for the former makes a nonsense of any notion of 'performance' pay – or even conditional pay.

Further, it is also obvious that an upper-level manager (especially a CEO) can make astronomical gains even if the corporation he is symbolically responsible for does *not* show significant appreciation of share value, or even shows relative depreciation of share values – that is, even if (in these given terms) the management could be thought of as 'performing' badly. The shape of markets determines share values to a large extent. In a bull market or a high tide of economic growth, share values can go up for modestly performing companies even if in relative terms (compared to the competition) a particular company's productivity and profitability falls.[12] In the long term this is, in fact, more likely to occur than not. Given that executive options are long term and given that they cost nothing for those who hold them, upper-level managers often stand to gain much from such market movements in a manner which is unrelated to the performance of the corporation (not to speak of the upper-level manager). Performances of companies are also likely to be related to the size of a company: smaller or more recently established companies are likely to show faster growth and therefore statistically better year-on-year performance, whereas a large and well-established company (say a FTSE 100 company) would be happy to hold its position and therefore doesn't show significant change in year-on-year performance.[13] Speculators work on this basis constantly. Also CEOs and upper-level managers are arguably best placed to have inside information about the future plans of the corporation and exercise their options conveniently, or to take advantage of option repricing.[14] This too complicates the matter of seeing conditional pay for upper-level managers in terms of options as being relatable to 'performance'.[15]

Also, even if we disregard all the above and continue to persist in believing that appreciation of share value is a pertinent measure of the upper-level manager's 'performance', it must be confessed that this may be a very lopsided index of 'performance' from the point of view of stakeholder interest. The only kind of stakeholder interest that this measure of 'performance' directly protects (and the only one for which adequate legal provision usually exists) is the shareholders'. It is generally argued that that in turn has necessarily beneficial effects on other stakeholders' – employees', consumers' – interests too. For instance, appreciation of share values and expansion of a corporation ensures greater security for employees and allows more employment to be created, and may bring prices down and allow for greater investment into the quality of the product and the satisfaction of consumers' needs. This seems logical but is regretfully not necessarily the case. The drive toward share-value appreciation from a managerial point of view has little to do with protecting the interests of all stakeholders: it usually results in target setting and temporary manipulation of expenses which are actually detrimental to the sense of security of employees, and depends on making employees more malleable to managerial demands.[16] This is a matter that I will come back to at a later stage – for a full appreciation of this also needs to take account of the role of the capitalist state. Nor is it by any means certain that the kind of proliferation of consumables and routinisation of consumer services imposed by such share-value appreciation drives in the name of meeting consumer needs is necessary or desirable (a debate that I won't go into now). At any rate, it might seem certain that share-value appreciation would be in the shareholders' interests – and certainly this is lopsided in itself – but ironically, a great deal of economic and business-management and legal thinking has found reason to be sceptical even of this. When Graef Crystal wrote his influential *exposé* of boardroom negotiations which result in excessive executive pay packets, *In Search of Excess*, he ostensibly did so because he felt that overpaid CEOs and other upper-level managers were systematically defrauding shareholders.[17] Crystal declared himself a selfless champion of shareholders. The debate about the conflict between ownership (shareholding) and control (management), and the nuances of agency theory (the costs that a corporation has to take into account for the performance of executive functions), have occupied countless pages.[18] Indeed, in following this debate one is persuaded to think, against one's better judgement, that only shareholders and managers are worth considering in capitalist corporations, and the most moral stances to assume is one that sees shareholders as being hard done by and considers that something has to be done about it. I have reason to be suspicious of this position, but I will come to that too in due course.

These more or less factual observations on conditional executive pay do, I hope, demonstrate how misleading the term 'performance-related' pay is here. But it isn't simply to demonstrate this that I have gone through a rather intrusive account of the matter – I have not lost the broad political philosophical focus on corporate capitalism. This issue of executive pay, and particularly the matter of conditional pay (masquerading as 'performance-related' pay) through stock options, is revealing of something crucial about the operations of contemporary corporate capitalism in the broadest sense. Most studies of this matter (confined to economics and business studies and judicial theory) are devoted to working out how to make this system work, *how to make these modes of conditional executive pay more directly related to measures of performance* – these studies possess an instrumentalist approach which is of little political philosophical interest. The political philosophical interpretation of these matters leads us in quite a different direction.

The obvious inference to draw from the above is that the attempt at making this structure of executive remuneration more coherent, of making executive share and option compensations more closely linked to any index of performance (especially if we try to discern excessive or extra performances) is unlikely to work because this structure is not designed for this. To a large extent, I suspect, such instrumentalist studies depend ultimately on some idea of creating models which would enable relatively sound financial projections to become possible and therefore render corporate performative criteria clearer. Both theoretical and pragmatic experiences have cast reasonable doubts on model-based instrumental thinking.[19]

The performances that upper-level management can provide, in its peculiarly dissociative and negative capacity, that have any effect on the body corporate as a whole (to borrow that term from Fayol) are in fact recompensed more than adequately by the base salary. The differentials between upper-level management's basic pay and any other level of employee's in a typical corporation is already a questionable acknowledgement of the importance allocated to managerial activity. If one wished to make the efforts of the body corporate as a whole more intensive (with a view to encouraging excessive and extra performances), a set of bonus-like compensations which would be retrospectively available to *all* levels of the corporation including management, and which would be conditional on meeting targets (not just the one of share-value appreciation) which acknowledge and protect the interests of *all* stakeholders, could easily be systematised and instituted. This idea is obviously speculative, and I don't intend to dwell on it here – my interests are not instrumental but exploratory at the moment – and the relevant questions are why does the above-described system exist, what is its underlying (not its ostensible) rationale, what does it reveal about the condition of contemporary corporate capitalism?

Continuing with the particular example of executive stock options, these cannot ensure any guarantee of performance because the fiscal movements through which they may become profitable are not conditional on any clear index of performance. They serve another purpose than the ostensible one in contemporary corporate capitalist organisation. This seems to tie in with the fact that they are offered as remuneration to that peculiar part of the corporation (upper-level management) which is in fact peculiarly dissociated from every other element within the particular corporation, which has a largely negative role, and which is sustained only by its doubtful claims to the contrary. The management that is not what it presents itself as being also serves another purpose than the ostensible one in contemporary corporate capitalist organisation. There is a play of shadows here: *the corporate stratum of upper-level management that is not what it claims to be is conditionally compensated for purposes that are not what they seem to be.* This conjunction of misdirections seems to me to be of the greatest interest.

What the gift of large numbers of executive stock options, which are clearly a no-loss proposition and which present remarkable opportunities for playing with shares without being trammelled by the disadvantages of actually investing in them, obviously can do and does is *provide an incentive toward financial speculation* (not 'performance'). Arguably this is so for most available kinds of executive share schemes. There is a wide gulf between financial speculation (which has to do with limited self-interests which are essential to corporate capitalism generally) and corporate performance (which has to do with stakeholder interests in the broadest sense and is significant to specific capitalist corporations). The final mark of the dissociativeness of upper-level management lies in the fact that the compensatory packages which are available to it draw it away from the latter (the specific performance of a particular corporation as a whole) and align it with the former (a speculative interest in the corporation in question). In this implicit drawing away, which is permitted and even encouraged by extant remunerative structures, from every element of the productive processes the dissociativeness and negativity of management is ratified.

But I need to be more precise: what sort of *alignment* is entailed here? The alignments that are established in the above-described system of conditional executive compensation are also the obvious ones: the stakeholder interests that the managerial possession of compensatory shares or options protects are obviously those of the shareholder. But I have touched on this already, and have mentioned how policy-makers and academics have devoted an enormous amount of research and contemplation to unravelling and dealing with the apparent conflict the above-described system initiates between shareholders (owners) and upper-level managers (controllers).[20] And in such discussions the shareholders turn out to be the victims (*à la* Crystal). What is misleading in this view is the peremptory fashion in which *all* shareholders are lumped together as 'the shareholder'. Just as all those who are called managers are not managers in the same way (only a few upper-level managers are involved in management *per se*), so too all shareholders are not *owners* in quite the same sense. At least the simplistic and all too familiar distinction between small shareholders (normally those who own less than 5 per cent of the total stock of a capitalist corporation) and principal shareholders (normally those who own 5 per cent or more) should be taken into account. In a public company (one on which there is an obligation that a certain number of shares be sold in the open market) the vast majority of shareholders are small shareholders. In a private limited company (where there is no such obligation) it is more likely that a small number of shareholders will all be principal shareholders, but not necessarily. Principal share-holders usually have corporatively and sometimes legally enjoined and agreed-upon controlling powers in companies which small shareholders do not.[21] In general, I think, it would be true to say that however black and white the so-called conflict of interest arising from a division of ownership (by shareholders in general) and control (management in general) might appear, the role of that elite of principal shareholders doesn't fit – it has a greyish muffled tone in all this. This grey area is often camouflaged by the sharper black and white of the general shareholder and the general management. But the general shareholder is overwhelmingly the great employed mass itself: people who give their savings to investment companies, people who take mortgages and have insurances or have to have insurances, people who go to banks, people who get salaries and sometimes use a bit of it to buy those discounted shares in the companies they work for, people who fear unemployment and want a nest egg, etc. – and many of these have company nametags with the word 'manager' in it and have never heard of stock options. I don't think these shareholders control anything. A close look at the muffled grey area is likely to be more productive at the moment.

It is very likely that a principal shareholder of a large corporation who is more or less removed from direct executive involvement in that corporation but has controlling interests therein – whose con-trolling interests may be expressed by involvement in boardroom decisions, or perhaps by occupying the position of an executive or non-executive director (one who therefore doesn't generally draw a salary from the company and cannot be considered an employee), apart from the legally determined privileges of being a principal shareholder – would have a speculative *view* of the corporation. Financial capitalists who have *only* a speculative interest in a company may well acquire the position of principal shareholders to obtain a suitable control for the sake of gains through speculation. Further, the speculative involvement of a principal shareholder in a corporation is likely to be enhanced if this shareholder has similar controlling interests in other corporations too (which is often the case where only professional investors or investment companies have the resources to buy shares at the required scale). By a speculative view or a speculative interest I mean that involvement in the fortunes of a corporation which restricts itself only or primarily to the status of the company in market terms (its profitability, its liquidity) and is unconcerned about its productive performances as such or in the overall stakeholder interests. This sort of reductive speculative involvement in a company which principal shareholders may have is actually a kind of refinement of the industrial capitalist's single-minded preoccupation with profit which Marx described[22] (or, alternatively, it might be thought of as a particular refinement of Weber's understanding of capital accounting which disregards substantive rationality). In the case of the industrial capitalist though, as Marx recognised, there was some sort of necessary contribution to the circulation of capital through production, and therefore some sort of commitment towards the integrity of that corporation too. Besides, the authority of individual or kinship-based ownership in corporations which dominated Marx's context gave industrial capitalists a much stronger extra-speculative interest in their corporations. The kind of principal shareholder described above – however this person (if it is a person) comes to occupy this position, even if he initially had an entrepreneurial role with regard to that company and has himself gone through various executive commitments at various stages – would, in the current organisation of significant capitalist corporations, have to relegate past commitments towards developing a more speculative *view* of the corporation by dint of occupying the position of principal shareholder. In other words, the principal shareholders of sufficiently significant and large capitalist corporations of our day are all more or less financial capitalists (whether they started off as entrepreneurs or industrial capitalists is irrelevant), who have refined the industrial capitalist's preoccupation with profits to a more consuming involvement in a speculative perspective. The industrial capitalist as owner who is preoccupied with profits would nevertheless be concerned with the activity of production and the composition of the corporation itself; the financial capitalist as owner is mainly concerned with the reduction of the corporation to a conglomeration of figures, which can be manipulated and massaged and altered and maximised, and has little regard for anything else.

To give that series of observations more flesh, and especially the observation that the more influential rungs of capitalist corporations (and therefore of contemporary corporate capitalism) are occupied by financial capitalists, I need to give a clearer sense of the process through which financial capitalists come to be where they are – and through which principal shareholders in significant corporations come to occupy their positions – and in which speculative involvement supersedes every other kind of involvement. I do this briefly in a suggestive rather than demonstrative fashion, by offering statements which can be tested (and which I am convinced would chime in with the reader's observations) rather than statements validated by empirical evidence (the more protracted route which isn't appropriate here).

The overall dynamic involved in contemporary corporate capitalism could be thought of as a gyre, a spiral that (paradoxically) both emanates out of and culminates in speculative activity or involvement. The whole fabric of corporate capitalism, insofar as this centres on capitalist corporations, revolves around and at the behest of a capitalist coterie, rather than class, which speculates, that is, initiates and keeps in motion financial movements. These financial movements are such that at the broadest and most cumulative level they keep markets alive, generate or dilute competitive directions, raise or break or merge or erase specific corporate sectors, and have a profound effect on the relative prosperity or poverty of regions, on social conditions and governance in the capitalist sphere of influence. Through the essential level of the organisation of specific capitalist corporations within this gyre, the general movement of the gyre is maintained; and the whole structure is driven by the power exerted by speculative interests at all levels. This controlling power of speculative interests at all levels is strengthened by the capitalist obsession – which I have remarked in the definition of capitalist corporations in the first part of this study – with a constant drive towards expansion, occupying space, growing.

So, for one involved in corporate activity, at the most concrete level, the movement upwards *within* a corporation is correspondingly linked to the movement of the corporation as a growing pro-gressing expanding structure which in turn is linked to an increasingly influential role in the speculative activities of corporate capitalism in the broadest sense. A typical corporate success story is of an entrepreneur who started a private company with some investors, became an industrial capitalist (executive and owner rolled into one), gradually acquired the role of overall manager of an expanded and subdivided corporation with other levels of management under him (which also involved therefore a gradual removal from direct executive involvement), who became a director of an ever larger and more diverse corporation (now almost entirely remote from executive functions) which at some stage went public, who thereafter came into a position whereby the corporation was so diversified and complex and extensive that his initial entrepreneur-ial connection with it became ever more remote and a speculative view of it prevailed, who by then was also in a position to invest his growing assets into other enterprises (by taking them over, merging them, or controlling them as autonomous corporations) to which he can have had no other than a primarily speculative interest. The ever growing remoteness from entrepreneurial origins and industrial executive preoccupations is supplemented by an ever growing closeness to that restricted point of view of speculative involvement. This flows into the concentrated point of the control of speculative interests at the tip of the corporate capitalist gyre. Other success stories or stories of failure merge into this. An entrepreneur may set up a small enterprise, reach a level of demonstrable success, and then get absorbed into a larger existing corporation which pays him well and perhaps makes him an upper-level executive whose speculative interests are given full support by certain shares or options rewards. Or otherwise an entrepreneur may start a small company, find a small niche, get challenged by a larger corporation and close down. Or alternatively the company could be taken over and dismantled. Or a sufficiently active employee may work his way up, get gradually removed from the (let's say) technical work he was involved in and gradually put to greater and greater degrees of managerial work, gradually reaching a level of management at which he finds that the best way to maximise his self-interests (perhaps a predisposition to his doing so was responsible for his rise in the first place) is by abandoning direct involvement in the workings of the specific cor-poration and its general stakeholder interests and by developing a speculative view of the corporation. Perhaps he finds himself holding lots of executive options or executive shares, and meets like-minded people in the boardroom. Or perhaps (to take a failure story) the talented worker who finds it difficult to dissociate himself sufficiently from the specific productive processes of the corporation and its general stakeholder interests gradually finds himself stagnating in a situation where none of his talents can be exploited further. All of these bits and pieces fall in together to contribute to the overall gyre of contemporary corporate capitalism wherein speculative interests ultimately hold sway. And it is in this obsessively expansive and profoundly influential spiral of corporate capitalism as a whole that, at a micro level, the alignment between the principal shareholder who necessarily has a speculative view, and the upper-level manager whose conditional pay structure is an incentive towards developing speculative interests, fits in comfortably. This alignment is not the result of a conspiracy theory – it flows from the systemic logic of corporate capitalism at large – and has developed through incremental and contingent measures that were and are often hidden behind convenient myths. Such convenient myths are the ones I have mentioned (the conjunctions of misdirections): the alleged superlative importance of upper-level management which is actually dissociated; the notion that executive share or options compensation has something to do with management while it actually has to do with speculation; the idea that there is some sort of uniform conflict in the corporate sector between ownership and control whereas the picture is far from being black and white; the idea that there are victimised shareholders who are generally ordinary working people while there are significantly different kinds of shareholders with significantly different powers.

The alignment of speculative involvement is, of course, not simply confined to upper-level managers and large investors in significant corporations (whether from within or outside). Within this alignment there is also naturally a whole army of servants who facilitate speculative activity under the incentive of developing their own speculative involvements. The chief butlers amongst these are probably the investment bankers or investment-banking partners who facilitate speculative deals and stand to gain a percentage of the proceeds from all the speculating parties concerned. Their minions are regiments of market-makers, arbitrageurs, corporate law experts, public relations mediators, etc. This is in itself a complex and fascinating subsector within capitalist corporate processes, but I do not intend to dwell on it here. It can be demonstrated with little

difficulty that the same sort of speculative incentives through conditional pay as for upper-level corporate managers are in operation
here, assisted by much the same kind of obfuscations.

Two questions remain before I leave this section: (a) why is it
convenient to have these myths (or, in other words, why does such
a complex machinery of misdirections about managerialism and
public shareholding persist or why is it sustained)? (b) what role does
the capitalist state play with regard to the above-discussed operations
of capitalist corporations? These need to be answered in order to lead
toward the political philosophical implications of the above.

The answer to the first question above has to do with political contingency. Speculative activities and involvements are naturally
indifferent, and often inimical, to most popular notions of social
justice and rational social ideology. The gains that certain parties can
make through speculative activities are spectacular, lead to concen-
trations of social capital, and are not necessarily related to
value-enhancing input. However value – and therefore ultimately
social wealth – is calculated, the onus of value-making is on either
those who contribute directly to a physical or intellectual productive
process (in spirit this has to be close to a Marxist labour theory of
value), or to the behaviour of consumers (marginal utilities) or to
both. But in this process there is no necessary value-enhancing contribution from speculators, whose activities are largely confined to
manipulating value-enhancing activities with a view to siphoning
off and concentrating social wealth (whereby limited self-interests
are served) and controlling the overall capitalist process. Undeniably,
to some extent speculative activities do serve to inject capital in
growing productive sectors, but the onus of getting such sectors
going depends on entrepreneurial activities which are extrinsic to
speculative activities, and their value-enhancing potential depends
on those who contribute to productive processes and consumers.
Speculative activities are not in themselves value enhancing; they
may be used to set up the conditions of value enhancement, but
only so long as the self-interests of speculative alignments are
thereby served. Corporate capitalism is a *perpetuum mobile* controlled
and sustained by speculative involvements, which in its reproductive
gyre-like spiralling perpetually serves the limited self interests of significant speculating actors – a speculating coterie. The disparity
between value-enhancing activity and speculation is (insofar as it is

contingent on the micro issue of executive pay) more or less the sort of disparity between the basic salary for managerial activity (which may be thought of as compensation for an intellectual contribution to the productive process, though usually overrated in those terms) and the conditional pay which masquerades as being 'performance'-related but is actually an incentive towards speculative activities. The best analogy for gains made through speculative activity is that of winning money through gambling: they both involve assessable risks, and they are both modes of wealth allocation that cannot be justified in terms of compensation or deserts. If speculative activity is often *not* like gambling that is only because there is a great deal of corruption involved in the practice of speculative processes: through insider dealing, through illicit information gathering, through the manipulation of different tax regimes and legal provisions in different countries, etc. Inevitably, it seems to me, once the speculative incentive of executive conditional pay is realised, there creeps into that whole system a taint of corruption. Speculative incentives with executive options and share schemes seem to be designed to encourage tacit insider dealing, despite the obvious legal provisions against this which are usually instituted.

Speculative activity is clearly contrary to existing notions of distributive justice. This is so whether one thinks of distributive justice in a liberal fashion as a meeting of just needs and just deserts,[23] or whether one considers the matter from a socialist perspective of at least basic or complex egalitarianism,[24] or even whether one contemplates this from what is now the prevailing conservative position of equality of opportunity. The last might appear to be the most easily reconcilable with the prevailing capitalist order of sustaining speculative interests, but this is not the case. In practice, an equality of opportunity could only be thought to be in operation if there is some initial position of parity from which opportunities can be availed of, worked for or not taken advantage of. The current speculation-centred workings of corporate capitalism are designed to ensure that no identifiable position of parity can be established; there would have to be a value-producing mass (producers and consumers) which does not get its just deserts and whose needs are not justly met for the appropriations of speculators to be absorbed. The systematisation of this is more refined in contemporary capitalism, but not hugely different from Marx's understanding of unfairness involved in the broad class stratifications into workers and capitalists, which necessarily generates an industrial reserve army and unemployment in industrial capitalism.

Since the operation and dominance of the speculative spirit of contemporary capitalism is not in consonance with existing notions of social justice, and therefore with any rational political ideology, it is politically expedient to have myths of the above sort to make it appear to be consonant. This could obviously be effected through either of two strategies: (a) by making speculative involvement appear to be more democratic than it is; and (b) by hiding a cold and politically measured apprehension of speculative practices behind more comfortable red herrings. Both these effectively occur in the widespread dissemination and acceptance of the above-mentioned kinds of myth.

The impression that the generalisation of 'the shareholder' produces in available ponderings in this area is one of the democratisation of speculative involvement, simply by repressing the significant differences between different kinds of shareholders and the different privileges and measures of control that these different kinds of shareholding have. That simple turn of phrase conveys the impression that everyone who is in some legalistic sense identified as a shareholder somewhere – which is the vast majority of all working people anywhere – are all colluding in this harmless game of speculating. Actually, the vast majority of working people who may invest their earnings through share schemes, pension schemes, mortgage schemes, insurance schemes, etc. – usually mediated by banks and investment companies in safe investments, and occasionally in more risky ventures by the adventurous – are not speculating at all. They are allowing speculators – that alignment of large shareholders (whether with inside or outside interests) in significant corporations, investment bankers/partnerships and their machinery, upper-level executives in significant corporations – to have free play with significant percentages of their earnings and savings. They are also helping this alignment to disburse the costs of maintaining the machinery that is devoted to supporting their speculative activities.

The carefully exaggerated importance of management/managers who are primarily involved in managerialism *per se*, which helps to shroud their dissociative relationship to productive capitalist processes and their ultimate negativity, is extremely useful in drawing attention away from the speculative involvements with which they are aligned. This diversionary effect is heightened by making that which enables this alignment with speculative interests to be created (that is, conditional executive pay) to appear to be a measure of something that it bears no relation to (that is, 'performance'). The effective purpose of these obfuscations are easily grasped if we think of them as producing two aspects of managerialism: an illusion (a mask) of upper-level management/managers as assuming overall responsibility to protect all kinds of stakeholder interests with regard to specific corporations; a hidden but more truly expressive visage of upper-level management/managers as agents aligned with speculative interests which they have every incentive to work for and which are ultimately indifferent to the health of and general stakeholder interests of specific corporations. The first aspect – the illusion, the mask – acts as a buffer which absorbs anything that might strike anybody as suspect about the processes and functioning of contemporary corporate capitalism. Any unease about anything, from micro issues to do with the malfunctioning of particular corporations to macro issues to do with the general behaviour of the capitalist corporate sector generally, can be directed at the mask. The mask of the responsible performing manager provides a place where blame may be allocated. All the iniquities and injustices of corporate capitalist organisation, all the frustrations and bloodthirstiness of those stakeholders who don't get what they want, can be thrown at this mask. The mask performs the same role that the foot soldiers of the roman legions did. Consumer problems can be blamed on management, employee dissatisfaction can be directed at management, 'the stakeholder' (including the small party of real speculators as wolves in sheep's clothing) intervenes, on the understanding that control and ownership have been divided, capitalist political parties and their officials join in with the populist pretence of doing what they are appointed to do (protecting the interests of the people who are all stakeholders in the vaunted 'stakeholder society'). But the mask is a mask – it makes very little difference to upper level managers/management what accusations are thrown at them – they know it is part of their job – something that has to be ... well, managed. They are also well aware that this doesn't matter because this is not the side that butters their bread. The hidden visage which is rather beautifully aligned with speculative interests knows that its bread is well-buttered despite or even because of all this.

The role of the capitalist state is generally to collude with the control of speculative interests in contemporary corporate capitalism, and to provide systematic support to all the mechanisms that enable the maintenance of such control – including systematic playing along with the myths. This is a matter that requires closer inspection and I shall come to that in the next chapter.

More immediately, and as much to maintain a sense of symmetry as a matter of interest, it is worth considering the role of the state with regard to the admittedly limited *leitmotiv* of this section – conditional executive pay masquerading as performance-related pay while naturally being aligned to speculative involvements. With regard to this issue there are three obvious ways in which the state plays a role:

(a) The first has to do with the control of the judicial apparatus that the state has at its disposal. If I assume that British Company Law is a representative instance from which the kinds of principle which generally govern corporate capitalist jurisprudence may be inferred, certain features of the law come to mind that are peculiarly felicitous for speculative interests. So, for instance, the definitions of affiliations to a corporation apart from those that attach to workers or employees (and in British law this is complicated by the existence of a separate legal code as Labour Law)[25] are so fluid and indistinct as to naturally facilitate the formation of speculative alignments of the sort described above. The status of the members (shareholders) of a corporation, of the executive and non-executive directors and shadow directors, of senior managers (from this level downwards an employee-likeness is legally established by the right to remuneration for services, though this is shouldered by legally enjoined extra-employee roles insofar as senior managers have large fiduciary responsibilities, that is, those that depend on trust), of promoters and auditors, of membership of the board, etc., is established to a large degree on simple declarative statements to that effect which are documented and agreed upon.[26] Unlike the employee whose status is established by the drawing up of certain contracts wherein obligations are predetermined and qualifications are accepted, the obligations of the above-mentioned levels of affiliation *follow from* their declared status as such and do not *determine* the declaration of the status itself. This might have little substantial effect on the manner in which a director and an employee can be legally held responsible for their actions with regard to a corporation, but it does have a substantial effect on the manner in which these positions come to be occupied in the first instance. The flexibility of the manner in which non-employee-like or extra-employee-like positions come to be held in a corporation (legally simply through declarative statements which are appropriately recorded) undoubtedly facilitates the creation of alignments which, happily for speculative interests, do not have straightforward and immediate legal implications. Company law has to depend on restraining the activities of such alignments after the fact, by stipulating against insider dealing, by trying to ensure against contraventions of fiduciary responsibilities and conflicts of interest, etc. But such after-the-fact restrictions can always be circumvented by finding the loopholes in any prescriptive statement of what constitute such infringements, or by the dependence that such legal strictures must have on precedents. Fortunately for speculative interests, existing legal precedents often work both ways, and new precedents are rarely set.

(b) The second way in which the capitalist state may support the above-described issues in capitalist corporations is by its budgeting powers within its area of authority. Budgeting powers are of course enforced by the judicial apparatus in place, but are distinct from these in being a legislative prerogative which is more within the control of a particular government and more conditional on its understanding of a given context. The particular aspect of budgeting which is especially significant to the micro issue of conditional executive pay as well as the related macro issue of the control of speculative interests is that which has to do with the establishing of suitable tax regimes for given contexts. A particular tax regime can be used to encourage an alignment of managerial parties to speculative interests by encouraging conditional pay as described above (say, by providing that executive options and share benefits would be taxed at a lower income tax rate rather than a higher capital gains tax rate), and may be used to encourage speculators generally by the provision of tax-free zones or tax havens (say, by providing for tax-free investment opportunities, or by trying to draw speculators from outside by providing for comparatively low upper-level income taxes). Both these have happened routinely in contemporary corporate capitalist contexts.[27]

(c) Capitalist states may tacitly facilitate the control of speculative interests by lending their support to the myths that obscure the extent of that control. The sense of democratising the possibilities of speculation can be promoted by the state through vague undiscriminating invitations for everyone to participate in a capitalist stakeholder society. When the puzzling iniquities of stakeholding in that abstract sense become all too apparent by evidence of growing inequality and rising poverty and fluctuating unemployment within the capitalist zone itself, and when these are thrown further into relief by the more unmitigable disparities that are constantly getting exacerbated between different countries and populations at a global level, different capitalist states and their mediating forums promote the vaguest and most wishy-washy of promises. It is among the latter that such catchwords as '*trickle-down* economy' and 'taking advantage of *globalisation*' find their place. When specific events threaten to dismay specific sets of stakeholders (consumers, small shareholders, workers) and reveal the unpalatable speculative interests behind them, the relevant capitalist state makes populist and obfuscatory gestures of fighting managerial incompetence or insisting on proper managerial 'performance', or at its most adventurous, makes a few tokenistic interventions in the organisation of large corporations. These are matters that are too familiar in the contemporary corporate capitalist ethos for me to have to cite specific evidence.

But the contribution of the state in contemporary corporate capitalism is not something that can be fully described in a short space, and it is to a fuller treatment of this that I turn in the next chapter.

9 Corporatism and the Corporate Capitalist State

To discern how the contemporary corporate capitalist state comes into the picture of capitalist corporate organisation drawn above, it might be useful to be reminded of the definition of the political state given in the first part. I distinguished the political state and the capitalist corporation there as intentional systems (drawing that term from Dennett) in the following fashion: the capitalist corporation is an intentional system with definite ends-orientations (profits), which acts as its own interpretive agent and acts upon itself accordingly; the political state is the interpretive agent for the people–land–resources it is with regard to (it is the people–land–resources in question which is the intentional system) with a view to determining what the ends-orientations therein might be and then acting upon the intentional system accordingly (which it is empowered to do by its monopoly on force).

There are certain inferences which can immediately be made from this and which I omitted to make before. The *degree of success* of a political state as *interpretive agent* with regard to the people–land–resources under its jurisdiction as intentional system would depend largely on the kind of relationship that exists between the former and the latter. This relationship could be determined to some extent by the manner in which a given political state comes to be established or appointed as such. If the mode of the establishment or appointment of a political state is such that it would have within itself an identity of interests with the various sectors and interests that compose the people–land–resources it is with regard to as a whole, one may surmise that its interpretive attempts are likely to be more successful. In this case success is seen in terms of the closeness of the connection between political state and people–land–resources, and therefore of the state's being able to have an authentic sense of what the people–land–resources intends and to act accordingly. This, I feel, would be the mainstay of any argument in favour of a purely democratic mode of establishing the political state or appointing those who represent the political state (whether that works in practice or not). Alternatively, some may argue that greater success in such interpretation is likely to occur if there is an overall and coherent and disinterested intellectual apprehension on the part of the political state of what the various sectors and interests of the people–land–resources are without any necessary identification with the various sectors and interests that compose the people–land–resources. Here, success is understood in terms of a nonpartisan view that enables the retention of certain ideologically determined directions in a fashion which is sensitive to an interpretive apprehension of the context it has to operate within. Such an argument entails the establishment of the political state or appointment of representatives thereof through some meritocratic process or identification of established authority (whether that works in practice or not). This could well be the justification that certain autocratic or theocratic or oligarchic or single-party-controlled political states may draw on (I don't mean to lump these forms of government together as being similar in any way except in being able to draw on this *form* of argument). In practice, the principle of disinterestedness (or of not having to identify too closely or completely with the people–land–resources as an intentional system) is one that no current form of democratic statehood can wholly eschew – and certain ideological orientations and an encouragement toward disinterestedness are usually ensured by such means as having a constitution and a certain degree of meritocratic contribution in state functioning (say, in the form of a meritocratically appointed civil service). To many, the necessity for a principle of disinterestedness seems to be as obviously desirable as a necessity for closeness to people–land–resources as an intentional system: for example, it is possible that a political state would find that *all* sectors and interests of the people–land–resources it is with regard to entertain a certain unpalatable prejudice (a xenophobic hatred of those who are considered to be 'foreigners' for instance), and it may be deemed self-evidently undesirable that the political state should identify with this pervasive prejudice.

The *degree of success* of a political state insofar as it *acts upon* the people–land–resources (the intentional system) it is with regard to would depend largely on the kind of state apparatus it has at its disposal (the machinery that ensures its monopoly on force, such as legislative and judicial machinery, military machinery, economic machinery, public relations machinery), and on the direction in which it wishes to take the people–land–resources as a result of its interpretive activity. The phrases 'acting upon' or 'directions' or 'ideological orientations' here should be understood in the broadest sense as having not only dynamic but also static connotations: so, a conservative agenda or a desire to maintain the status quo in this context is also a direction or ideological orientation which needs to be acted upon. The question of what constitutes success in this regard is more clear cut than in the matter of what is a successful interpretation of an intentional system: success is in the implementation of whatever action the political state determines to take as a result of its interpretive attempts concerning the people–land–resources it is with regard to. I don't think any further qualification can be offered about the nature of the state apparatus apropos different forms of government – any form of government can have a strong or weak state apparatus.

The most optimistic expectations that are conceivable for the corporate capitalist state at an advanced stage of capitalism are probably those that were offered by 'corporatist' political theorists in the late nineteen-seventies and nineteen-eighties. Political reflection on 'corporatism' (with the fascist associations of the term shorn off) was initiated largely through the writings of Claus Offé and Phillipe C. Schmitter.[1] A succinct summary of the principal ideas of 'corporatism' is given by Cawson and Saunders: they think of it as a mode of resource allocation, distinct from such modes of resource allocation as the 'market mode' (which depends on some objective principle, irrespective of whether the principle in question is as vastly different as Adam Smith's invisible hand or Marx's law of labour) and the 'bureaucratic mode' (where resources are allocated politically by state institutions which are separated from civil society). The alternative 'corporatist mode', they maintain, is characterised as follows:

> Corporatist decisions are neither imposed by objective laws nor by a determinate political authority. They reflect the outcome of a bargaining process between corporate interests, which implies the assumption that each party is able independently to exercise some form of sanction. Power is thus neither pluralistically dispersed, nor concentrated, but polycentric within an overall hierarchy. The private economy cannot operate independently of the state, but the state does not control private capital. (1) The state intervenes to safeguard and protect capital accumulation [...],

but it must legitimate its intervention to both capital and labour [...]. Such intervention is not pursued by means of bureaucratic strictures, but by the establishment of ad hoc agencies on which the interests of labour and capital are directly represented. (2) The characteristic pattern of legislation is discretionary and enabling: the agency is given powers to intervene in a manner which discriminates between capitals or between sectors, rather than as in the bureaucratic mode via a universally applicable code of rules. Economic planning in a corporatist system is essentially indicative, whether in the form of specifically negotiated planning agreements, or via the co-ordination of information to feed into the economic calculations of individual corporations.[2]

The essay from which I quote this is primarily concerned with the different kinds of interest representation that occur within the state at central (or national) and local (or regional) levels – but that needn't concern us here.

The approach of 'corporatist' theorists agrees with the definitions of political state and capitalist corporation given above: there is an implicit recognition of the different intentionalities involved. Its optimism lies in envisaging, within the context of corporate capitalism, the development and institutionalisation of certain forums for negotiating and bargaining between the two main intentionalities involved, which would be able to bring together and mediate between a wide range of different and even contrary interests (capitalist and labour, regional and central, and other different sorts of interest group). Here the political state itself is seen both to maintain its ideological commitment to advance capitalist corporations and the activities of the corporate sector and to defend the broader and often opposed interests of the polity at large, by (a) *delegating its responsibility as interpretive agent of people–land–resources as intentional system* to independent negotiating bodies (with suitable representation of relevant interest groups), which could undertake negotiation and bargaining with a view to reaching definite sanctions, and by (b) *retaining its prerogative to act upon the intentional system of the people–land–resources* insofar as it is committed to using the machinery at its disposal to implementing the sanctions so reached. The ability to delegate the responsibility as interpretive agent to independent negotiating bodies and to ensure that the relevant interests are adequately represented therein suggests that an identification with different interests and sectors already exists within the composition of the political state and its representatives – which clearly indicates the existence of a democratic mode of establishing or appointing the state. The commitment enjoined here on the political state to act upon the sanctions reached through bargaining and negotiation ensures the possibility of strengthening the existing democratic mode. This implicit identification of democratic process and corporate capitalist political state is one of the theoretical strengths of this approach, for such identification is often unwarrantably or erroneously taken for granted. Overall, the corporate capitalist state retains an interventionist role coherent with its status in the economic sphere, but without any direct alignment with either the corporate sector or any particular sector in the people–land–resources it is with regard to, and always with democratic sanction. In theoretical terms the 'corporatist' vision appears to be plausible, and in the late seventies and especially in the eighties capitalist boom liberal 'corporatist' theorists were optimistic that their vision was either in the process of being realised and instituted or that this was imminent, despite the scepticism of a few Marxist theorists.[3]

By the late eighties and early nineties though, it became clear that corporate capitalist political states were not moving towards 'corporatism'. In an interesting study of the matter, *Corporatist Decline in Advanced Capitalism* (1993), Mark James Gobeyn observed:

> Essentially, corporatism, with its emphasis on centralized, harmonious, consensus-oriented bargaining arrangements between the state and the economy's producer groups, seems to be on the decline in Europe. [...] Emerging in [capitalist] societies, then, are more selective sectorial corporatist bargaining arrangements accompanied by more market-based forms of labour-management relations. This trend towards instability within and/or dismantlements of corporatist institutional arrangements quite obviously weakens the aforementioned assumptions of many liberal corporatist theorists concerning the apparent durability and likely predominance of these arrangements throughout advanced capitalism.[4]

In short, it becomes apparent by this time that in fact the bargaining position of all but the corporate sector is growing weaker and that correspondingly that of the corporate sector is growing stronger. Gobeyn's analysis of this does not actually examine the role of the political state in this in a straightforward fashion; he more or less assumes that this is coeval with what could be considered a weakening of the state or a diminishing of the state. His analysis concentrates on the economic factors: in his context, a combination of increasing unemployment (and a related weakening therefore of trade unionism), increased mobility of capital, the reduction or erasure of trade barriers and tariffs, and growing international investment opportunities.[5] These economic considerations can however be translated into broader systemic terms that are pertinent to the generalisations presented above. From the point of view of this study, what Gobeyn effectively says in identifying these contextual economic factors as being responsible for the failure of the 'corporatist' vision, is that: (a) under certain circumstances (like increasing unemployment) the representatives of certain interest groups (like trade unions for workers) may not have the requisite bargaining and negotiating position compared with the representatives of opposed interest groups (say, managers' associations for corporate capitalists/speculators) within the negotiative/bargaining and sanction-making independent body to which the political state delegates the role of interpretive agent – and in such a case the political state would be in no position to do anything about this apart from honouring its commitments to carrying out the sanctions of that body, even if thereby a particular interest group gains undesirable and unfair advantage; (b) the political state is limited in its powers to the people–land–resources it is with regard to and which it has under its jurisdiction, whereas the interest groups who might operate within this jurisdiction can nevertheless draw upon resources and support from outside that jurisdiction (mobility of capital, etc.).

It appears to me that while the contextually relevant factors cited by Gobeyn are significant, the failure of the 'corporatist' ideal was essentially implicit in its conceptual assumptions. This becomes clear if closer attention is paid to the role of the corporate capitalist political state, and the assumptions regarding this that are made in 'corporatist' thinking. Since this is illuminating for an understanding of the contemporary corporate capitalist state it is worth dwelling on.

In fact there is one crucial assumption in the conceptualisation of the 'corporatist' ideal, and this is an assumption of *balance* – which is analogous in many ways to Marx's assumption of an equilibrium in unravelling how the reproductive processes of industrial capitalism may conceivably carry on in an expanding spiral. 'Corporatist' theorists assume that the different interest groups which engage in negotiating/bargaining do so in a manner which is balanced in the sense of all parties representing themselves truthfully and completely and each party having a sufficient understanding of the interests of all the other parties. There is little leeway for misrepresentation, partial representations, obfuscations, confusions, subterfuge, hidden interests, manipulations, etc. within the understanding of such negotiating/bargaining. It is assumed that the relative influence of the bargaining and negotiating positions of all parties within a sanction-making body are balanced; that their mutual dependencies and interdependencies are such that no dominant interest group is able arbitrarily to have its own way. It is precisely the lack of such balance that makes Gobeyn's point about unemployment relevant. It is also assumed that the corporate capitalist state is able to retain a necessary distance or sense of balance with regard to all interest groups and is invulnerable to one or the other of the 'economy's producer groups' (to use Gobeyn's words) for its own resource needs. In practice this has proved to be very unlikely – a point which I touch upon later. It is assumed in too clear cut a fashion that *all* interest groups and sectors are able to find adequate representation and expression. Within that, too little allowance is made for the general interests of the great mass of differently employed and located people under the jurisdiction of a political state which may not be identifiable as being within the purview of any specific sector or group with representatives; too little allowance is made for the conflicts of interest and overlapping interests which may exist between extant sectors and groups. The glossing over of these disruptive possibilities in the conceptualisation of 'corporatism' seems to me to be of a similar variety – and therefore I present these as being overlooked by a crucial and tenuous assumption of *balance*.

These theoretical and rather abstract reflections on the role of the contemporary corporate capitalist state address what is arguably the most idealistic and optimistic conceptualisation thereof. The tenuousness of this gives some indication of what sort of very unideal roles the corporate capitalist state may assume if it cannot aspire to this. The role that the contemporary corporate capitalist state is more likely to, indeed must and does, assume, where the kind of misdirections and obfuscations prevail which I have described above (those designed to enable speculative interests/involvements to flourish), is quite different from the 'corporatist' idea.

To allow speculative involvements to be dominated and maximised by a small number of self-interested alignments is so contrary to popular notions of social justice that it is impossible for any political state to be seen to condone it, let alone actively further it, as a political ideology and agenda. The political state is by definition an interpreting and acting agent with regard to the intentional system of the people–land–resources as a whole that is under its jurisdiction; and the dominance of such speculative interests is antithetical to any intentionality that may be seen to pertain to the people–land–resources as a whole. So the contemporary corporate capitalist political state which finds itself enmeshed in an ever-expansive and inescapable systematisation of speculative interests and involvements in contemporary corporate capitalism is inevitably put in a position of Sartrean 'bad faith' – of having to present itself in a way that undercuts its *raison d'être*, that is contrary to what it inevitably is.[6] To come to grips with what this position of 'bad faith' entails for the corporate capitalist state, three issues need to be clarified: (1) *how* does such a state deal with this self-contradictory position? (2) *why* precisely does it do so, why doesn't it use the substantial state machinery and legislative prerogatives at its disposal to establish a position of 'good faith'? (3) *what* does the state actually contribute to the schema of contemporary corporate capitalism? I proceed to address these as the *how*, the *why*, and the *what* issues.

THE *HOW* ISSUE

The means which enable corporate capitalist states to deal with its position of 'bad faith' are easily recognised in most corporate capitalist contexts of our time. Again, I offer the following observations as general systemic features of such contexts and do not attempt to present any extensive demonstration of them; instead I rely on their familiarity to confirm the observations. There are, in brief, two means – which coexist and support each other – through which the contemporary corporate capitalist political state reconciles itself (and more) with the current condition of corporate capitalism: one of these could be thought of as an assumed *transparency*, whereby the state apparently willingly relegates its control or inter-ventional prerogatives on economic spheres of political interest, and prudently allows (and enables) corporate capitalism to have free play in the markets; the other mode could be thought of as *mirroring*, whereby within economic spheres of political interest over which the state cannot relegate its control or interventional prerogatives, and within the structures of political state organisation itself, an effort is made to emulate the practices of capitalist corporations.

Announcements of the corporate capitalist political state's deter-mination to be transparent can always be recognised as such in retrospective.[7] The determination to be transparent is not, as it might be expected to be or as it might be presented as being, a passive affair: the political state is designed to interpret intentional-ity and act accordingly, and its cause of transparency must also appear to be an interpretive strategy and a mode of action. So such transparency cannot be effected in any sort of realisation of *neutrality* (to take the libertarian or neo-liberal term which I will come to in due course)[8] – nor for that matter is it the harbinger of a *withering away of the state* (which is the flip side of the same concept and which I have discussed already)[9] – but has to be implemented as a matter of policy. This is a self-erasure that occurs in a buzz of activity. It might be announced as a policy of privatisation, whereby as many sectors under state control and financing as possible are sold off to corporate capitalists. It has to be suggested in this process that in doing this the intentionality of the people–land–resources that the state is with regard to is being carried out – a matter of careful argu-mentation, manipulation, statistic throwing, authoritative testifying, etc. There have to be gestures of the state protecting the interests of the people–land–resources and keeping certain reserved interven-tional prerogatives in the agreements and contracts which seal such sales. The indelible fact that such transfers – such policies of pri-vatisation – are in fact a complete shift of relevant intentional prerogatives (from that which is the state's responsibility of serving the intentions and interests of the whole people–land–resources, to that which is a capitalist corporation's or group of such corporations' single-minded intention and interest to make profits irrespective of people–land–resources) has to be somehow shrouded and obscured, even if momentarily. The underlying fact that the capitalist corpo-ration's movements – indeed corporate capitalism's generally – are already governed by limited speculative involvements has to be magicked away from popular attention. The latter is, of course, facil-

itated by the fullest determination on the part of capitalist corporations not to draw attention to this; the state simply has to fall in
with the myths and established modes of misdirection and obfuscation already in operation. Other policy decisions are implemented by
the corporate capitalist political state to back up moves like privatisation, usually by the exercise of its legislative powers. This can
manifest itself in the state's adjustment of the relevant tax regime
to encourage corporate capitalist activity to the maximum, such as
investment tax saving schemes and other tax incentives (I have
touched on this already). The corporate capitalist state finds the
policy of reducing the taxes to be a most effective short-term
populist measure, and particularly useful since it chimes in with the
devolution of responsibility which comes with transparency.
Populist budgeting may also typically see some extraordinary
investment being made in that restricted sector which the state
cannot afford to relegate completely to the capitalists (like health,
or education, old-age and disability provision, and policing, though
these too may gradually be effectively privatised in insidious ways).
It is well known that the budgetary legislative powers for corporate
capitalist states has become less a matter of economic control and
more a matter of making political gestures. Commodity price-fixing
within budgetary periods is always therefore left to be ultimately
conditional on market behaviour. In fact, the further the contemporary corporate capitalist state consolidates its position, the less it
may take its budgetary prerogatives seriously, leaving significant
budgetary decisions (for example, letting the banking sector take
over interest rate setting on borrowing and lending). In short,
policies which may be offered as *privatisation, cutting taxes, reducing
welfare expenditure by making welfare spending more efficient and
effective, creating investment opportunities by providing tax incentives* are
some of the measures which mark the contemporary corporate
capitalist state's determination to be transparent.

The above kind of determination to transparency is generally
attended by a determination to mirroring in the corporate capitalist
state. This is, of course, no more than another sort of self-erasure,
another kind of hiding away of 'bad faith'. The idea is that if the
state emulates in a superficial fashion the behaviour and mores of
capitalist corporations – and keeps doing this insistently and continuously – the perception of a clear and incontrovertible divergence
of intentionality represented by the state and contained in the
capitalist corporation (and therefore in corporate capitalism) will at

least be blurred, and will perhaps gradually begin to get overlooked all together. If the superficial behaviours of political state and capitalist corporation seem to be indistinguishable, then the underlying rationales which distinguish them will get dimmed, and with any luck will disappear entirely. And the more these underlying rationales cease to be distinct or distinguishable, the more *natural and/or obvious* would corporate capitalist superstructures and the dominance of limited speculative involvements appear. The result is a wholesale import of corporate managerial discourses (with all their superficiality and ability to misdirect) into the sphere of state activities, within state organisation, within those sectors (welfare sector, government protected industry) which have to remain under state control – simply because the latter are too overtly conceptualised to protect the interests of the people–land–resources as a whole. This is what I call here mirroring. It is a kind of superficial rhetorical manipulation, which resonates with all the sophistry of classical rhetorics. It is implied in thinking of state–people relationships as corporation–client relationships, in seeing the economic investments of the state as being essentially of a similar nature to the investments of any capitalist corporation, and subject to the same rules. It is contained, for instance, in the calls for superior managerial 'performance' in state-controlled welfare and public services, and in the measurement of such 'performance' in terms of cost-effectiveness, if not profitability. It is implicit in political processes and state activities which have increasingly to present themselves in terms of public-relations, image-making, vote *banking*, spin-doctoring, advertising. And so on.

THE *WHY* ISSUE

Most of what could be said here I have already stated in passing above, but it might be worth going through the following points briefly here even at the risk of some repetition. Some of the obvious reasons for the corporate capitalist state's being prepared, or perhaps obliged, to assume a collaborate role with the processes and speculative involvements behind corporate capitalism are the following:

(a) The scope of corporate capitalist processes, ever expanding as it is, has in the post-colonial and post-world-war period extended beyond the scope of the jurisdiction of any single political state or even any specific alignment of political states. More importantly, within this increasingly international domain (the ambition of this internationalism is contained in the term 'globalisation'), the processes of corporate capitalism from the micro level (e.g. the manner in which labour–management relations are regulated) to the macro level (e.g. the manner in which dominant speculative involvements manipulate global markets) are much better coordinated than is possible for any particular alignment of political states. Such processes of coordination have been enabled by the formation of mergers and oligopolies (or at least trading agreements) amongst significant capitalist corporations; by the development of technological resources devoted to gathering information about different markets and stockholdings, sorting and making such information accessible, and transmitting it expeditiously; and by the development of systems for efficient long-distance transactions to take place. Naturally these developments in the corporate capitalist domain put the individual political state in the position of the supplicant. While the state can bring its legislative apparatus to bear on economic activity within the people–land–resources under its jurisdiction, it cannot do so effectively (even in collaboration with other similarly situated political states) at an international level. There are two options open here: either the political state can devote its efforts to trying to persuade capitalist corporations and the speculative interests behind them to focus their activities in some way within the people–land–resources under its jurisdiction (in effect this would become a corporate capitalist state); or the political state can choose to isolate itself from international corporate capitalism, to maintain suitable control of its domestic economy, and perhaps to initiate economic exchanges and agreements with other states which choose to do the same (roughly the situation that characterised the former communist bloc). However, the fact remains that an alignment of political states simply cannot be as well coordinated as international corporate capitalism: the former is divided by having primary commitments to the intentional systems of different peoples–lands–resources, while the latter is united by the cohesiveness of its international organisation and by the ultimate ends-orientation of speculative involvements. And a controlled domestic economy cannot compete with a free-flowing international economy. So assuming the role of the supplicant, trying to persuade capitalist corporations and speculative interests to locate themselves within its people–land–resources of jurisdiction, is the easier option for a given political state – and the reason why the corporate capitalist state is such as it is becomes clear. Some of the ways used to persuade capitalist corporations and speculative interests to locate themselves among the people–land–resources under a political state's jurisdiction are: to offer investment and speculation opportunities which are identified with that people–land–resources (this is where privatisation comes in); to offer investment and speculation incentives (a suitable tax regime and clearly defined but not-too-interventionist juridical and legislative frameworks help); to offer investment and speculation advantages (an efficient stock exchange, technological expertise, cheap labour, etc., may all do that); to offer an ideologically friendly environment for investment and speculation (a state which symbolically *believes* in corporate capitalist processes by emulating them can go a long way here).

(b) Corporate capitalist processes have primarily affiliated themselves to and located themselves within political states where the prevailing mode of establishing or appointing the state is democratic – or, more precisely, depends on a system of multi-party democracy. A multi-party democracy presents certain obvious strengths, and also certain obvious vulnerabilities.[10] The vulnerabilities are such that corporate capitalists will always be able to find significant positions of political leverage within the political state. A multi-party democracy naturally allows for political alignments to be formed by conflicting and different interest groups. At the very least, in a multi-party democracy corporate capitalists can always present an influential and well-resourced political front (more so than most, possibly all, other interest groups). More likely, corporate capitalists can render their interests more invincible by aligning themselves within a large number of conflicting and different political fronts in a multi-party democracy, thereby ensuring support from the political state, irrespective of whoever gets established or appointed as state representative. This sort of multiple alliance is enabled because of the differentiated levels of political parties and the political state, and the often independent financial and resourcing arrangements and accountability which exist at party and state levels. There is usually a great deal of haziness about the manner in which a political party and the political state that is effectively composed of that party are held accountable. I should indicate here that this should be read as an argument not against democracy *per se*, but against the prevailing practice of democracy, and I have speculated on the possibility of reconceptualising democratic practice so as to counter these vulnerabilities elsewhere.[11]

(c) I have no doubt whatever that genuine rational confusion about political intentionalities, and about ideological convictions (and more spectacularly misconceptions), have also guided the contemporary corporate capitalist political state to assume its transparent emulative role. There are undoubtedly political ideologues and activists and other participants who *believe* in the 'natural' justice of free markets and speculative involvements, in trickle-down effects and a richer globe, that greater human 'happiness' and 'freedom' ensue from these than from anything else, and so on, more as articles of faith or as being *faits accomplis* than as a rational political choice (which brings us back and looks forward to the question of the disabled political will).

THE *WHAT* ISSUE

What does the state actually contribute to the schema of contemporary corporate capitalism?

Collaboration, of course, but I hardly need to go any further into that.

The corporate capitalist political state also provides democratic legitimacy for corporate capitalist processes and for the underlying speculative interests. This involves a curious misplacement from the manner in which the democratic process should be understood. The democratic process, as I have observed above, is meant to establish or appoint the political state or representatives thereof who would thereafter be the interpretive and acting agent of the intentional system that is the people–land–resources under its jurisdiction. The democratic process could be thought of as creating within the established or appointed political state a certain empathy with all sectors and interests of the people–land–resources in question, and the state could therefore be expected to perform its interpretive and acting functions that much more coherently with the interests of the people–land–resources as a whole. The legitimacy that the democratic process thereby gives to the political state's future interpretations and actions occurs in the announcement of the people's belief (by voting or whatever electoral procedure is in place) that the prospective state is qualified to fulfil its interpretive and acting functions. Normally it is understood that such a seal of approval can be withdrawn from a political state composed in a particular way in favour of one with a different composition by enabling the repetition of the democratic process at fixed or necessary periods. It should also be understood that the legitimacy that the democratic process confers is only within the frame of the intentionality of people–land–resources as an intentional system, and to nothing else, and certainly to nothing that contravenes the spirit of the wholeness of that intentional system and its interests.

The scope and breadth of corporate capitalism and the hold that speculative involvements have on economic movements has, as I have argued above, created a mesh which may put the political state in the position of the supplicant. And, as I have also maintained above, the form of multi-party democracy is such that it is easiest for corporate capitalists and speculators to exploit its vulnerabilities and exert a certain political leverage, or in general to associate themselves with it. It seems inevitable that for the contemporary corporate capitalist state to follow a feasible economic programme, a close collaboration with corporate capitalist processes (including transparency and mirroring) would be entailed, and that all interest groups and party formations which can realistically hope to contribute to democratic government and provide practical manifestos to that effect would accede to that. Necessarily therefore the interest groups and sectors and parties which seem to be realistically available for democratic choice are already, under the circumstances, coopted into the great system of corporate capitalism. This does not mean that the establishment or appointment of such parties as political state is an endorsement of corporate capitalism (since there is little choice) – in fact insofar as democratic processes express anything in such establishment or appointment it is with regard to itself as an intentional system, and that simply cannot coincide with the intentional systems pertinent to corporate capitalism in itself – but the appointment of such parties can be *represented as* or rather *misrepresented as* a democratic sanction for corporate capitalism and the underlying speculative interests themselves. And indeed this happens constantly, and through this curious mislogic the corporate capitalist political state seems to accord a kind of democratic legitimacy to corporate capitalism itself.

But that still doesn't complete the picture of the corporate capitalist state's contribution to the overall schema of corporate capitalism. It only elucidates the role that the political state plays in mediating between corporate capitalism at large and the people–land–resources under its jurisdiction, a sort of internal picture. Arguably the corporate capitalist political state makes an even more significant contribution at an international level, through international political alignments and regulatory bodies. That however is a matter of some complexity that needs a separate focus – and I devote the next chapter to it.

10 Corporate Capitalist States and International Relations

The following discussion of the role that contemporary corporate capitalist political states play in the arena of international politics is limited precisely to that and doesn't venture into a broader consideration of the theory and practice that pertains to that arena. However, such a discussion can hardly be undertaken without some understanding of certain basic features of international politics. Relatively recent discussions of international politics and international relations have been hugely facilitated by Kenneth Waltz's systems-oriented neorealist work in the area, *Theory of International Politics* (1979), not so much for the veraciousness or persuasiveness of his formulations as for the convenience of having these formulations to work with or against. Indeed much of the theorising about international relations that has taken place since – structuralist approaches, deconstructionist Third Debate contributions, regime-theory interventions, ethics and order-centred discussions – has been routinely presented as modifications or rejections of Waltz's formulations.[1] The advantages that Waltz's international political system construction presents are an apparently universal applicability (thus inviting a more context-sensitive challenge), a penchant for distinguishing and holding apart ideas and areas clearly for the sake of neatness (thereby naturally drawing out the protests of those who can discern complex interconnections, and can reconcile themselves to a more hazy picture), and a dismissiveness regarding the constraints of international law (which understandably rouses those who have some conviction in the effectiveness of the latter). In drawing out the basic features of international politics, which I need to do in order to focus on the above issue, I also take advantage of Waltz's formulations. Before getting down to this, I should also clarify that the following discussion, though informed by an awareness of events in the field of international politics, is not developed in terms of a systematic analysis of or demonstration through empirical evidence. The discussion is developed as a series of projections and inferences that become possible given the foregoing discussion. What is clearly missing here is a historical perspective of the matter of international relations, and a sufficient account of ongoing events. I leave to the reader the effort of testing the inferences and projections offered in terms of empirical evidence.

The first concept that needs some elaboration within the frame of international politics regards the status of the political state therein. So far I have understood the political state as an interpretive and acting agent with regard to the intentional system of the people–land–resources under its jurisdiction. This appears to restrict the conceptualisation of the political state entirely within domestic or internal precincts. The question that naturally arises here is whether this continues to be a pertinent mode of defining and understanding the political state when we come to the arena of international politics. Waltz, in his quest for systemic and compartmentalised neatness had placed the domestic (or internal) system and the international (or external) system as separate and non-overlapping systems. Waltz's systemic methodology consists primarily of two levels of discernment: a level of units and a level of interactions between units that as a whole constitute a system.[2] Since I intend to examine the systemic methodology from a political philosophical perspective at a later stage I don't dwell on the nuances of this here. With this systemic methodology in hand, Waltz asserts that the units which pertain to the domestic system and the units which pertain to the international system are of a different nature, and therefore interact in distinctly different ways. The pertinent units for the domestic political structure are constitutive groups which are differentiated by their functions (that may presumably get stratified into classes or castes or other kinds of functional groups). Since such units are differentiated, their relationship to each other is hierarchical, and there is overall coordination and stability (they complement rather than compete with each other). The pertinent units for the international political structure are sovereign political states which are, as units, essentially alike (hence the assertion of the principle of self-determination and autonomy or sovereignty, and the principle of the equality of states in international politics). Since the units are alike, their relationship to each other is competitive (rather than complementary), and what prevail in the system of international politics are somewhat fragile balances of power, assertive self-interests, and potential conflicts. The arena of international politics is, so to say, *anarchic*. In Waltz's terms:

Differences between national and international structures are reflected in the ways the units of each system define their ends and develop the means for reaching them. In anarchic realms, like units coact. In hierarchic realms, unlike units interact. In an anarchic realm, the units are functionally similar and tend to remain so. Like units work to maintain a measure of independence and may even strive for anarchy. In a hierarchic realm, the units are differentiated, and they tend to increase the extent of their specialization. Differentiated units become closely interdependent, the more closely as their specialization proceeds. Because of the difference of structure, interdependence within and interdependence among nations are two distinct concepts.[3]

Waltz had anticipated some scepticism about his identification of political states as like units in the international political structure,[4] and trenchant arguments have been presented against such an identification.[5] The point that seems not to have been sufficiently addressed with regard to these formulations (even if we broadly accept the methodology), and which is in fact crucial to this study, is the precise place of the political state in the domestic structure and the relationship of that to the precise place of the political state in the international structure. For Waltz, the political state does not actually seem to have any presence in the domestic political structure and is omnipresent primarily in the international political structure; these are just two different structures and the political state appears significantly in one of them. The relationship between the two is more or less taken for granted, but in a far from clear fashion, by the undefined and fuzzy understanding of 'nationhood' which links 'national' and 'international'. In fact, it seems to me that Waltz's overzealous holding apart of the domestic and international political systems is not feasible because there is a contiguity in the status of the political state from the one to the other, thus linking them in inextricable – perhaps even undifferentiable – ways.

The political state, as I have maintained so far, is defined by its interpretive and active functions with regard to the intentional system of the people–land–resources within its jurisdiction, and is established and appointed as such (irrespective of how competently or inadequately these functions are performed, and what the mode of such appointment or establishment might be). This is true not only at the domestic but also at the international level. If a political state is recognised as an independent and self-determining and sovereign entity by other political states, and enters into associative or conflictive relationships with other states on those grounds, it is only because of and insofar as it is established or appointed as an interpretive and active agent for the people–land–resources it is with regard to. *As such therefore the legitimacy of the political state is the same at both domestic and international levels, and it is incumbent on the political state to interpret and act upon the intentionalities of the people land resources it is with regard to at the international level just as within the domestic level.* This is an unnegotiable principle. Waltz's notion that in the international political system states are free-wheeling units whose behaviour can be understood only through an understanding of their systemic relations to each other simply doesn't take account of this obvious fact – indeed nor do most of Waltz's supporters and detractors who deal with international relations at a theoretical level.

The second general issue in international relations that I need to elucidate is one that I have touched on briefly already (in the context of Waltz's formulations): the peculiar connotations of the concept of 'anarchy' in this area. 'Anarchy' is rather a dramatic term for this concept, which refers to no more than the observation that there is no superior power to political states in the arena of international politics, no top-down mode of regulating and controlling and coordinating the relations and interactions between political states, no interpretive and active agent with regard to any intentional system consisting of different political states. The regulatory modes which guide international politics are therefore conceived to be unlike those modes of political regulation which are to be found in political theory and philosophy, which are primarily concerned with an internal or domestic situation, or consider such a situation to be of primary interest. The somewhat superlative term 'anarchy' of international politics is, I suspect, merely used to emphasise the difference and even oppositeness of this sphere of political conceptualisation, the stuff of which is ideology, order, organisation, etc. The international political theorist's embracing of such a concept as anarchy is a sort of defiant recognition of the absence of conventional political conceptualisation at this level. The fact that one of the earliest and clearest modern conceptualisations of political statehood, in Thomas Hobbes's *Leviathan*, actually moves straight from the pragmatic considerations of authority within a state to mystical considerations of authority in the kingdom of God, and finds no space for an intermediate consideration of inter-state politics (or the concept of a super-Leviathan) seems to set the tone for an inadequate political philosophical focus on this area.[6] Naturally the theorists who choose to focus on international politics against the grain of the Hobbesian trend find themselves drawn towards that area which precedes or is definitively outside conventional political philosophical conceptualisation, such as a state-of-nature hypothesis or a condition-of-anarchy hypothesis. Even while following this somewhat defiant philosophical symbology, such theorists do, of course, recognise that the arena of international politics is a *happening* one, all too real and pragmatic (so much so that international relations is a comparatively young discipline, and largely and till very recently undertheorised), and therefore far from being as unanalysable and unformulable as a condition of true anarchy – or for that matter a hypothesis of a pure state of nature – would have to be. Consequently the anarchy of international politics usually includes either certain principles of spontaneous or automatic regulation (this is where Waltz's appeal to the historically located ideas of *realpolitik* and balance of power come in),[7] or alternatively certain consensually or even discordantly asserted and codified systems of constraints (conventions, norms, laws, rules, etc.),[8] or perhaps some mixture of both.

Now, while I have some sympathy with this general concept of anarchy as outlined above, and with the existing theoretical formulations of regulation which pertain to international politics, the latter seem to be me to be inexplicably limited. It strikes me as odd that thinking regarding the kinds of regulation that exist within the peculiar sort of anarchy of international politics has been so single-mindedly devoted to such regulation as being exerted either in a top-down fashion or in a horizontal fashion. Such thinking has been too preoccupied with the *absence* of superior power or the *presence* of some overarching system (which therefore is a preoccupation with top-down regulation); or too focused on the mechanics of consensual or discordant constraints or on competitive principles (which could be understood as horizontal regulation). Despite ample empirical observations demonstrating the efficaciousness of *bottom-up* regulation in international politics, this seems to have received scant theoretical attention. And yet it seems to be obvious that bottom-up regulation is possibly the most significant factor in the practice of international politics. As I have maintained above, a political state has a contiguous function at domestic and international levels, and at both levels is defined and understood as the interpreting and acting agent for the intentional system of the people–land–resources it is with regard to. *In principle, such negotiations or agreements as a political state enters into with other political states at the international level has still to be guided by interpretation of the intentionalities of the people–land–resources it is with regard to and its commitment to act upon these.* It is possible, of course, that certain autocratic or strongly ideologically oriented states may act on initiatives (international or domestic) that show little evidence of being consistent with the intentionalities of the people–land–resources. But that does not disturb the principle – for even if some state does so, it still does so because it is identified as a state, and its actions are legitimised, by this principle. If indeed a political state continues in practice to flout this principle, this would provide a very good argument for that status and that legitimacy to be removed from those who constitute that political state by the people–land–resources in question, by whatever means. If a particular political state finds another political state acting upon an intentionality which is such that it affects the intentionalities of its own people–land–resources, this would provide a good argument for hostilities to be initiated. And so on – I don't think the bottom-up regulation can or should be disregarded.

The third general concept in international politics which needs some attention is that of the constraints (conventions, norms, rules, laws, etc.) which regulate (and paradoxically even describe) the so-called anarchy of international politics. Any adequate consideration of this could, however, lead to the labyrinthine philosophical underpinnings of international law, international regulatory organisations and their functions, international negotiative forums and their conventions, international economic institutions and the relative standing of different political states therein, etc. – all matters which I do not intend to go into in this study. At the most general level, and as something that is directly pertinent to the present focus on corporate capitalist states in international politics, I would like to draw attention to a crucial distinction in this area noted by Terry Nardin in *Law, Morality and the Relations of States* (1983). Nardin sees international relations, insofar as they are not purely conflictual, as guided not so much by the anarchic competitive *realpolitik* of Waltz and neorealists as by certain constraints that attach to different kinds of international 'association'. Nardin's notion of association is given as an open-ended concept, capable of accommodating both divergent and common interests. To be able to do this he draws a distinction between two kinds of association, labelled 'purposive association' and 'practical association', which is best given in his own words:

> Those who are associated in a cooperative enterprise to promote shared values, beliefs, or interests are united by their convergent desires for the realization of a certain outcome that constitutes the good they have come together to obtain. Association of this kind is what [...] I [identify] as 'purposive association',

and:

> Association on the basis of an authoritative practice, on the other hand, is appropriately called 'practical association,' because in this case the associates are related in terms of constraints that all are expected to observe whatever their individual purposes may be. Often there is no shared purpose uniting those whose conduct is governed by an authoritative practice such as a morality or a system of laws, and in such cases there is no basis of association other than those common constraints.[9]

This account of association appears to me to be useful both for its brevity, and because it doesn't in itself depend on any formulation or systemic thinking which may contradict the qualifications on the status of the political state and bottom-up regulation that I have made above.

Nardin's concept of association and the distinctions therein lead to an interesting thesis that forms the body of his book. He observes that in the course of the twentieth century (up to the present time) purposive association has gradually gained ascendancy over practical association. This is marked, for instance, in the progression from what the League of Nations stood for, a practical association of political states, to what the United Nations has now come to stand for:

> the institutionalized embodiment of an international society united by a determination not only to fend off disruptions of international peace and to preserve the security and independence of its associates, but also to promote the realization of the social

and economic welfare of its constituent societies – to do this not merely as a means to international peace and security but as an end in itself.[10]

Nardin believes this shift from the conceptual predominance of practical to the conceptual predominance of purposive reasoning to be flawed because the proponents of the latter:

> neglect to consider the implications, for their own proposals, of the fact that international society is distinguished from a state of extreme conflict not so much by the degree to which its members are moved to cooperate in the pursuit of common interests as by the degree to which they understand themselves to be members of a society defined by common rules, moved sometimes by common and sometimes by divergent interests.[11]

The demonstration of this thesis is Nardin's thing, and I leave it to him (it seems to me that on the whole his demonstration is sound). Given the distinction between the two kinds of association there is a ring of something familiar about the observation. International politics is commonly seen (by media political analysts and foreign affairs experts, by political ideologues on one or the other side of any fence, by historians) to operate at a double level: at an ostensible level that asserts certain purposive ends (in ethical terms usually, such as a cause of freedom, or humanitarian values) and invites or engages in association in those terms; and at a more or less covert level that is consistent with pragmatic common or divergent interests (usually economic interests). So, while a United Nations peacekeeping army or a NATO allied force may be deployed ostensibly for certain ethical or humanitarian ends, it is always worth looking for the economic interests and ideological alignments underlying that move; when the International Monetary Fund or the World Bank makes a loan to a needy political state, it is always worth examining the ideological and economic implications of the conditions which attach to such loans; when the World Trade Organisation admits a new member to its fold, it is always worth asking why it has chosen to do so at that particular moment; when Britain plays up the rhetoric of an ethical foreign policy or American marines are sent off to 'intervene' against this or that 'rogue state' for the sake of 'democracy and world peace' and inflict some 'collateral damage' or neutralise a 'totalitarian regime', the underlying economic and ideological possibilities are always worth investigating. The pragmatic considerations of international politics are commonly understood to be fronted by pronouncements of a purposive nature. In our time such pronouncements have become increasingly enshrined in international institutions (World Bank, UN, NATO, WTO, IMF, etc.), so that, as Nardin rather unconvincingly observes, purposive association seems to supersede practical association.

It is impossible to examine this observation further than Nardin has done by staying within the orthodox field of the theory of international relations. In fact the roots of this situation cannot be fully grasped unless we take account of the complex linkages between the domestic and the international, between the political sphere and the economic sphere, and (for our time) the links of all of these to contemporary corporate capitalism. And this brings me back to the issue in hand: the role of contemporary corporate capitalist political states in international politics.

I have argued above that the legitimacy and status of the political state as a sovereign and equal entity at the level of international politics is determined in the same way as at the domestic level. I have also argued that at least one of the regulatory modes that works in international politics is bottom-up – some sort of accountability on every political state towards fulfilling its interpretive and active commitments to the domestic sphere.

The contemporary corporate capitalist political state is such because it colludes with corporate capitalist processes. I have examined why and how it does so in some detail in the previous sections. When such a corporate capitalist political state finds itself within international politics it has to do essentially what it has done at the domestic level. This means that the entire agenda which is devoted to playing supplicant to and colluding with corporate capitalism, to trying to increase and intensify and concentrate the interests of large capitalist corporations and significant speculative involvements within the area of its jurisdiction, is transferred to that state's activities at an international level. The corporate capitalist political state tries, in other words, to use or manipulate international relations with a view to further facilitating and encouraging corporate capitalist interests that already exist within the people–land–resources under its jurisdiction to grow and stay there.

The corporate capitalist political state also carries to the international level its uncomfortable position of bad faith, which can now be seen as bad faith not only to the peoples–lands–resources under its jurisdiction, but also to all the other peoples-areas under the jurisdiction of other political states from which it hopes to wrest or cajole concessions that would serve corporate capitalist and speculative interests generally – and of course particularly if located within its own precincts. This translated and rather exacerbated position of bad faith has to be managed at the level of international relations itself. The bottom-up regulation which exists, the fact that the gaze of the people–land–resources is constantly fixed on the machinations of the corporate capitalist (or indeed any) state, makes the need for such a management of bad faith all the more urgent.

To put it briefly, the contemporary corporate capitalist political state acts as the agent of large capitalist corporations and speculative interests in the area of its jurisdiction, and therefore as the agent of corporate capitalism generally. Typically the following are some of the characteristics of the foreign policy that a contemporary capitalist political state may follow:

(a) The formation of alignments and agreements with other corporate capitalist political states which are similarly situated in economic and ideological terms, with a view to identifying common and complementary trading areas, relaxing or gradually removing trade barriers, and creating a more uniform legislative and legal environment across corporate capitalist political states. From a political point of view this is as much a matter of caution as an encouragement to the expansionist nature of corporate capitalism. Such measures do of course encourage the expansionist tendency of corporate capitalism to consolidate itself: there is freer movement of capital, there is potential for mergers between corporations and the formation of monopolies or oligopolies which draw upon a larger labour market and cater to a larger consumer market, and that in turn provides the opportunity for onslaughts to be made by capitalist corporations and underlying speculative involvements with superior resources against markets which are still outside such a zone and perhaps still restricted. From a political point of view the similarly situated corporate capitalist political states which enter upon such agreements and alignments are simply performing a risk-minimising function; they are trying to ensure that nothing would be lost for any of them by opportunistic movements of corporations and speculative interests to capitalise on legislative and legal differences. At least those corporate capitalist states that have reached a similar capacity for maintaining the locations of significant capitalist corporations and speculative involvements within their precincts collectively ensure that they would try to maintain that position or strengthen it.[12]

(b) The maintaining of a policy of appeasement and self-preservation with regard to corporate capitalist political states which are ideologically similarly located but in an economically stronger position – i.e., those that have been more successful in getting significant capitalist corporations and underlying speculative interests to be located within their precincts. For the policy of appeasement and self-preservation to work out to the satisfaction of both sides (economically stronger and economically weaker but ideologically similar corporate capitalist states) there has to be some perception on the part of the economically stronger state that the position of the economically weaker state is not too distant from its own, that within a predictable timespan the latter might reach a position of parity with the former, and that given that eventuality (and given the nature of extant and opposed ideological and economic zones) it is prudent to be appeased and to preserve such economically weaker political states on their own terms.[13] If such a perception does not exist, it is very unlikely that the economically weaker corporate capitalist political state would be able to get away unscathed from the economically stronger political state – appeasing the latter would probably involve making trade and legal–legislative concessions which would in the long term be detrimental to its people–land–resources (insofar as significant outside corporations and speculative interests may weaken indigenous corporations and speculative interests). And this is because of the next point.

(c) Attempts to extort or force concessions from other political states which may be ideologically similar but significantly weaker economically, or which may be ideologically differently organised and therefore try to protect their peoples–lands–resources from an unrestricted influx of outside capitalist corporations and speculative interests within their precincts. Such concessions may take the form of coercing such political states to come into line with the legal and legislative provisions and trading advantages which the corporate capitalist political state offers capitalist corporations and speculators within its own precincts, even if this is deemed to be disadvantageous for the political states which are being so pressured or even if they consider this to be ideologically and otherwise undesirable.

Such coercion may take the form of economic sanctions, conditions imposed on loans at times of need or calamities, covert or overt political interference, the manipulation of the international media to use international opinion, outright military aggression or the threat thereof, etc.[14]

(d) Since the above policies are effectively evidence of bad faith not just against specific peoples–lands–resources which specific corporate capitalist political states are with regard to, but against the people–world–resources generally, and since there is both a certain degree of horizontal accountability (in terms of international conventions, laws, norms, etc.) and more significantly an unavoidable measure of bottom-up regulation from the very peoples–lands–resources that political states are with regard to, the true nature of such foreign policies have to be shrouded in misconceptions and misdirections too. The true nature of such foreign policies is in fact only a thinly shrouded affair: it is simply that such foreign policies reveal that contemporary corporate capitalist political states are often no more than agents for significant capitalist corporations and their underlying speculative involvements. But this cannot be too blatantly revealed; a condition of bad faith is always an embarrassment if too obviously exposed. Besides there is no need for such exposure to take place; this bad faith can be conveniently shared and dispersed. So the contemporary corporate capitalist political state carries on its international agenda at all fronts – whether as alignments or agreements with like partners, as appeasement and self-preservation with superior partners, as coercion and aggression against weaker or different states – through such international regulatory bodies and negotiative forums and aids organisations as exist, or by creating such forums in agreement with its partners.[15] Powerful corporate capitalist political states carefully build up modes of influence (by bullying, by sanction, by superior resourcing ability) within such bodies and forums and organisations which in practice defeat any notion of the sovereignty and equality of states that such formations have to maintain in principle. In such formations purposive principles are instituted, which seem to supersede practical ones, which can be manipulated to disguise the international policies which the corporate capitalist political state is likely, is in its own way obliged, to follow in its bad faith. It is the business of the foreign affairs department of a well-placed corporate capitalist political state to be able to present its policy of alignment, appeasement and especially aggression as serving some universal ethical or humanitarian purposive cause. It is the business of the foreign affairs departments of other corporate capitalist political states that are similarly located and in partnership with that state to accept and endorse this presentation and to aid its alignment-seeking, appease-ment-seeking or especially aggression-instigating gestures.

I think it is commonly accepted that an aggressive or coercive stance assumed by one political state towards another, which compromises the sovereignty and equality of the latter in international politics even though it has the full endorsement of and legitimacy bestowed by its pertinent people–land–resources, is an imperialist stance. Such an imperialist stance may manifest itself in terms of direct conquest, or in terms of indirect administrative and political control, or in other even more subtle modes of undermining a political state's status as such. There are different possible reasons why any political state may assume an imperialist stance: to serve certain economic vested interests, to serve certain culturally determined value systems, or to serve certain theological or political ideological alignments. At any rate, if that appears to be an acceptable understanding of the matter, it seems to follow that all contemporary corporate capitalist political states are, just by dint of being so, inclined to be imperial-ist. And they are inclined to be imperialist to serve the economic vested interests of significant capitalist corporations and speculative interests with which they collude at a domestic level and for which they serve as agents at the level of international politics. The logic of corporate capitalist processes, the systemic imperatives of corporate capitalist organisation, renders it necessary for all corporate capitalist political states to be imperialist towards political states that are either ideologically and therefore economically differently organised from itself, or are simply economically weaker than itself. The imperialist proclivity of the corporate capitalist political state is part of the overall process and organisation of contemporary corporate capitalism. In spirit this observation is of course similar to the link made between late nineteenth-century imperialism and industrial capitalism by Lenin or Hobson.[16] However, in that context the relation of the capitalist political state to the processes of industrial capitalism was such that there seemed to exist a much stronger *political imperative* from *specific capitalist and imperialistic states*, which somehow overshadowed or controlled and contained the industrial capitalist processes and interests. (Waltz makes the most of this apparently strong and specific political imperative to suggest that Lenin and Hobson had in fact reductively brought two different systems – the political and the economic – together.[17]) In the contemporary context, it seems to me, the imperialist tendency of corporate capitalist political states cannot be ascribed to the political imperatives of specific corporate capitalist states, but is more uniformly a condition which every corporate capitalist state has to subscribe to to some degree (depending on their relative economic strengths), a condition which *derives* from the processes and organisation of corporate capitalism in general.

With those few observations on the role of corporate capitalist political states in international relations I feel I have a serviceable overview of contemporary corporate capitalism. The throwing of a grid, the tracing of a picture starting from a suitable social outcome (the rise of managerialism here) which was the matter of this part has been achieved to a plausible degree, at least insofar as space permits, providing a sort of thumbnail sketch which can never satisfy but can only be thought of as serviceable or plausible. Despite the many gaping holes, this will serve to lead back to the substance of political philosophy, the issue of political means and ends. Underneath the above-traced rationale of the organisation of contemporary corporate capitalism, the carefully constructed misdirections and obfuscations and myths that operate therein, the main actors and interests which sustain this system, there is of course that which all this is with regard to – the mass of 'ordinary' people (living under certain states and ultimately in the world, working for governments and corporations or being unable to find work, consuming the produce of corporations and investing modestly, voting in elections and trying to respond to world events, abiding by the legal and political dictates of their contexts, accommodating themselves to or reconstructing social environments, being misguided or being enterprising, being acted upon by the above-described system and the main actors therein). To try to focus on this mass in terms of the above picture would be to unleash the concerns of political philosophy, and it is to political philosophy that I turn in the next and final part of this study.

Part III

The Disabled Political Will and Anti-Political Philosophy

11 The Mechanics of Disablement

The picture of contemporary corporate capitalism that I have drawn in the preceding part has several features that are worth noting:

(a) Such a picture (of a fairly wide scope) cannot be supported by any comprehensive accounting of the mass of available information which is pertinent to it: there is too much pertinent information to be taken into account. Nor can such a picture discuss sufficiently all relevant and authoritative ideas from all the disciplines that are implicated in it: that too would be an inexhaustibly protracted affair. Clearly the above picture is a sketchy and erratic affair, often joining the points of its emphasis in intuitive ways, leaping across boundaries with less than sufficient circumspection, and understating in the process such important considerations as the place of technology and technological innovation, the nature of consumerism, the nuances of global poverty, the claims and commodifications of identity, and so on, in contemporary corporate capitalism. What I hope may sustain that picture are the two following considerations: one, that it presents a construction which is internally coherent and consistent, and avoids self-evidently untenable assumptions and implications; and two, that along with a few illustrative and extremely selective references to pertinent information and ideas it optimistically remains open to testing in terms of such other information and ideas as may be brought to bear upon it. This may of course lead to a need for the refutation or modification of the picture, but I feel convinced that it would lead to its confirmation in essence – or that at any rate the picture would be able to accommodate other such information and ideas within itself and in its own terms. Perhaps, in consideration of its obvious limitations and its open-ended presentation (open to testing) this should be thought of not so much as a picture as a model which may aid contemplation of the nuances of contemporary corporate capitalism from a political philosophical perspective.

(b) Although this might not always be self-evident, the above picture (or model) of contemporary corporate capitalism does, I believe, consistently maintain a political philosophical perspective.

This is not because it follows certain acknowledged modes of political philosophical analysis (the fact that it doesn't is what renders its political philosophical perspective non-self-evident) nor because it lays out a political philosophical conceptualisation (definitively concerned with understanding a given state of collectivity so as to determine ends and means) – it is because the picture provides an 'object' which is amenable to the application of political philosophy, which can, so to say, be subject to the gaze of political philosophy.

If I had developed this picture around certain assumed first principles (egalitarianism, freedom, justice, or whatever, and with whatever emphasis) its political philosophical intent would have been declared and self-evident. Even if I had assumed certain first principles for its contemplative procedures (a version of what constitutes rationality, or what are the conditions of communication, or what entails the attribution of values, and so on) its political philosophical intent would have been *more* evident. In fact, such preconditions are usually so entrenched in political philosophy that, in the course of the above presentation, I might already have drawn upon philosophically loaded value judgements, unitary models of reasoning, etc. – or, at any rate, the reader might have felt encouraged to do so. But as a whole I feel the above picture presents a philosophically neutral and contingent description of a given state of affairs. There is no immediate political commitment formed in maintaining that in this state of affairs things are often not what they seem to be, or that things are such as they are. Nevertheless, I also feel that this hasn't simply been a descriptive act in a sociological spirit – it is in fact geared towards the application of political philosophy. This is a matter that needs some elucidation, and some backtracking.

The picture of contemporary corporate capitalism described in Part II above, even though not self-evidently enunciating or espousing political philosophical commitments, is immediately of interest from a political philosophical perspective. It is of political philosophical interest for one main reason: *it offers no location within itself from which a political will – to which political philosophy is closely aligned and with which political philosophy is closely concerned (all ideas I have touched on in Part I) – of whatever variety may be exerted.* This of course needs further elucidation, and I shall proceed to that soon. But it is also something that is intuitively evident, that pops out for those

concerned with political philosophy even from the merest discernment of the picture, so that any deeper contemplation of this is
primarily a matter of analysing this enigmatic phenomenon.

Let me go over the ground of that seemingly obvious feature in a bit
more detail. Recalling certain points I had made in Part I may
facilitate this. The following description of the political will was
offered there:

> The active principle which enables the political state as
> explaining–predicting agency to act upon (be effective on, to
> direct) the intentional system – the people–land–resources – it is
> with regard to (or which it explains, tries to predict) could be
> thought of as *political will*. The political will of the political state
> is more than simply a monopoly on force: *it is an intentional use*
> *of the power it has by dint of such a monopoly, for whatever ends it*
> *wishes to achieve and in terms of whatever understanding it has as*
> *explaining–predicting agency, with regard to and with effect upon the*
> *people–land–resources under its jurisdiction (or the intentional system).*

I also clarified that this doesn't mean that a political will is only
exercised or manifested in a progressive/regressive or revolutionary
state, but also in a conservative state which actively promotes the
need for retaining a state of affairs: a political will can be both for
change and stasis. I also extended the scope of the understanding of
political will in the following manner:

> The political state is undoubtedly best placed to exercise a political
> will over its sphere of influence (the intentional system it is with
> regard to), but conceivably oppositional and/or supersedent
> and/or competing political wills can be expressed and perhaps
> even exercised both from within and from outside that sphere of
> influence.

Thus a non-state-sponsored collectivity of some description (a trade
union, a non-governmental body, an interest group or association,
a political organisation outside legislative precincts, etc.) may express
an independent political will, as may individuals, with whatever
success, *within* the zone over which a political state has jurisdiction.
Or another political state, an international association or interest

group (e.g. an international environmental lobby or human rights organisation), an international legal or economic regulatory body, etc., and even externally located individuals, may also express a political will from *outside* with effect on the same zone. Finally, I presented the idea of the political will as distinct from the active principle which actuates capitalist corporations (in that it is its own interpreting–predicting agency and acts upon itself with a predetermined ends-orientation), which I had called a *capitalist drive*. I observed that though the capitalist drive can have significant political effects and necessitate certain kinds of exertions of political will, 'the capitalist drive is not in itself coincidental with political will or vice versa; the explaining–predicting agencies and the intentional systems concerned in these active principles, their intentional impetus, are significantly different'.

The supplicant corporate capitalist political state that protects and is protected by speculative interests and affiliated alignments both in domestic and international politics, that mirrors and simulates corporate structures within its own organisation and acts as an agent for speculative interests on the international stage, cannot be said to be performing and acting upon interpretations–predictions of the intentional system of the people–land–resources it is with regard to. Speculative interests, as I have observed above, do not cohere with any conception of social ideology or justice in themselves, and therefore cannot be thought of as consistent with any exercise of political will. At best, speculative activities can be thought of as indifferent to any polity, and may lead incidentally – but not intentionally – to certain effects, beneficial or otherwise, on some collectivity. Speculative interests are indifferent to political will, irrespective of the kind of political effects that they may exercise, and are central to capitalist corporate organisation mainly because they embody the principle of the capitalist drive. Since the principle of the capitalist drive does not coincide with the principle of the political will, the political state that sustains itself and is sustained by, that protects and is protected by, that promotes and is promoted by speculative alignments, that moreover surrenders its definitive prerogatives as a political state to the movements and locations of speculative interests and surrenders even its organisational criteria to those of such alignments, cannot be regarded as doing what defines it as a *political* state. It does not matter whether representatives of such a corporate capitalist state formation *believe* that supporting the capitalist drive in this fashion is politically expedient, or how *convinced* they may be that certain speculative interests framed within the structure of international corporate capitalism do serve political ends. This is not an article of faith; it is a rational matter. The political state cannot be thought of as such if it becomes a coextension of the corporate sector and its underlying speculative interests; the only way in which a political state can hope to make use of speculative activities and movements in the interests of the intentional system it is with regard to is by controlling speculative interests by the exercise of a political will. The political state would have to accommodate speculative movements and activities, control (both in the sense of enabling and restricting) speculative interests within its conception and understanding of political means and ends that in turn are derived from its interpreting–predicting engagement with the intentional system it is with regard to.

At any rate, it seems to me to be fair to say that the kind of corporate capitalist political state that has been delineated in the above-drawn picture (or model) is not a *political* state at all, it is better understood as a corporate capitalist *non-political* state. It is a state wherein the capitalist drive has cancelled the political will, where the political will has been effectively disabled.

Significantly, the disabling of political will involved in that picture does not end there. There is little space for the expression of oppositional and/or competing and/or supersedent political wills from internal or external alignments or entities in this picture. Several features enumerated in the above picture contribute to this. The international scope of speculative movements and activities which sustain speculative interests; the manner in which supplicant corporate capitalist states conduct themselves as agents, create alliances and coerce possible oppositional or non-capitalist zones, and influence the conduct and formation of international regulatory organisations; the kind of resources that international corporate capitalist organisation has at its disposal – all these mean that non-conciliatory external political wills can simply be overshadowed and consumed out of existence. The effectiveness with which perspectives are played on in corporate capitalist organisation – whereby things are often not what they appear to be, significant interests are hidden behind obvious sounding myths, misdirections and conflations are propagated and repeated and argued for till they acquire the function of truisms, obvious centres of power and manipulation are either unavailable or available only in a symbolic fashion – creates an air of ambiguity and murkiness which it is almost impossible to cut through with any certainty, let alone act against. The fact that the political state, which is in the first instance the repository of political will and acts as a locus of oppositional/ competing/supersedent political activity, has itself assumed the character of non-political state in corporate capitalism, has become a mere cog in larger and hazier processes (of course, while vehemently protesting that this is not the case), is itself a not insignificant factor in the disabling of other political wills. To a large extent, it might be said, oppositional/competing/supersedent political wills are disabled by not knowing what to oppose or compete with or attempt to supersede in a *political* sense or with *political* effect.

The effects of this in political conceptualisation and activism that characterise the contemporary world are all too evident. Sociologists and anthropologists who have concerned themselves with the con-solidation of advanced corporate capitalism under the all-encompassing term 'globalisation' (and with a suitable sense of corporate capitalism's confidence in its unassailability) have often observed that globalisation seems to be attended by the growing pre-dominance of identity politics.[1] That the expansionism of corporate capitalism, which is more or less synonymous with globalisation, has been the *cause* of the persistence and exacerbation of identity politics even in its least palatable forms has been mooted less often, though the idea is not unfamiliar.[2] It is easily grasped that such identity politics can be manipulated and commodified to extend the ends of corporate capitalism, and ultimately to serve speculative interests. However, it has generally been easier to argue that the growth of identity politics is the result of a greater degree of individual freedom and self-possession which corporate capitalist organisation for various reasons allows (in essence a desirable state of affairs, but amenable to some unfortunate conflicts). It seems to me quite possible that this is another misconception that could be unravelled – but I won't actually engage with this here because it is beside the point. It is beside the point since, insofar as identity *politics* can be thought of as politics, it is the assertion of a particular notion of *collectivity* (in identity terms such as culture, race, nation-ality, gender, sexuality, etc.), and the circumstance that the identity terms appear to delineate the individual physical and social entities who claim to promote the interests of that collectivity does not mean that conceptions of individuality and individual freedom and self-possession are thereby promoted. That identity politics has become the last bastion of *political* conceptualisation and activism seems to me to be the clearest symptom of the efficaciousness of the disabled political will. It is patently obvious that identity politics, despite making laudable and inevitable contextual interventions, is in the larger picture a self-defeating politics. There are two primary reasons for this. One, the rationale of an identity politics is an exclusive one, it is a rationale which allows political positions only to those who can acknowledge those identity features as being their own and excludes all others who can't (others may sympathise, but they cannot but be others). This, in turn, diverts attention away from all those potent factors that have a broader impact (even on those within the identity-based collectivity) than this narrow view of collectivity can comprehend. Two, the rationale of identity politics is such that it may always potentially *defeat* even its own collectivity, fragment itself, gradually erode its own political stance. No particular selection of identity features can ensure homogeneousness in other possible identity features, and the logic of identity politics can extend to every kind of identity-characteristic. It is inevitable that the most laudable and necessary of identity politics, such as is involved in the women's movement, would have to take account of internal divisions – would break into homosexual and heterosexual women's movements, and black and white and other racially and culturally distinct and often opposed women's movements, and so on. I do not say this to denigrate the indubitably significant achievements of such identity politics: my point is that identity politics does gradually erode its political will, fragment, and fit in neatly and comfortably with the disabling of political will involved in contemporary corporate capitalism.

Of the conception of individuality and individual freedom and self-possession in the context of corporate capitalism I have quite a lot to say below.

Not least considerable among the explanations of the disabled political will that the above picture presents is the effect of the formidable edifice of philosophical ideas and concepts which have been constructed in support of this state of affairs and which have been assimilated within it. This is not simply the province of those who pass for philosophers: indeed the sources of these ideas are often sociologists and economists and management theorists and others, and the ideas in question have been assimilated in management, economic, sociological, etc. discourses. These are nevertheless philosophical ideas in that they have a conceptual efficacy that cannot be confined to those particular disciplinary areas or restricted to such disciplinary activities. This edifice of ideas is closest in spirit to political philosophy in that it self-consciously presents (constructs, even invents) a tradition for itself from within the precincts of political philosophy. That these philosophical ideas have played a substantial part in the construction of the above picture is a fact that I have gestured towards above but haven't dwelt on. This part is devoted to the philosophy which has grown to justify the current condition of corporate capitalism, been assimilated within it in various forms, and has most effectively contributed to the disabling of *our* political will.

The present part does not examine *all* philosophical ideas that are concerned with contemporary corporate capitalism: the focus here is specifically on those philosophical ideas that support the condition of contemporary corporate capitalism as presented in the above picture, that are assimilated in contemporary corporate capitalist organisation and constituent discourses, and that contribute to the disabled political will which prevails therein. Though such philosophical ideas do present themselves in the spirit of political philosophy and construct or invent a tradition for themselves within political philosophy, it seems to me that they should not strictly be called political philosophy. A philosophy which is designed to take politics away from the realm of philosophising, which is designed to disable the political will and thereby render all attempts at thinking about ends and means redundant, cannot be called a political philosophy – it is more appropriately thought of as an anti-political philosophy. I mean *anti-political* philosophy (the philosophy which is anti-political) rather than *anti-political-philosophy* (which suggests opposition to political philosophy in itself, rather than a conceptual opposition to politics). This part is primarily about the particular sort of anti-political philosophy that has grown in concert with the growth of advanced corporate capitalism.

In addressing this I necessarily look into a range of anti-political philosophical concepts and texts. Each of these have distinctive nuances and emphases which are worthy of attention, but more interestingly they often present essentially similar positions, and these positions are often developed through similar modes of argument. A brief preliminary account of the shared or recurring positions and modes of argument in such anti-political philosophy will undoubtedly both save me the trouble of unnecessarily repeating myself later, and help in presenting arguments in a concise and suitably comparative fashion.

I might as well clarify what my main contention is here before giving such an account: *invariably the positions that are taken in such anti-political philosophical statements are tenuous or insufficiently developed, and this is usually because the modes of argument that are employed to develop these positions are often (more often than not) philosophically inadequate. I have yet to come across a statement of an anti-political position in support of contemporary corporate capitalism that can, in the development and espousal of that position, be considered to be philosophically adequate.*

A brief preliminary account of the shared or recurring positions in such anti-political philosophy (the modes of argument underlying these are delineated after that) is given in the three following points:

i. Anti-political philosophy generally depends on the assertion of *appropriate philosophical first principles*, which are unnegotiable and indelible under *all* circumstances, or which are in some sense universal. The process of philosophical enquiry which tries to develop a system or develop a critique of a system by starting from philosophical first principles is, of course, deeply rooted in practically all political philosophy, and as such is not a characterising feature of anti-political philosophy. Anti-political philosophy specifically assumes such first principles as enable the development of systems (or of critiques of alternative systems) which are close to or almost identical to those claimed by contemporary corporate capitalism. Typically such first principles have to do with some notion of individuality and humanity, usually such as would enable the assertion of the inviolability or the discreteness of the individual or the absolute possession of the self. The appropriate first principles are usually given as such not because they can be proved in themselves (they couldn't be *first* principles if that were the case) but because they seems to be so self-evident or obvious or universally acceptable as not to require validation. If an anti-political philosophical statement can find an appropriate first principle which *is* universal, and manages to demonstrate that systems such as are coherent with contemporary corporate capitalism follow inevitably and consistently from it, that statement would be considered a strong one. All philosophies that draw on philosophical first principles of any sort naturally try to persuade others that a strong case is being made. In arguing against such first-principle-based efforts several strategies are available:

One, that at any given moment it is possible to find not one or two but several such apparently universal and self-evident first principles, which may lead in quite different and perhaps even contrary directions if developed separately. There is, in other words, a certain degree of arbitrariness involved in the selection of any first principle at the expense of others that might be available. In the context of anti-political philosophy (which is the focus here) this argument is not directed specifically against it: this is an argument which can be directed at practically all political philosophy as it is pursued now. I have considered elsewhere[3] (albeit rather inadequately) the manner in which the arbitrariness of first principles in political philosophy can be negotiated and don't intend to take the broader implications of this argument any further here. But in discussing below anti-political philosophy based on first principles, I do often have recourse to comparison with what appear to be contrary first principles.

Two, that principles which are presented as first principles in specific philosophical statements are not really first principles at all – that there are considerable exceptions where they wouldn't hold, or that they are simply nonsensical themselves. My reservations about first principles asserted in anti-political philosophical statements are primarily of this category.

Three, that even though the first principles that are asserted do seem to hold universally or to be universally acceptable, the systems and critiques of systems that are developed on their basis are not consistently done and/or do not follow inevitably. This too forms a significant part of my objections to anti-political philosophy based on first principles.

ii. A philosophical position that is especially pertinent to anti-political philosophy which supports contemporary corporate capitalism is one that asserts the *pre-eminence of automatic or spontaneous or nonvolitional processes* (by definition the assertion of such processes ultimately defeats any possibility of the exercise of political will). The emphasis here is on the *preeminence* of such processes, for again practically all political philosophy has to accept the unavoidability of *some* such processes (the role of 'nature', whether understood as human nature or natural forces, for instance), and has to find ways to accommodate them or adapt to them or control them. The assertion of the preeminence of such processes is typically not given, as being self-evidently the case – this is not, as far as I am aware, presented as a first principle itself in anti-political philosophy. Usually arguments are presented to prove that the preeminence of such processes is the case, though once such arguments are presented and the case is so to say made, it is often thereafter assumed that such processes are a priori. In expressing scepticism about anti-political philosophy that asserts the preeminence of such processes I address the arguments presented to *prove* that such is the case.

iii. The final recurring philosophical position of interest is one that is most closely connected to contemporary anti-political philosophy, and has seldom figured in traditional political philosophy. In this it is asserted that *systems* (such as those that underlie the conduct of organisations, social existence generally, and conceptualisation itself) can be instituted or can somehow come to exist or are in existence which are indifferent to all partisan interests, are pervasive or universally effective, and are impregnable to manipulation. Accommodation, adaptation, construction and necessary change can be conducted or can occur within the precincts of such systems, but the system itself would – once in existence – be essentially unchanging (hence the disabling of political will).[4] In the anti-political philosophy that supports corporate capitalism, such systems are felt to be in existence already or to be imminently available. This philosophical position is not necessarily developed in terms of either first principles or automatic processes (though both may be called upon), but is argued for in terms of the plausibility of examples of such hypothetical systems or the actuality of instances of such existing systems. In examining these below I question whether such systems are in fact plausible (if presented in hypothetical terms) or actual (if presented as existing).

The tenuous modes of argument that repeatedly appear in the development and presentation of the above anti-political philosophical positions can be conveniently presented in the form of loosely (not rigorously) logical statements. This is convenient because it helps me to make two points more or less simultaneously. One, general logical statements such as those given below clearly cannot be considered to be true or applicable in any universal law- or rule-like sense – they can only be possibly true or applicable under specific conditions which have to be fully enunciated. Two, their use by anti-political philosophers, as we shall see, is tenuous because in the statements of such philosophers such general logical statements are used *tacitly* as if they have a rule- or law-like validity – special conditions which may make such logical statements true or applicable are usually not given, and are presumed to be unnecessary. To a large extent the three philosophical positions briefly outlined above are developed in terms of, and ultimately depend on, the misuse of such general logical statements.

The general logical statements that do not have a law- or rule-like validity and are misused repeatedly (in that they are used as if they do) in anti-political philosophy are as follows. If 'A', 'B', 'C', etc. are some such thing as factors or entities or ideas under philosophical examination, which appear in given states of affairs, and the appearance of which can be explained by and/or can imply some such collection of propositions as 'a1', 'a2', 'a3', etc. in the case of 'A', or 'b1', 'b2', 'b3', etc. in the case of 'B', and so on, then:

a. *Contained overdeterminism*
   If 'A' can be explained primarily through one proposition 'a1' (or a few such propositions) then other possible explanatory propositions 'a2', 'a3', etc. can be considered to be secondary or irrelevant.

b. *Translative overdeterminism*
   If the appearance of 'A' can be explained through 'a1', 'a2', a3', etc. for a particular state of affairs, the appearance of 'A' can be explained with the same propositions in any state of affairs where such an appearance occurs or becomes evident.

c. *Associationism*
   If it so happens that in a given state of affairs 'A' and 'B' are generally found together and 'A' and 'C' are not generally found together then in that state of affairs 'B' and 'C' would also generally not be found together.

d. *Exclusionism*
   If 'A' and 'B' are contrary or opposed to each other, a state of affairs in which 'A' prevails or dominates must be one from which 'B' is excluded, and vice versa.

e. *Oppositionism*
   If 'A' has certain implications 'a1', 'a2', 'a3', etc. and 'B' has certain implications 'b1', 'b2', 'b3', etc, and if 'A' and 'B' are opposed or contrary to each other, then all the implications 'a1', 'a2', 'a3', etc. must be opposed to all the implications 'b1', 'b2', 'b3', etc.

f. *Transpositionism*
   If a certain verisimilitude can be found between *some* of the factors
   'a1', 'a2', 'a3' which explain 'A' and *some* of the factors 'b1', 'b2',
   'b3' that explain 'B', 'A' and 'B' could be taken to be the same or
   overwhelmingly similar (despite their different designations).

These might seem rather abstruse and a bit removed from this
context and the present argument, but I am confident that their
relevance will become clear as I progress with the elucidation of
specific anti-political philosophical ideas below (and in doing this,
where such a tenuous logical statement is tacitly used in a law- or
rule-like fashion I will mark it out). The fact that such general logical
ideas are demonstrably misused in anti-political philosophy,
however tacitly and unobtrusively this may be done, lays such
philosophy open to a stylistic charge of positivistic excess. This is
especially ironic because anti-political philosophers often object
vociferously to all sorts of positivistic excesses.

   At any rate with this preliminary account of the matter at hand I
am set to examine specific anti-political philosophical statements in
greater detail. Below I confine myself to those statements that are
most closely connected with the development and consolidation of
advanced corporate capitalism – i.e., mainly with such statements
as were produced around and after the Second World War.

The thinking of Karl Mannheim and Karl Popper, insofar as their
efforts have political implications, prefigures many of the characteristics of anti-political philosophy in our age of advanced corporate
capitalism, and therefore presents a suitable starting point here. I do
not believe either of them were wholly anti-political philosophers
themselves, but their ideas have anti-political tendencies. This is
more the case for Popper, who has gradually come to be regarded as
one of the progenitors of modern anti-political thinking, and who
regarded anti-political thinkers (particularly the truly anti-political
philosopher whom I address soon, Fredrick Hayek)[5] with sympathy.
This is apparently not the case with Mannheim (whose emphasis on
social planning during and after the war is suggestive of the
contrary), but a careful consideration of the development of his ideas
does reveal a distinctive sort of anti-political outcome. In fact, I am
aware that there might be some resistance to lumping Mannheim
and Popper together in this fashion, not least because they were so

ostensibly opposed to each other's positions.[6] On the surface, it is difficult to think of two thinkers of the time who are more apparently contrary in their approaches to philosophy: where Popper's understanding of politics focuses on a notion of individuality Mannheim's focuses on an understanding of collectivity; where Popper espouses the desirability of piecemeal social engineering Mannheim champions the need for holistic social planning; where Popper presents his ideas as emerging by the negation of extant wisdom Mannheim presents his as emerging primarily from a synthesis of relevant extant wisdom; Popper's agenda seems to be optimistically conservative while Mannheim's appears to be cautiously constructivist. But these obvious oppositions are, as I have already suggested, on the surface. In appearing to *contradict* each other they effectively succeed in *complementing* each other.

12   The Anti-Political
       Self-Defeat of Mannheim

Mannheim's first principles – the perceptions which he asserts as being so self-evident as not to need proof, which he simply asserts, and which form the beginning point of conceptual understanding and construction for him – are twofold. The first could be put as follows: the world as it *is*, the lived world, the social world, in all its minutiae and in its wholeness, is in a state of constant flux, a constant fluid movement. The flip side of this first principle is that all *perceived* order in the world, all efforts at rendering the world understandable, all modes of organisation that attend our existence in this world are primarily due to conceptual efforts. This should not be confused with any simplistic notion of the world existing in the mind or in concepts alone: for Mannheim the world, and we in the world, indubitably exist, but this existence of the world and of us within it is lived and grasped and acted upon and continues because conceptualisation (spontaneously or wilfully) occurs in proactive ways and imposes order on the fluid world. An attempt to discern how conceptualisation occurs, and to what effect, is what occupies Mannheim; his writings are largely devoted to understanding this or being able to describe it as completely as possible in a typically sociological spirit. This is evident in his early views on structures and history, and the connected ideas of rationality that he developed within it and dwelt on with greater emphasis in his later works. In the revised section of his doctoral dissertation, published as 'On the Logic of Philosophical Systematization' (1922), he argues for the *constitutive* primacy of systematisation in the world: systematisation underlies conscious existence and the consciousness of existence in the world insofar as this can be grasped:

> Systematization is constitutive to such an extent that anything 'given' (this term still understood in a subjective and genetic sense) – any 'fact of experience' (in the broadest sense) – must already belong within one of the existing systematizations, in so far as it is theoretically grasped at all. [...] We must consider sys-

tematization as a constitutive form, since a theoretical object that is not systematized is altogether inconceivable.[1]

The depth of Mannheim's emphasis on conceptual effort (in the special sense of having constitutiveness attached to it) is easily gauged from this presentation of the primacy of systematisation as a conceptual mode with regard to and within the flux of the world. Mannheim's idea of history is presented in a similar mould: 'Historicist theory fulfils its own essence only by managing to derive an *ordering principle* from this seeming anarchy of change – only by managing to penetrate the *innermost structure* of this all-pervading change',[2] as is his understanding of rationality and irrationality[3] (which I comment on specifically below), and (as we shall see) his approach to knowledge itself and its metatheory – the sociology of knowledge.

The second first principle that Mannheim asserts is best given in his own words from *Ideology and Utopia* (where it is stated most succinctly, though this is far from being the only place where it is stated):

Strictly speaking it is incorrect to say that the single individual thinks. Rather it is more correct to insist that he participates in thinking further what other men have thought before him. He finds himself in an inherited situation with patterns of thought which are appropriate to this situation and attempts to elaborate further the inherited modes of response or to substitute others for them in order to deal more adequately with new challenges which have arisen out of the shifts and change in his situation. Every individual is in a two-fold sense predetermined by the fact of growing up in a society: on the one hand he finds a ready-made situation and on the other he finds in that situation performed patterns of thought and of conduct.[4]

In brief, the second first principle simply asserts the unavoidable and inevitable sociality of individuals (there are no individuals without collectives), and therefore the individual conceptual effort cannot but emerge from within and in terms of a collective conceptual background.

According to Mannheim's first first principle the condition of the world, within and with regard to which conceptualisation takes place, is one of constant movement. This movement would probably *be* anarchic and certainly *seem* to verge on anarchy if non-conceptually left to spontaneous devices, or if inadequately conceptualised. This movement could be harnessed into different sorts of coexisting and simultaneous patterns – could be discerned as and then moulded into *processes* – only if the conceptualisations which exist within it and with regard to it attain a suitable degree of comprehensiveness and coordination. The idea is that processes are *discerned* and if discerned can also be acted upon, and that the constitutiveness of conceptualisation or systematisation (which is therefore coincident with both discernment and action at a fundamental level) allows for this. To reach a suitably comprehensive sociological conceptualisation that would be able to coordinate within itself all the relevant partial conceptualisations that already exist in different spheres of knowledge is what Mannheim understands to be the direction of a *sociology of knowledge* (thus, Mannheim sees a sociology of knowledge as subsuming all related knowledge and information within itself).[5] The contemplation of that which actually seeks to modify society in necessary and desirable ways, once some sort of comprehensive sociological conceptualisation is grasped, is what he presents later as *planning*.

To be able to reach towards a conceptual position from which a sociology of knowledge in Mannheim's sense can become possible, and from which planning in that sense can be anticipated, it is necessary that a reckoning be made of the state of conceptual understanding and achievement that already exists. This entails a thoroughgoing assessment of the socially, economically, politically, philosophically, historically, psychologically, etc. contingent condition of the contemporary world; a deliberately comprehensive attempt to gain a necessarily collective understanding (since this follows from a first principle too) of the conceptually constituted contemporary ethos. It is to this rather mind-boggling endeavour – or rather to the consideration of how such an endeavour could be undertaken – that Mannheim's principal works are devoted: *Ideology and Utopia* (1929), *Man and Society in an Age of Reconstruction* (1935), *Diagnosis of Our Time* (1940), and *Freedom, Power and Democratic Planning* (posthumously published in 1950).

In all of these Mannheim investigates the degree of rationality and irrationality that is manifested, and the balance between rationality and irrationality that is evident, in the different constitutive conceptualisations that are available. In *Man and Society* Mannheim describes two kinds of rationality and irrationality: substantial and functional. These are given as follows:

> We understand as substantially rational an act of thought which reveals intelligent insight into the interrelations of events in a given situation. Thus the intelligent act of thought itself will be described as 'substantially rational', whereas everything which either is false or not an act of thought at all (as for example drives, impulses, wishes, and feelings both conscious and unconscious) will be called 'substantially irrational';

and:

> Whether a series of actions is functionally rational or not is determined by two criteria: (a) Functional organization with reference to a definite goal; and (b) a consequent calculability when viewed from the standpoint of an observer or a third person seeking to adjust himself to it.[6]

On the whole Mannheim believes that the development of a *sociology of knowledge* or the application of *planning* should involve a maximisation of substantial rationality. Significantly, however, he does not always seek the preponderance of rationality in all processes, he seeks a suitable balance: there are *necessary irrationalities* (such as may be embedded in human nature, rooted in the ineradicable and powerful depths of the unconscious) which actually assist the effort of conceptualisation and can be peculiarly useful at times.[7] On the whole, the factors that guide Mannheim's assessment of existing conceptualisation in the contemporary world are as follows: (a) the determination of substantial irrationalities that have come to exist, with a view thereby to discovering how these can be reduced so that on the whole substantial rationality will prevail; (b) to find out where there are gaps in the comprehensiveness or totality of conceptualisation, since he holds such gaps responsible for a prevalence of substantial irrationality, with a view to sealing such gaps so that the direction of comprehensive conceptualisation can be taken; (c) to discover means for balancing out and using necessary irrationalities.

With these first principles, ideas of process, and notions of rationality and irrationality in hand, Mannheim's diagnoses of the contemporary *Weltanschauung* fall into place. Each phase of Mannheim's conceptual efforts is an attempt to diagnose the prevalent substantial irrationalities which are evident in a given context (despite the appearance of functional rationalities which maintain a momentary stability and hold the potential anarchy of substantial irrationality at bay), and is followed by suggestions of possible correctives (whereby a greater and lasting stability which is coherent with substantial rationality can be envisaged, and perhaps ensured). Thus in *Ideology and Utopia* he concerns himself with the substantial irrationalities which, in his time, were contained in political pursuits centred on those two terms:

> The concept of 'ideology' reflects the one discovery which emerged from political conflict, namely, that ruling groups can in their thinking become so intensively interest-bound to a situation that they are simply no longer able to see certain facts which would undermine their sense of domination;

and:

> The concept of *utopian* thinking reflects the opposite discovery of the political struggle, namely that certain oppressed groups are intellectually so strongly interested in the destruction and trans-formation of a given condition of society that they unwittingly see only those elements in the situation which tend to negate it. Their thinking is incapable of correctly diagnosing an existing condition of society. They are not at all concerned with what really exists; rather in their thinking they already seek to change the situation that exists.[8]

What needs to be noted here is that Mannheim's understanding of these terms differs from those usually found in socialist, liberal, conservative or fascist political thinking of the time. It was generally understood that an ideological concept or utopian vision is the end result of certain rationalistic processes, which could then be questioned accordingly and dismissed or accepted. Mannheim however defined these terms so that they become implicitly and inevitably aligned with certain substantial irrationalities. So, for Mannheim, these terms and their particular nuances needn't be weighed and tested at all because they are indicative of substantial irrationality simply by being designated as such and could be rejected outright. Further, this mode of definition, whereby substantial irrationalities are revealed, but which is indifferent to the specific kinds of ideological concepts and utopian visions which exist, could be thought of as missing the point: arguably Mannheim is not really talking about the commonly accepted connotations of ideology and utopia at all, but is appropriating those terms to designate certain preconceived ideas about substantial irrationality that he considers to be the order of the time. Moreover, having done this he goes on to suggest that what usually passes for ideology and utopia in current political thinking is consistent with his unusual definitions. (In this Mannheim makes his thinking subject to what I have called *transpositionism* in the previous chapter.)

Similarly, in *Man and Society* Mannheim identifies three conditions of the contemporary world which have vitiated attempts at substantial rationality: these are (a) the fundamental democratisation of society, (b) growing interdependence within society, (c) a general disproportion in the development (primarily intellectual) of different sectors in human society.[9] In combination these have worked to defeat such modes of social harmonisation and control (thus attempts at imposing substantial rationality) as were in evidence at the time: the self-regulatory decentring of power involved in laissez-faire liberalism, and the extreme centralisation of power involved in dictatorial regulation. In his time (at the moment of ongoing conflict and impending chaos) the failure of these seemed to Mannheim – as indeed to many – to be self-evident; understandably Mannheim's efforts were devoted not so much to arguing why he considered them to have failed, as to diagnosing the self-evident failure as one to do with substantial irrationality arising from the given conditions of contemporary society. The combination of the above three conditions is unlikely to cohere in purely self-regulatory liberalism, Mannheim observes, and yet centralised dictatorial regulation is directly against the spirit of fundamental democratisation.

A prolonged charting out of different phases of Mannheim's diagnoses of substantial irrationalities in the contemporary situations he encounters is unnecessary: these form the most familiar of his diagnoses and are sufficiently indicative of his analytical methods. Apart from the instance of *transposition* above, and despite the cautious quest for balance that Mannheim constantly demonstrates, there are other slighter logical problems with his analytical methods. An overfondness for finding neat dualisms is characteristic here (laying him open to the charge of subscribing to both what

I have called *oppositionism* and *exclusionism* above). However, there is nothing in this so far which suggests that Mannheim could in any way be associated with anti-political philosophy which disables the political will. On the contrary, in fact, insofar as these lead to a search for substantial rationalities, and since Mannheim follows them up with recommendations of correctives to institute substantial rationality – since he doesn't diagnose the malaise without considering the medicine – it seems more than likely that Mannheim could only be regarded as a political philosopher who enables the political will. Curiously, however, a closer look at the correctives that he proposes given the above diagnoses reveals a somewhat different outcome.

The corrective to the substantial irrationalities of ideological concepts and utopian visions as defined by Mannheim is the development of a comprehensive *sociology of knowledge*; the remedy for the substantial irrationalities of decentralised liberal self-regulation and centralised dictatorial regulation given the conditions of contemporary society as Mannheim understands these is a commitment to cautious and holistic *planning*. Two epistemological conditions determine (not necessarily self-consciously) the description of these correctives as given by Mannheim:

(a) The rather tenuous employment of *transpositional*, *oppositional* and *exclusionist* analytical procedures in understanding contemporary society leaves Mannheim with a dwindling field of extant conceptualisations that he considers to be promising. The position is as follows: since neither this perspective nor that perspective (utopia or ideology, liberal self-regulation or dictatorial regulation) can be accepted there has to be a third or alternative perspective; since both perspectives are understood as *oppositional* and *exclusionist* (an understanding which is aided by appropriate *transpositions*) a third or alternative perspective cannot really emerge by negotiation or compromise between them as they are given; since such perspectives are irrational in a substantial fashion (they all have a comprehensive wrong-headedness about them) the entire potentially comprehensive fields of their application would have to be revisited, reconsidered, reassessed. In an almost absolute sense, to get to a suitable alternative perspective which would act as a corrective, Mannheim suggests, the whole business of conceptualising in a comprehensive fashion would have to start anew and be sceptical of all conceptualisations that exist.

(b) Since it follows from the assumed first principles that conceptualisation is constitutive, and that all change (correction, modification, or revolution) is fundamentally a conceptual effort, it is to the cultivation of suitable conceptualisation that we should turn in all spheres to provide suitable correctives. Such conceptual efforts cannot be deemed to be conducted satisfactorily unless they attain to sufficient comprehensiveness. At the same time, this comprehensiveness is such that it should not wholly undercut the first principle of constant flux (for that would lead to a static society). Moreover, since it is a condition of conceptualisation that it is collective (again as a first principle) such conceptual efforts cannot be deemed to be fulfilled unless a suitably collective self-understanding, divested of all narrow self-interests, has been established. In brief, what is fundamentally needed is a conceptual effort that leads to a complete picture but paradoxically a complete picture without closure (which is open-ended).

In outlining both the comprehensive *sociology of knowledge* and the holistic concept of *planning* Mannheim subscribes to these epistemological conditions in different ways. The sociology of knowledge, as Mannheim presents it, is a vast conceptualising enterprise that would subsume within itself and be able to evaluate all existing knowledge. It would attempt this by exercising a scientific sociological methodology with regard to all given knowledge, such as would entail a constant taking into account of concrete details, a progressive establishing of actual links and renunciation of the purely speculative links and hypotheses, so that ultimately there would emerge 'a sociological technique for diagnosing the culture of an epoch'.[10] The discipline of such a *sociology of knowledge* would ensure that a *realistic* perspective of the world (as opposed to utopian or ideological conceptualisations) would be sought,[11] and that such a view would be comprehensive or total insofar as it rises above all the partial views which prevail.[12] Such a *sociology of knowledge* is not a corrective in itself, but without it, Mannheim feels, correctives cannot be conceived or instituted. Correctives, therefore, become imminent *after* the conceptual effort to erect such a *sociology of knowledge*,[13] and some sort of concrete action would be found within such a constitutive conceptual effort itself only in the future – and it cannot be enunciated till then:

What the sociology of knowledge seeks to reveal is merely that, after knowledge has been freed from the elements of propaganda and evaluation, it still contains an activist element which, for the most part, has not become explicit, and which cannot be eliminated, but which, at best, can and should be raised into the sphere of the controllable.[14]

The notion of holistic *planning*, which Mannheim increasingly championed after the late nineteen-thirties, is given at a similar level of ambition, tentativeness and incompletion – with a similar air of describing what it may consist in without being able to ascertain concretely what it may lead to. The notion of *planning* is after the fact of a *sociology of knowledge* in a specific way. In *Man and Society* Mannheim places *planning* as after the fact of a certain sort of conceptual effort which has to do with the understanding of what he calls the *principia media* of an epoch. The idea of understanding an epoch, the state of the world, a state of affairs in terms of *principia media* consists in (a) understanding a specific fact or event and the general principles underlying it in a balanced fashion so that both the general and the particular implications are suitably apprehended; (b) being able to find patterns of organisation between and through the employment of such *principia media*; (c) a commitment to understanding the multiplicity of patterns of such *principia media* which every epoch must inevitably have.[15] This elaboration of understanding is in fact very similar to the conceptual effort envisaged as a *sociology of knowledge* in *Ideology and Utopia*. It differs only in being so formulated that it appears to be more pragmatically oriented (and it is probably for this reason that Mannheim didn't call it a construction of a *sociology of knowledge*) – it leads to something (effective *planning*) rather than seeming an end in itself (which can reveal the pragmatic prospect only in the future). Where a *sociology of knowledge* appeared tendentiously to be largely in the intellectual sphere, a predominantly conceptual effort, which would lead to action at the point of its comprehensive fulfilment, thinking in terms of *principia media* is a kind of action in itself, is conceptualisation as action, wherein 'thought is not an independent self-contained and abstractly intelligible fact but is intimately bound up with action'.[16] Conceptualisation as thought and action thus has immediate effect in Mannheim's *planning* – but he does not thereby abandon the holistic quest and expected fulfilment in the future:

> The most essential element in the planned approach is, then, that it not only thinks out individual aims and limited goals, but also

realizes what effects these individual aims will in the long run have on wider goals. The planned approach does not confine itself only to making the machine or organizing an army but seeks at the same time to imagine the most important changes which both can bring about in the whole social process.[17]

In this pragmatist spirit, Mannheim's discussion of *planning* consists not of an overview of an extant state of knowledge, but of known ways of making pragmatic interventions in economic, cultural, political and broadly social processes, through an assessment of different sorts of social control of which there is experience and in terms of what he understands as the prevailing state of society (the three conditions enumerated above). That, Mannheim suggests, is the basis of pragmatic intervention in the present and a first step toward the comprehensive *planning* which can only come to exist in the future.

A consideration of these ideas leads me directly to a statement of the reason why Mannheim inadvertently, almost against the grain of his own thinking and despite appearing not to, falls in with anti-political philosophy, complements anti-political thinking rather than contradicts it, contributes to a disabling of political will. *What is clear from the above is that for Mannheim all modes of political conceptualisation and action, all modes of determining ends and means, all politically intentional interpretations and explanations in the present are restrained in favour of realisations and clarifications which can only occur in the future. That in itself is, of course, not particularly disabling if the conditionality on future realisations, etc. is not overstated. After all, the future is unavoidably implied, just as the past is, in the present. But Mannheim's projected future of realisations and clarifications is particularly disabling because it presents no promise of ever becoming the present. The negotiation between first principles and microcosmic insights and total perspectives, between comprehensive or total conceptualisation and the given state of continuous flux in the world, between the difficulty of getting over one mode of constitutive conceptualisation and establishing another, between substantial irrationalities which can only be fully evident in the present and substantial rationalities which can only become confirmed in the future, between the constitutiveness of collective conceptualisation and the unavoidable dynamism of constant change and the need to accommodate it – all these mean that the future will always be the future and*

*the present will always be awaiting the clarity that is to come in the future.
Or, in other words, Mannheim disables the political will by constantly
deferring something within political philosophy, by the constant post-
ponement of political philosophy within an endless process of sociological
understanding (irrespective of whether it is more intellectually efficacious
or more pragmatically oriented).* Thus, despite his best intentions,
Mannheim's thinking becomes assimilable into the anti-political
disbelief in the possibility of determining ends and means and
exercising a political will; it becomes symbolic of the self-defeat of
political philosophy. This is marked by his growing closeness to
some of Popper's anti-political philosophical precepts (which I
discuss in detail in the next chapter) in his later reflections on
democratic planning – though Mannheim, even at this stage, never
allows his thinking to coincide with Popper's.[18] To the end,
Mannheim stuck to the notion of planning.

The endless deferring of effective political philosophy to the future
predictably leads to the final cop-out of Mannheim's later thinking
(despite standing by a need for planning), it leads to the most
explicitly politically disabling of positions – a pragmatic religiosity.
In his final attempt at reorienting his notion of planning while
retaining the first principle of flux in the context of western liberal
democracy (as this began to take shape after the Second World War)
in *Freedom, Power and Democratic Planning*, Mannheim recommends
the following concretisation of the ultimate end – a final reconcili-
ation with the contemplation of a future that never comes, a
perfection that is never reached – necessarily a metaphysical end:

> Certain unchanging aspects of the human mind seem to indicate
> the need for transcendental religious foundation in society; and
> several factors make this need even more urgent in our present
> situation. There exist some archaic patterns in the human mind
> and in the nature of human action that lead to the quest for
> certainty and deeper foundations. [...] calm assurance that the
> highest thing in life is communion with One to whom we can
> speak and who will respond with unfailing understanding and for-
> giveness is so deeply ingrained that despondency would reign if
> this religious belief were lost. Only through satisfaction of these
> deep-rooted aspirations (that there is a Purpose to what we are
> doing and that there is a Personal Power to whom we can appeal)
> can man develop the sense of belonging in a world where he can

find his place and where there is an order that supports him and dispels his anxieties.[19]

Interestingly, Mannheim's religiosity is presented not actually as a matter of faith, but as a pragmatic need for faith. Religion would divert people, he suggests, from seeking final resolutions by providing a sort of subterfuge – the mirage of an unquestionable higher power – by which to reconcile themselves to the given situation and make the best of it. This might seem to contradict the optimism of Mannheim's *sociology of knowledge* or the idea of *planning*, but it seems to me that this is a logical outcome of the political philosophical self-defeat that was written into their future-gazing construction. The blatant recommendation that people stop efforts at substantial rationality as an end in itself is actually an acknowledgement of the apprehension that it cannot be effectively realised under the conditions that he had himself laid out – it can only be deferred. Mannheim ends up by thus underlining his anti-political philosophical surrender.

13 Popper's Anti-Political Philosophical Tendencies

The self-acknowledged failure of the development of Mannheim's search for a suitable social and political order coincides rather neatly with Karl Popper's critique of such searches. Karl Popper's tentatively anti-political philosophy – this is tentative rather than fully fledged – is developed through a series of critiques, and is presented more as a matter of guarding against certain ideas than as a commitment to conceptualising or not conceptualising political means and ends. Thus, the two main statements of Popper's social and political thinking are primarily attacks on certain political philosophical ideas: *The Open Society and Its Enemies* (1945) details the shortcomings of a series of political philosophers who had, not unlike Mannheim, recommended holistic social transformation (focusing mainly on Plato, Hegel and Marx), and *The Poverty of Historicism* (1957) presents a more succinct statement and critique of the general ideas (rather than of details and specific thinkers) associated with the same theme. It is not my intention to address the specific ideas that Popper objects to (let's call this the sphere of Popper's *negative* thinking), but I would like to emphasise that this forms the bulk of Popper's efforts in this direction. However, I have two brief points to make in glossing over the negative thinking, which effectively leads me to his *positive* thinking – it is on the latter that I focus here, with the understanding that the positive can, for Popper, be apprehended through the negative. The two points apropos Popper's negative thinking are:

(a) The method of developing political philosophical perspectives primarily through a critique of an existing set of ideas necessarily falls back on what I have called *associationism* above. Since Popper finds that from Plato onwards certain historicist principles are associated in different ways by different philosophers with attempts at holistic conceptualisation, and that these are in turn associated with utopian thinking, and all of these in turn with authoritarianism, and in turn with collectivism, he more or less assumes that there is some sort of necessary relationship between these, and often presumes such an association even where it isn't evident. And similarly, he assumes a necessary relationship in the perception that anti-historicism is often associated with anti-utopianism and with liberalism and with individualism. The argument is given with the understanding that such associations have been made in given examples, and is followed by an attempt to explain how this association comes about after the fact; but the argument seldom takes the path of demonstrating that these ideas are implicitly such that there would inevitably exist a necessary relationship. In other words, Popper gives, often rather tenuously, a law-like validity to the instances of association that he discerns and thinks of these as necessary relationships, whereas it is quite possible that though such associations *have* been made, they are not *necessarily* made. Further, rather like Mannheim, Popper too is given to finding neat dialectical positions, which fall in with a questionable *oppositionism* and *exclusionism*. Popper's sphere of negative thinking is too neatly arraigned against the conglomerate of holistic thinking, and utopianism, and historicism, and authoritarianism, and their opposites (anti-utopianism, individualism, liberalism, etc.) are too completely excluded from that sphere. There is little space for a complex cross-linking of ideas here: Popper assumes without much reflection that individualism cannot be a holistic concept, that liberalism cannot be utopian, that authoritarianism cannot be anti-historicist, etc. simply because he is not (or doesn't admit to being) aware of instances where such untidy associations have been made.

(b) Popper's sphere of negative thinking (as I have asserted already) is obviously underlaid by a sphere of positive thinking, even if the latter is only available in an implicit fashion, is only inferable and not stated. It is hardly conceivable that Popper could offer an effective critique of any set of ideas without espousing some set of ideas himself, in terms of which the critique appears as critique. However, he presents these positive ideas with such circumspection and makes them so conditional on the shortcomings that he sees in certain areas of political philosophy that one might have doubts as to their independent status. It seems possible that Popper only espouses certain ideas because he disagrees with their opposites: that in fact the sphere of his positive thinking is the product of opposition to the sphere of his negative thinking, the product of *oppositionism*. As it happens though, this is not the case. Popper provides enough of a philosophical apparatus (from first principles to concepts of process and rationality) and enough of a sense of context and contingency to enable his sphere of positive thinking to have an independent status.

The first principle that characterises much of Popper's positive thinking and is most closely associated with anti-political philosophy thereafter (and is particularly resonant given the discussion of Mannheim's assumption of collectivism) is that of the primacy of individualism. The assertion of the primacy of individualism makes a puzzling appearance in the course of the discussion of Plato in *The Open Society*, where its status as a first principle is somewhat obscured. This appears in the midst of charting out the ostensibly oppositional position to what Popper argues is Plato's holistic, historicist, collectivist, totalitarian, utopian conceptualisation – that is, a piecemeal, anti-historicist, individualist, democratic and pragmatic conceptualisation. Popper somehow assumes that Plato's particular form of utopian thinking sets the pattern for all utopian thinking thereafter (thus ironically giving Plato credit for hitting upon a Platonic essential form of the idea of utopia), and proceeds to present the oppositional position at a level of generality which is tenuous (from the righteous perspective of 'most of us, especially those whose perspective is humanitarian').[1] The assumption that Plato's particular argument can give an insight into collectivism in general, and that this needs to be countered by an assertion of individualism in general, is clearly a case of what I have called *translative overdeterminism* above – and effectively it is a puzzling statement of the matter. It is also puzzling because the assertion of individualism simply isn't clear enough in the almost purely *oppositional* manner in which it is presented here. When Popper proceeds to elaborate on the second of what he contends are the three main demands of a 'humanitarian theory of justice' ((a) 'the equalitarian principle proper, i.e. the proposal to eliminate "natural" privileges, (b) the general principle of individualism, and (c) the principle that it should be the task and purpose of the state to protect the freedom of its citizens')[2] he does so self-consciously in terms of sorting out oppositions – and feels some sort of justification of individualism is reached by joining it with altruism.[3] None of this however quite tells us what Popper thinks individualism consists in; what exactly is its status in the context of the rest of Popper's so-called humanitarian theory; what, in brief, does Popper mean by individualism? *The Open Society* doesn't quite answer this question: individualism isn't explained, its place in a piecemeal, anti-historicist, pragmatic, etc. conceptualisation isn't elucidated – it is simply more or less assumed that it is associated with the latter and opposed to holistic, collectivist, utopian, etc. conceptualisation and must therefore be better. But that simply isn't a sufficient argument: that something isn't good doesn't necessarily imply that its opposite would be better.

A clearer notion of what the primacy of individualism means for Popper (irrespective of what it is in opposition to) is available in his philosophy of mind, especially in certain sections of the portions penned by Popper in *The Self and Its Brain* (co-written with John C. Eccles, 1977). Here, after discerning three modes of conscious knowledge – that which exists at a level of materiality (he calls this World 1), subjective knowledge (World 2), and objective knowledge (World 3), and recognising that 'fully conscious intelligent work largely depends upon the interaction between World 2 and World 3'[4] – he charts out the process whereby the intelligent stage, which distinguishes humanness, comes into being. This entails a beginning from the biological principle of individuation, progression through various teleological stages determined by evolutionary needs, and culminating in the following surmise:

> the human consciousness of self transcends, I suggest, all purely biological thought. I may put it like this: I have little doubt that animals are conscious, and especially that they feel pain and that a dog can be full of joy when his master returns. But I conjecture that only a human being capable of speech can reflect upon himself. I think that every organism has a programme. But I also think that only a human being can be conscious of parts of this programme, and revise them critically.[5]

It seems to me that this first-principle understanding of humanness as consisting in self-understanding – where the *self* is already bio-logically individuated, and the understanding of self is therefore presumed to be the individual self – is what constitutes the primacy of individualism for Popper. That this conjecture within the precincts of the philosophy of mind becomes for Popper a political first principle is immediately confirmed after this statement, where (for the only time in *The Self and Its Brain*) he bounds off into the realm of political conviction:

The most widespread aim in such a plan of life is the personal task of providing for oneself and for one's dependants. It may be described as the most democratic of aims: remove it, and you make life meaningless for many. This does not mean that there is no need for a Welfare State to help those who do not succeed in this. But even more important is that the Welfare State should not create unreasonable or insurmountable difficulties for those who try to make this most natural and democratic of tasks a major part of their aims in life.[6]

Along with Mannheim, we may feel tempted to argue, and rightly, that self-knowledge is inevitably an awareness of being with others and therefore being in a collectivity, that Popper's own emphasis on the need for speech in self-knowledge and the recognition of dependants as an aim which follows is evidence of that. Be that as it may though, the *content* of Popper's assertion of the primacy of individualism as a political first principle is revealed.

Parallel and opposed to Mannheim's first principle of the flux of the world and consequent constitutiveness of conceptualisation, Popper's understanding of the relationship between conceptualisation and the world may also be thought of as a first principle. As a first principle, in contrast to Mannheim's, this could be stated in general terms as follows: *the world is subject to certain constitutive laws and processes (it is not in itself simply a state of flux) which it is the task of conceptualisation to understand and come to grips with (so conceptualisation is* conditional *and not* constitutive*). Since conceptualisation is always conditional on given abilities to engage with the world, and since the world can only be engaged with a bit at a time and within the limitations of ability and need, conceptualisation is always inevitably a limited and incomplete process.* This first principle contains a significant corollary: like Mannheim, Popper doesn't presume to address that which is outside the conceptual (in that sense the emphasis on conceptualisation, the sense of being contained in the conceptual, is assumed with equal strength by both): the world can be understood only through conceptualisation. The difference is that whereas Mannheim believes that for us the world *is* conceptual, Popper is convinced that the world is always *more* than what is conceptually available. This becomes the basis of Mannheim's quest for comprehensiveness in conceptualisation, and Popper's call for the awareness of the limits and conditionality of conceptualisation.

This first principle is clearly implied in Popper's reflections on scientific exploration, developed most cogently in *The Logic of Scientific Discovery* (1959) and extended to various spheres of thinking (analytical and social and political philosophy). It is in understanding scientific exploration, wherein the engagement of conceptualisation with the world occurs with the most lucid sense of trying to unravel and understand the laws and processes that constitute the latter, that the encompassing nature of conceptualisation and all its limitations become manifest. Understanding scientific exploration for Popper is mainly a matter of establishing suitable modes of *testing* scientific formulations so as to make sure that acceptable relationships between conceptualisation and the world are established by these (by drawing on the internal coherence of formulations, by drawing on empirical evidence, by ascertaining coherence in the world of experience).[7] The limitations of conceptualisation with regard to the world are revealed as the limitations of scientific formulation – which can never be fully ascertained (tested for every possible context and condition),[8] and are always open to modification or change or rejection if at any moment tests which make such formulations untenable are found (this is the gist of Popper's famous notion of *falsifiability*).[9] Out of this sense of the limitation of conceptualisation emerges Popper's notion of *conceptual processes*, as distinct from the *natural processes* of the world. In brief, since conceptualisation is always limited and open to testing but never conclusively verifiable, it would always have to evolve ways of dealing with falsification by reformulation and renovation – so conceptualisation should not be thought of as a quest for holistic understanding but as a process consisting in an endless positing of hypotheses, testing thereof, provisional acceptance thereof, and when necessary (when falsified) rejection thereof, and replacement thereof by new hypotheses, and so on. The conceptual process of scientific exploration, notes Popper, is necessarily without beginning or ending.

What this position also does however is to commit Popper to conceptualisation in itself, and in this, despite the obvious differences, Popper is not that far from Mannheim's belief in conceptual efforts. Like Mannheim, Popper also thereby acknowledges a sense of being enclosed in conceptualisation – which, even in the most ostensibly ends-oriented of conceptual efforts in the sciences, becomes no more than an endlessly self-contained and self-perpetuating affair. And in this Popper also interestingly comes close to Kuhn, who is often understood as espousing an opposing philosophy of science. Kuhn was convinced that science is a matter of reluctantly (and rather arbitrary) shifting paradigms within human conceptualisation;[10] Popper's interesting metaphor for scientific exploration captures a sense of the shifting and the arbitrary in conceptualisation too:

> The empirical basis of objective science has thus nothing 'absolute' about it. Science does not rest upon solid bedrock. The bold structure of its theories rises, as it were, above a swamp. It is like a building erected on piles. The piles are driven down from above into the swamp, but not down to any natural or 'given' base; and if we stop driving the piles deeper, it is not because we have reached firm ground. We simply stop when we are satisfied that the piles are firm enough to carry the structure, at least for the time being.[11]

It is the observation that we stop when we are satisfied and not because we actually reach any truth which gives Popper's view of scientific conceptualisation – and therefore of conceptualisation generally – its arbitrary edge and self-containedness.

Popper thinks of this model of scientific investigation as one that is pertinent not only to the pure or natural sciences but to all rational thought. The first principle involved here (conceptualisation is limited) is given general efficacy and extended to other areas of knowledge; and the model of scientific exploration becomes representative of rational exploration generally. Thus Popper extends the notion of the falsifiability of scientific formulation to analytical philosophy at large by proposing that falsifiability could become the answer to Hume's scepticism about induction[12] – a translation of ideas which other analytic philosophers have often challenged.[13] More significantly in this context, Popper presents this model of scientific exploration as the basis of sociological and political conceptualisation too. The section entitled 'Aftermath' in the second volume of *The Open Society* is largely a summary of his objections to holistic utopian thinkers for having failed to understand the truly rational method of social theory and practice, i.e. 'the *social aspects of knowledge*, or rather of scientific method',[14] followed by recommendations for bringing such sociologies of knowledge in line with Popper's understanding of scientific exploration, with the realisation that '*A social technology is needed whose results can be tested by piecemeal social engineering*' (Popper's italics).[15] In other words, social and political theory/practice should be a continuous conceptual process which, in the spirit of the scientific conceptual process, would offer hypotheses (social technological formulations) which could be accepted in a provisional manner and tested (through social engineering) with a full apprehension of their inevitable limitations and possible falsifiability.

The above account of Popper's first principles and the frame of positive ideas with social and political effect which devolve from that is sufficient to reveal his anti-political philosophical tendencies. Before elucidating that, it should be noted that the anti-political tendencies are foreshadowed already in the fact that Popper typically carries out a *translative overdeterminism* in extending his inferences from a philosophy of scientific exploration to give them general validity, and in considering his model of scientific exploration as the exemplar of general rationality. Popper doesn't draw a clear argument to justify this, he depends on plausible sounding assertion. The plausibility of such an assertion derives to a large extent from an existing predisposition in sociological and political disciplines towards modelling themselves (often tenuously) in terms of scientific methods, and to a certain extent from the persuasiveness of his negative thinking (his often sound objections to what appear to be associated with opposite tendencies – he naturally makes the most of neat *oppositionism* in this, by dividing all conceptual effort into either the magical or the scientific). But he doesn't sufficiently consider the possibility of having modes of rational conceptualisation that may be irrelevant and inapplicable to the natural sciences but quite tenable in social and political matters; and certainly in philosophy or mathematics alternative rational models are legion. Indeed, it is ironic that Popper seeks to make his philosophy of science grounds for restraining certain kinds of social and political action and recommending others, when it is arguable that this philosophy of science has no practical implications for the conduct of the natural sciences themselves.[16] If the field of scientific practice is to be philosophised in a way that does not interfere with it, what justification is there for using those philosophical precepts to interfere in a range of different fields?

To move on though, in consonance with the above first principles and corollaries, Popper maintains that the *only* kind of social and political existence which can be endorsed is one in which certain forms of *democratic institutions* prevail wherein what he considers to be *piecemeal social engineering* can be constantly encouraged and pursued. The two italicised phrases in that sentence designate Popper's chief positive political ideas, and require some elaboration.

Democracy, for Popper, constitutes a set of well-tried and tested modes of equalitarian control, designed to maintain the primacy of individualism, which are simply opposed to any form of tyranny:

> the theory of democracy is not based on the principle that the majority should rule; rather, the various equalitarian methods of democratic control, such as general elections and representative government, are to be considered as no more than well-tried and, in the presence of a widespread traditional distrust of tyranny, reasonably effective institutional safeguards against tyranny, always open to improvement, and even providing methods for their own improvement.[17]

Popper thinks of democratic institutions as providing *a structure* (hence institutionally framed) through which the primacy of individualism would be maintained by permitting a multiplicity of interests to be accommodated and promoted, through consensus and compromise; as also naturally offering the means for change and regulation within itself through the democratic processes which it contains and adheres to; and as preventing, through the same means and by dint of its institutional status, the predominance of specific collective interests or holistic transformative efforts to take place. As envisaged here, such democratic institutions need not be good in themselves, but would always allow for what is democratically deemed to be desirable to be tried out, adopted, modified, or dispensed with: 'The democratic institutions cannot improve themselves. The problem of improving them is always a problem for *persons* rather than for institutions. But if we want improvements, we must make clear which *institutions* we want to improve.'[18] From a social and political point of view, what such democratic institutions would facilitate is piecemeal social engineering (as opposed to holistic utopian engineering), that is, focused attempts at addressing specific problems, which would never aspire to go beyond the *specific*, and never seek anything other than solutions for manifest *problems* (not attempt to reach towards a *good* which is not in itself a solution to a problem). Thus coherence with the first principle,

which sees inevitable and insurmountable limitations in conceptualisation, would be maintained:

> The characteristic approach of the piecemeal engineer is this. Even
> though he may perhaps cherish some ideals which concern
> society 'as a whole' – its general welfare, perhaps – he does not
> believe in the method of re-designing it as a whole. Whatever his
> ends, he tries to achieve them by small adjustments and re-adjust-
> ments which can be continually improved upon. [...] He knows
> that we can learn only from our mistakes. Accordingly, he will
> make his way, step by step, carefully comparing the results
> expected with the results achieved, and always on the look-out for
> the unavoidable unwanted consequences of any reform; and he
> will avoid undertaking reforms of a complexity and scope which
> will make it impossible for him to disentangle causes and effects,
> and to know what he is really doing.[19]

Or more pithily: 'The piecemeal engineer will [...] adopt the method
of searching for, and fighting against, the greatest and most urgent
evils of society, rather than searching for, and fighting for, its
greatest ultimate good.'[20]

The anti-political implications of these two key ideas as presented
by Popper are discerned as follows. An outstanding feature of
Popper's presentation of democratic institutions and piecemeal
social engineering, which are indeed consistent with his first
principles of the primacy of individualism and the limitations of
conceptualisation, is that these do not seem to recognise the possibility of the *interconnectedness or interlinkedness of social and political
phenomena (including problems)*. Deriving as Popper's ideas do from
the contemplation of natural science, this is curious, because
scientists always recognise, even while artificially maintaining disciplinary boundaries, the basic interlinkedness of natural
phenomena from micro to macro, from special to general, from
particular to essential fields. In social and political thinking the
interlinkedness of pertinent phenomena (in terms of economic
determinations, in terms of societal stratifications, in terms of
discursive strategies, etc.) have been the mainstay of intellectual
exploration, and even if it might be pragmatically necessary to
address separate problems in themselves, it is impossible for either
the theoretician or the practitioner to forget it. Even if the perceptions of such interlinkedness are conceptually manifested in such

tenuously reductionist notions as a conspiracy theory (one cause or agent can be held responsible for all the problems), or such simplificationist notions as an anarchist agenda (if everything is destabilised something new may emerge), to overlook interlinkedness on those grounds cannot but be the most ill-conceived *oppositionism*. At the very least, social and political conceptualisation, however limited and prone to fallibility they might be, are implicitly grounded on notions of interconnectedness in their very rootedness in notions of society and polity. Importantly for us, *so are all political institutions*. For instance, the political state of whatever nature (and especially the democratic state), as I have presented it above, is not appointed to represent a particular kind of problem – it addresses a complex and interconnected set of problems and expectations pertinent to the people–land–resources it is with regard to (and has to conceptualise this by interpreting and acting upon that intentional system as a whole). Even if ministries are established to address specific categories of problems and issues (agricultural, industrial, foreign affairs, monetary affairs, etc.) it is inconceivable that these ministries can exist and conduct their business in any sort of splendid isolation. It is similarly very unlikely that a political state which is aware of other political states can be indifferent to this awareness. It might be argued that Popper's notion of piecemeal social engineering may work at least pragmatically by focusing on particular problems in a realistic fashion, if not in any understandable philosophical sense – but even practical efforts in Popper's terms are unlikely to succeed if all potentially or tendentiously holistic conceptualisation is abandoned. To be consistent with his own model of scientific exploration he has to at least allow for the tendency of holistic conceptualisation, the aspiration of holistic conceptualisation, at the very least insofar as *we are satisfied with it* (just as testing of a scientific formulation may stop when we are satisfied). But Popper doesn't allow even for this in his oppositional and exclusionist zeal.

In fact the only possible consequence that any attempt to adhere to Popper's social and political thinking can conceivably have would be as repressive as the kind of tyranny that he condemns most vociferously – a comprehensive disabling of political will in all the senses outlined above. It seems to me quite possible that Popper didn't realise this, for he undoubtedly intended well. *To treat social problems separately and political institutions discretely, and to discourage all efforts at holistic conceptualisation and understanding, and all attempts to act upon ideals which emerge from the latter, would be a formula for developing a society with myopic political vision. No sense of political means and ends – whether of a conservative variety, or such as champion incremental change, or such as recommend comprehensive change – can be conceived under these circumstances, let alone acted upon. But that doesn't mean that social injustice would disappear: it would simply mean that a status quo would prevail, where only specific symptoms might be perceived without any apprehension of the complex underlying causes. Only one organ can be treated at a time, but without examining, insofar as that is possible, the whole organism. There would only exist an impression of the endless bustle of dealing with minutiae.* Popper's social and political concepts seem to me to be the formulae for disabling the political will; this becomes clear when they are put into perspective (as I have attempted above) as a sphere of positive ideas constructed on certain first principles. It is understandable that Popper should become the harbinger of the kind of anti-political philosophy which coheres best with the corporate capitalism of our time, wherein the political will is most systematically disabled.

Nevertheless, I still maintain that Popper had only anti-political philosophical *tendencies*; his is not an anti-political philosophy in full bloom. This is because Popper, like Mannheim, believes in the enclosure of conceptualisation and in the efficacy of conceptual efforts (though these are limited and fallible). He does believe in the possibility of rational conceptualisation, and in the ability for change to be wrought (in modest degrees) through such effort, and that change cannot be effected in any other way – indeed that conceptualisation is the only way in which we engage with the world, and that we all have a commitment to enlarging our conceptual faculties. This, despite the limitations and cautions that are emphasised, enjoins a voluntarism in social and political conduct that is consistent with an ability to exercise the political will. That Popper considers this to be the case, rather against the grain of the rest of his thinking, is clear in his chief objection to historicist thinking. Actually there is some confusion here: Popper associates historicist thinking with utopianism, holistic planning, etc., and (in typical *oppositional* fashion) recommends that any social and political conceptualisation (*The Poverty of Historicism* makes a list of the different possible kinds) which derives itself from and places itself in terms of historical processes should be eschewed. Clearly, however, this somewhat exaggerated position should not be interpreted as a wholesale rejection of historicist understanding – Popper's own explanation, for instance, of Plato's utopianism depends on his being able to contextualise Plato, and his understanding of the emergence of the open society is given in terms of historical process in Volume 1 of *The Open Society*. It seems to me more accurate to understand Popper's objections to historicism as reservations about historicist *determinism*, and his qualms about the latter follow not so much from the associations he tenuously makes but from the fear that such determinism limits the possibilities of conceptualisation and conceptual efforts (effectively restrains the possibility of the political will):

> Only a historicist who takes an optimistic view of social development, believing it to be intrinsically 'good' or 'rational', in the sense of tending intrinsically towards a better, towards a more reasonable state of affairs could offer [hope of a better world]. But this view would amount to a belief in social and political miracles, since *it denies to human reason the power of bringing about a more reasonable world.*[21]

It is also Popper's optimism about the possibilities and efficacy of conceptualisation and his conviction that we have no choice but to act through conceptual efforts, which leads to his rhetorical call for more and more daring ideas at the end of *The Logic of Scientific Discovery*: 'Bold ideas, unjustified anticipations, and speculative thought, are our only means for interpreting nature: our only organon, our only instrument, for grasping her. And we must hazard them to win our prize.'[22]

Popper only had anti-political philosophical tendencies. For a full flowering of anti-political philosophy we have to turn to Hayek.

14   Hayek and the Mature Anti-Political Philosophy

The impression that Hayek's and Popper's thinking shares common ground,[1] which they themselves promoted, derives from the apparent similarity of their first principles – Hayek too subscribes to the primacy of individualism and to the limited and fallible quality of any conceptualisation of the world. At that superficial level of statement there does seem to exist a likeness between Popper's and Hayek's positions, but that is where the resemblance actually ends, for the inferences that Hayek makes from these first principles are quite different from Popper's.

Strictly speaking, Hayek's understanding of individualism is not really as the *primacy* of individualism, it is as the *absoluteness* of individualism. In presenting his notion of individualism Popper had in mind its primacy as opposed to the secondariness of collectivism, but Popper didn't dispense with collectivism all together. Collectivism is permissible and even necessary, Popper suggests, but only so long as it doesn't infringe on the primacy of individualism, so long as individual freedom and democratic equalitarian principles are not compromised. Hayek's assertion of the absoluteness of individualism is actually an assertion of the irrelevance of collectivist considerations in political and social conceptualisation. Hayek's notion of the absoluteness of individualism is not, of course, a denial that people live with regard to and communicate with each other, and participate in a process of civilisation (such a denial would negate even anti-political philosophy); the absoluteness of individualism consists in an arbitrary and deliberate *conviction* (hence a matter of faith) that *all* that an individual can and should really be concerned with is the well-being and aspiration of the individual self, and that *any* notion of collective conceptualisation and action for collective well-being which follows a route that is inconsistent with that is irrational and irrelevant. Consequently, collectivity does not have to be considered in social and political thinking at all; all that is needed is a sufficiently strong and determined view of the inviolability of the individual (and this includes the inviolability of individuals by other individuals):

What is essential to the functioning of the process [of civilisation] is that each individual be able to act on his particular knowledge, always unique, at least so far as it refers to some particular circumstances, and that he be able to use his individual skills and opportunities within the limits known to him and for his own individual purpose.[2]

Further, since the recognition of communicative and civilisational processes is inevitably collective (social) in some sense, and is difficult to reconcile with the kind of absolute individualism that Hayek asserts, he finds it necessary to define collectivity in a manner which effectively effaces itself, wipes itself away. This is ingeniously done by defining collectivity (or the only permissible understanding of collectivity) as an almost accidental coincidence of individual perspectives – collectivity becomes a sort of mathematical function of different individualities put together, which inexorably remain individual:

This view does not, of course, exclude the recognition of social ends, or rather the coincidence of individual ends which makes it advisable for men to combine for their pursuit. But it limits such common action to instances where individual views coincide; what are called 'social ends' are for it merely identical ends of many individuals – or ends to the achievement of which individuals are willing to contribute in return for the assistance they receive in the satisfaction of their own desires. Common action is thus limited to the fields where people agree on common ends. Very frequently these common ends will not be ultimate ends to the individuals, but means which different persons can use for different purposes.[3]

Such is Hayek's first principle of individualism (quite distinct after all from Popper's), and his inference therefrom about the nature of permissible collectivity (which is effectively a denial of collectivity). I think this sounds implausible even at this initial point as a perspective from which to approach social and political considerations, and it seems to me almost inevitable that Hayek will have to contradict himself if he continues to engage with social and political issues – as indeed he does. Such an absolute presentation of individualism as a determinant of social and political conceptualisation seems to invite what in Chapter 12 I called *contained overdeterminism*.

That this occurs in untenable ways in Hayek's thinking becomes clear in due course.

Hayek's tendency towards *contained overdeterminism* arising from his faith in absolute individualism is evidenced in his presentation of what is effectively his (and parallel to Popper's) second first principle: a belief in the limitations and fallibility of conceptual efforts with regard to the world. Interestingly Hayek is given to presenting this as not a first principle at all, but as deriving in some way from the first principle of absolute individualism:

> [Individualism] merely starts from the indisputable fact that the limits of our powers of imagination make it impossible to include in our scale of values more than a sector of the needs of the whole society, and that, since, strictly speaking, scales of values can only exist in individual minds, nothing but partial scales of values exists, scales which are inevitably different and often inconsistent with each other.[4]

The limitation and fallibility of conceptualisation, the argument goes, derive from the fact that only individuals can be said to conceive, and reflect the narrow ambits (limits) within which individuals live and with which individuals are concerned. This is questionable as an argument at various levels. The notion that 'strictly speaking, scales of values only exist in individual minds' is deeply puzzling: *strictly speaking*, the individual mind may not have any understandable existence as such, insofar as thought is not understandable (and scales of values are not understandable qua values) except in some sort of communicative form (a language perhaps, if one wants to be concrete), and whether any communicative form can be thought of as an individual affair is very doubtful indeed. That leads into the labyrinthine considerations of private language which Wittgenstein, for instance, considered and abandoned.[5] If we momentarily get rid of the rather arbitrary notion of the absoluteness of individual minds, there is no reason why, through an exploration of communicative modes and exchange, a *collective* effort between many and even all individuals to discern a universal scale of values (with some necessary conditions) could not exist such that it supersedes the limits of individual experience. To take a different tack, even if we grant that conceptualisation (and the subscription to values) is primarily determined by individuals for themselves, there is no *necessary* reason why this conceptualisation (and individually chosen scale of values) should be thereby limited. It is of course true that individuals necessarily exist within a limited ambit of needs and place and time, but it is quite possible that their thoughts needn't be (that an individual may hit upon universally efficacious thoughts and values may be debatable, but not conclusively discountable). Arguably, the processes of universalisation that rational thinking in any communicative form offer *may* allow even individuals, with their limited ambit of experience and concerns, to reach effectively universal levels of conceptualisation and scales of values. The most accurate statement from this perspective would be that this is unlikely, but not necessarily impossible. I don't think Hayek's argument to *prove* that conceptualisation has to be limited can be taken seriously (it is no more than the consequence of a *contained overdeterminism*); the idea can however simply be accepted as a first principle, for certain political exigencies – something like, for instance, that it is politically inconvenient to have to admit at any point that any individual point of view can be universally efficacious, even hypothetically. Instead of saying this is not possible, we can (with Hayek) assert as a matter of principle (a second first principle) that we choose not to accept such a possibility. What is of immediate interest here is that this second first principle concerning the limitations of conceptualisation is also (despite appearances) significantly different from Popper's parallel second first principle.

The difference is this. Where Popper is, as I have observed above, fully cognisant of the inescapability of conceptualisation, and is optimistic of the possibilities of conceptual efforts, and leaves some space for the exercise of a voluntaristic political will, Hayek *seeks* to restrict conceptual efforts. The natural or material processes that distinguish the world from conceptual processes for Popper are ultimately only available *through* conceptual processes (hence even science is an autonomous conceptual process); whereas for Hayek *natural or material processes are so overwhelmingly and inescapably there that conceptual processes should simply accommodate and adapt to them and not try to overreach them.* It is with this in mind that Hayek, in fact, argues that conceptualisation is less important and effective than unconceptualised action.[6] It is because of the difference from Popper in this respect that Hayek is able to realise anti-political philosophy to the fullest, while Popper rests with at expressing anti-political philosophical tendencies.

The most strikingly anti-political corollary of these peculiarly Hayekian first principles is his controversial view of adaptive evolution (taken up gleefully, as observed above, by the anti-political organisation of corporate capitalism, especially in managerial discourses and consonant economic and political discourses). Hayek's idea of adaptive evolution – which is carefully distinguished from biological evolution – is not particularly complex: since conceptual efforts and aspirations are (given his first principles) necessarily within the sphere of individuals only and are therefore limited, they cannot be used to explain how institutions and societies as a whole arise and change; in fact under the circumstances it has to be the case that the appearance of institutions and social and institutional changes are not the result of any singular or motivating or purposive conceptual effort (certainly not human, and nor for that matter divine), that is, they are not the result of design and planning, at all; such appearances and growths and changes are in fact due to an incremental process of selection and adaptation from a large number of competing and coalescing individual perspectives and aspirations and efforts. That at any rate is the gist of the idea that Hayek presented most lucidly in the first instance in *The Constitution of Liberty*,[7] and developed and repeated with increasing vehemence in his later writings.[8] This differs from biological evolution in not being grounded in physical manifestations, but it is also analogous to biological evolution in interpreting social and political processes as not being a matter of any voluntary aspiration or any political will but as being a matter of following an evolutionary mechanism which is indifferent to such aspiration or will. But that in itself is not an anti-political view: it is an interpretation of social and political processes which may be said to compete with such other interpretations as the liberal notion of social contract, or the socialist understanding of class conflict. To argue that this is how social processes *are* (which is what Hayek's adaptive evolution does until this point) does not imply that this is how they *must continue to be*. What Hayek does thereafter however, and in doing this he brings his anti-political philosophy to maturation, is precisely that: he argues that that is how it *must continue to be*.

The reason why Hayek believes that the mechanism of adaptive evolution must be retained and indeed nurtured, why he is convinced that any attempt to exercise a collective political will or social aspiration must be restrained so that individuals may continue to exert their narrowly focused efforts for individual ends and thus fall in spontaneously with larger evolutionary processes – the reason has to do with Hayek's understanding of what he rhetorically calls 'freedom'. The wedding of individualism and conceptual limitations in the theory of adaptive evolution occurs in the name of freedom (which completes the scaffolding on which the anti-political philosophy that justifies contemporary capitalism continues to rest) and is presented by Hayek in the following argument. In the first instance, Hayek understands 'freedom' as being no more than an immediate corollary of the first principle of absolute individualism: since the only conceptual position that Hayek can acknowledge is that of the individual, he has to ensure that this conceptual position is *fully* acknowledged, and this full acknowledgement amounts to his understanding of freedom. In this the insistence on freedom is no more than another way of insisting on absolute individualism: it is an atomisation of individuals from each other and from collectives of any sort. It is given by Hayek as the need to ensure that individuals are not 'coerced' by others[9] – but *coerced* in Hayek's sense is an exaggeration, for what he means is that individuals should be restrained from any mode of influencing each other and that individuals should be protected from any kind of influence of a group or collective, unless this influence coincides entirely with the individual's utterly self-oriented (selfish?) aspirations. However gentle such an influence might be, however grateful an individual may be for it, however willingly an individual may wish to relegate or modify his aspirations because of it, Hayek would think of such collective or group influences as being coercive. The exaggeration in using 'coercion' here is unquestionably for *oppositional* effect – to associate the atomisation which is implicit in a notion of absolute individualism with something that is traditionally (morally and socially) valued, like *freedom*. Freedom for Hayek is simply a synonym for absolute individualism in the first instance: the pleasing conjunction 'individual freedom' doesn't, for Hayek, mean that there are other kinds of socially and politically efficacious freedom, it is a means of discounting what may pass for other conceptions of freedom.[10]

Once this rhetorical tactic is in place, Hayek goes on to present another understanding of 'freedom', this time drawn primarily from his other first principle. The argument – again a simplistic one – goes as follows: since conceptualisation *per se* (which for Hayek is essentially individual conceptualisation anyway) is inevitably limited and fallible as a first principle, it is best not to be dictated to by conceptualisations and well-conceptualised aspirations of any sort. Hayek suggests that freedom in fact is the condition that refuses to be dictated to by the conceptual. Freedom lies in not trying to conceptualise or to conceptually determine social and political matters. That naturally raises the question: what then would *be* that in which such unconceptualised freedom could be realised? At this point Hayek brings up his notion of adaptive evolution: freedom would consist in not engaging in conceptual efforts but in doing as individuals what one wishes to do to fulfil individual aspirations and leaving the rest to the mechanism of adaptive evolution, which would gradually and more or less spontaneously provide the necessary framework (in the shape of suitable institutions) to accommodate individual endeavours and give them a form that would not disturb such endeavours, as a more conceptually determined institution would. There is still, he argues, the free-flowing self-regulating world outside the limits of conceptualisation which determines the structures of much of our social and political institutions; all that needs to be done for freedom as given here to be realised in social and political terms is to surrender to its indifferent processes and make the best of them:

> To the empiricist evolutionary tradition [...] the value of freedom consists mainly in the opportunity it provides for the growth of the undesigned, and the beneficial functioning of a free society rests largely on the existence of such freely grown institutions.[11]

In other words, not only is adaptive evolution observed as forming the basis of political and philosophical development, it is recommended that every effort should deliberately be made to ensure that it *continues to stay so* – and with this the full theoretical structure of Hayek's anti-political philosophy falls into place. As a theoretical structure it undoubtedly has the allure of a neatish jigsaw puzzle; as a theoretical structure it is also inadequate in its foundations and in its argumentative processes, as I hope I have shown; and as a theoretical structure it remains inadequate even at this point. Is this understanding of freedom as drawn from the second first principle – and now clearly more than an *oppositional* rhetorical ploy – a concept of freedom at all? This is a question worth posing here. That individuals can do broadly what they wish to do for their satisfaction so long as they don't conceptualise beyond themselves, and so long as they don't conceptualise much at all, is arguably not freedom at all. It seems to me much more plausible that the individual's being given the choice to do things that he desires would not seem to be freedom unless he conceives of it as such, and he cannot conceive of it as such except in collective terms (the recognition of it being such from others, and the recognition of it with relation to others, and in others). It is unlikely that a person on a large and uninhabited desert island, a Robinson-Crusoe-like character, would consider himself free in any socially or politically understandable sense. It is also unlikely that a person who is simply not noticed whatever he does would think of himself as free. It is quite possible that a person who fulfils his every aspiration but cannot get anyone else to acknowledge this achievement wouldn't feel free. It is also quite possible that a person who finds himself able to fulfil whatever desire he has so long as this does not in any way extend to others (to be shared or discussed) may not consider himself to be free. Further, it is also worth asking ourselves: can a restriction not to *conceive* certain things (let alone act upon them) be considered a recommendation that is consistent with any rational sense of freedom? Not to be allowed to think differently from a given ideology is easily understandable as unfreedom. By the same logic, to be discouraged from thinking of comprehensive planning and designing social institutions (especially when this is devoted to some notion of a social good) must also be a condition of unfreedom. And further, yet another question may militate against Hayek's theoretical structure: is there sufficient evidence that institutions that have spontaneously and adaptively evolved (if indeed they have) are in fact as accommodative of absolute individualism (which is synonymous with freedom for Hayek) as he suggests? If it is assumed that some of the institutions of liberal democracy (and their customs and traditions) have evolved in such a manner, it must also be assumed that so have the institutions which are consistent with repressive theocracies and military states and monarchies, as have those which perpetuate sexist and racist and casteist prejudices, and so on, all of which pertain to our world. Under the circumstances, to leave political and social matters to spontaneous processes, and never to rise above the atomised individual – the most debilitating form of disabling that the political will can undergo – seems a pre-eminently risky proposition.

The inadequacies of Hayek's anti-political theoretical structure (a self-defeating holistic conceptualisation itself no doubt) seem to me to be all too obvious, and might well have been apparent to Hayek too. Hayek's anti-political philosophy as philosophy is fraught with problems from first principles to inferences to conclusions. What Hayek tries to do, apart from providing persuasive rhetorical ploys and the allure of the jigsaw puzzle that somehow fits to sell his theory, is to extend this theoretical structure to real-world problems and issues with a view to providing resolutions. And it is because he is able to give his doubtful theoretical tenets (his anti-political philosophy) this pragmatic orientation that he is so wholeheartedly taken into the bosom of contemporary corporate capitalism. It accords too well with the disabling of political will that occurs in contemporary corporate capitalism for Hayek to be disregarded in such a context. An examination of the pragmatic inferences that Hayek drew from his theoretical construction explains why he is so valued in such a context. Such an examination also reveals the way in which the philosophical inadequacies get transmitted and exacerbated and open up fissures of internal contradiction in the pragmatic sphere of political and social activities.

Central to Hayek's consideration of pragmatic social and political matters is his understanding of political states and the market mechanism, and his version of the opposition between them. This doesn't simply derive from the theoretical construction outlined above (though he carefully maintains consistency with that), it is more clearly the result of a *transposition* of an analytical method that pertains to his economic theories. This is therefore more illuminatingly approached in terms of his earlier attempts at reforming monetary theories – a brief outline of the analytical method (rather than the economic formulations and conclusions) of Hayek's *The Pure Theory of Capital* (1941) will serve to make my point. *The Pure Theory of Capital* is laid out in three distinct parts. The first part is a critique of existing theories of capital: it is plausibly argued that existing theories of capital have limited their scope by considering the components and process of capital circulation in too fixedly quantitative a fashion (quantifying too rigidly the monetary form of capital, the fixed and variable capital, the interim transitory forms of capital, the relation of capital to time, the assumption of equilibrium) from a prospective or retrospective perspective (but not from the in-process perspective of the *present* and protean forms of capital). In effect the very idea of capital has assumed the shape of a fixed entity, the transformations of which are prospectively calculable. Hayek contends that this is not the case, that capital is constantly changeable from a quantifiable point of view according, for instance, to the instability of the monetary form itself, the ambiguities of the character of non-permanent resources that are involved, and the effect that attempts at predicting the behaviour of capital has on the process itself with regard to which prediction is attempted. To rectify the shortcomings in existing theories of capital therefore, it is argued, a more complex picture needs to be drawn with a larger number of variables. This is what occupies the second and third parts of the book. Interestingly, however, when Hayek launches on reconstructing a theory of capital, he reverts to methodological positions which are subject to the same objections as those that he had raised in the first part: and they are surprisingly reminiscent of the weaker aspects of Marx's method. He starts by considering a simplified system in which circulation of capital takes place, and by enumerating the variables within that system that need to be accounted, and then moves on to a more complex system, the circulation of capital in which is described by differentiation from the simple system. This is a matter of analytical convenience though, and whatever qualms one may have about its being self-contradictory can be overcome by the clarity and methodological neatness of this analytical process. What is of greater interest from the perspective of this study is that the methodological convenience is given certain real-world-like analogues: the simple system of capital circulation is given as analogous to a strongly centralised state-controlled economy; and the complex system of capital circulation is given as analogous to an uncontrolled free-market economy. *Both are actually methodological idealisations to provide a basis for working out economic formulations at this stage, but the analogues are worth noting because somewhere along the line Hayek forgets that these are simply analogues for methodological convenience, and idealised at that, and begins to believe that they are adequate accounts of the behaviour and tendencies of political states and markets respectively.* That this might occur is evident in *The Pure Theory of Capital* itself, where Hayek rather unnecessarily and tenuously strives to make these idealised analogous models consistent with his first principle of absolute individualism. He makes out that a strongly centralised state is like the domination of the conceptualisation of an *individual* mind, and the free market wherein firms and corporations compete is like the confrontation of different individual conceptual positions. So, in introducing his method for the analysis of the complex (hence

more 'real') circulation of capital, he summarises the two methodological models thus:

> The case of a centrally directed communist society which we have
> been considering has shown us the rôle that is played by the two
> basic factors (*i.e.* the various opportunities to invest and the time
> preferences of the persons concerned) under the (analytically)
> simplest conditions, that is when all resources are under the
> control of a *single mind which uses them in the service of a coherent
> system of ends.* Here we shall move one step nearer to reality by
> considering the case where the command over the existing
> resources is distributed between *a multitude of independent persons,
> each of whom uses his share of them in the service of his individual
> system of ends* and all of whom are in a position to exchange on a
> market.[12] (my emphases)

In this, the *transpositional* tendency of the economic analytical
models (as analogues) to become equated with real world political
formations is all too clearly revealed, though there is still a sufficient
apprehension of the analytical idealisations (removals from 'reality')
involved. This also reveals the dangers of the process of *transposition*
from economic to social and political thinking, should it take place
(as indeed it does in Hayek's anti-political philosophical writings).
The economic analytical intentionality (the fact that these models
are intended for economic analysis) here ensures that this is not a
sufficient consideration of either the political state formation or the
politics of free-market formations (where politics has to do with the
consideration of ends and means with regard to a collectivity). The
first principle predisposition to seeing both in terms of *individual*
positions (which is acceptable as forming part of an economic
analytical method, but not from the perspective of political
philosophy) effectively means that this approach would also be
unequal to grasping the nature of either political state (as interpreting and acting agent with regard to the intentional system of
people–land–resources) or the capitalist corporation (which might
in legal and economic models be logically considered a kind of
super-individual, but which exercises conceptions of size and control
which are not encompassable within any political philosophical
concept of individual).

When Hayek performs this *transpositional* step in his anti-political
writings (beginning with *The Road to Serfdom*, most elaborately in

The Constitution of Liberty, and continually thereafter) it is noticeable that he doesn't actually engage with the philosophical or sociological aspects of either the state or the corporation. He takes it for granted that the methodological models for economic analysis will serve political philosophical considerations of real-world formations too. This understandably runs into all kinds of problems. With the *transpositional* perspective Hayek had *constructed* (in accordance with his first principles) the state as that which is most closely associated with planning and coercion and the market as that which is naturally disposed to freedom (the same as absolute individualism here) and adaptive evolutionary processes. By assuming these transpositional constructions Hayek commits himself to minimising the function of the state and maximising the space for free-market operations. But this accommodation of transposition from economic methods within his anti-political philosophical structure (built up from first principles) sits uneasily there. How, after all, is one to demonstrate that institutions and attitudes which are traditionally and conventionally associated with the political state (and Hayek finds his theoretical structure supporting traditions and conventions) are *not* in accordance with an evolutionary process (if that is accepted)? And how, for that matter, is one to demonstrate that free-market formations (which can scarcely be said to exist in any pure sense in the modern world) have risen from such an evolutionary process? Hayek wisely doesn't try to: instead he argues, in keeping with his now fully blossomed anti-political spirit, that if these real-world formations cannot demonstrably be shown to accord with his theoretical constructions, *they should be made to*. He devotes himself less and less to justifying his theoretical assertions and more and more to trying to make plausible pragmatic interventions on their basis with political and social effect.

As regards the state, Hayek tries to demonstrate that *if it is to keep to his notion of freedom and adaptive evolution it must oversee its own gradual dissolution* (an obviously tautological statement, for if the process of adaptive evolution really exists then the state doesn't have to be and cannot be consciously self-directing in this fashion). In pragmatic terms Hayek sees this process of gradual dissolution, ironically reminiscent of Engels's withering away of the state, as a studied reduction of all coercive powers in the state – that definitive monopoly of force – except those which are absolutely necessary. That exceptional field of necessary coercion which would still be maintained by the state is encoded, for Hayek, in a judicial system.

Hayek's arguments about jurisprudence are riddled with holes. The idea that there has to be necessary coercion is itself so problematic, given Hayek's first principles and theoretical construction, that he feels the need to focus on this especially.[13] Here he goes around in circles: to make sure that the realm of necessary coercion is maintained in a judicial system, without however thereby giving the state extraordinary powers to intervene in the workings of absolute individualism and adaptive evolution, he argues that the judicial system itself has to evolve adaptively and that the state should have no effective role in its determination apart from policing (as one who maintains it without impinging upon it). This is a difficult position to maintain on various grounds. Judicial systems *have been* and *are* generally (even in liberal democracies) such as do not simply *adapt* themselves to social and economic processes, but actively *respond* to such processes. Responding is quite different from adapting. A response implies the possibility of the exercise of a political will (which usually the state puts forward and implements as interpreting and predicting agency). The law is far more consistent with the dynamics of the political state's role as interpreting and acting agency with regard to the intentional system of people–land–resources – typically laws are constitutionally enjoined, open to emendation through state-governed processes and sanctions, and the result of fairly comprehensive planning. Laws are generally subject to application according to context and open to reinterpretation based on precedent. There is little that is a priori about judicial systems qua systems, and it is impossible to see such systems as indifferent to the dynamics of statecraft. From a liberal democratic point of view the best one can hope for is that the judicial system will reflect democratic interests which the state represents, but obviously the state may not represent these adequately at all times, and the state can use the law repressively if it doesn't. There is no effective way of controlling this apart from the retention of democratic processes on which the appointment or establishment of the state depends. Judicial systems and political state processes are inextricably entwined.

It is tempting to go into some of the absurdities of detail that Hayek comes up with here, but that would require as voluminous a space as Hayek's writings occupy. At any rate, what Hayek comes up with after these fumblings is that the state should confine itself in a minimalistic fashion to the policing of such adaptively evolved judicial systems, and should otherwise determinedly restrain itself from intervening in market processes – should indeed relegate every other sphere which has traditionally come under the precincts of state control to the spontaneous regulation of the market mechanism.[14] The lack of understanding of what a political state *is* and a lack of clarity regarding what the role of capitalist corporations in a free market might be (a direct result of the *transposition* discussed above) is reflected in the ad hoc notion that state processes and market processes are somehow coincidental and can be interchanged. This is a confusion, as I have maintained in the previous parts, that has dogged sociology and been embraced all too cheerfully in contemporary corporate capitalism. It is the conflation that allows managerial discourses and speculative interests free play, places the contemporary capitalist political state in its supplicant's emulating and mirroring place, and puts the seal on the prevailing disablement of political will in corporate capitalist contexts.

There is another caveat that Hayek makes regarding the political state that is worth mentioning here: he suggests that the democratic state is not democratic so much by dint of the manner in which it is appointed or established, as by its ability to fit into the role of policing and enabling adaptive evolutionary processes and institutions to flourish and absolute individualism (freedom) to prevail. Thus in *The Constitution of Liberty* Hayek points out that what is understood as liberal democracy – i.e. majority rule (whether through clear majorities or proportional representation) – is in fact against the grain of freedom, since inevitably in such government certain collective interests are likely to dominate.[15] In his later writings, as the vaunted socialist threat seems to recede, Hayek increasingly warns that it is the practice of liberal democracies wherein corporate capitalism is sustained which would ultimately compromise what he considers to be individual freedom.[16] At the same time, apart from enumerating what the minimal state should do, he does little to clarify what alternative modes of democratic process could be instituted to ensure the appointment or establishment of a suitable political state. A little reflection shows that this is not at all surprising given the Hayekian perspective: it merely confirms the paucity of Hayek's understanding of the state by underlining his sense of the *unimportance* of the state. If the state is merely going to be a functionary of a preordained (in some evolutionary way) judicial system and little more, and if everything else is left to absolute individualism and the market mechanism, it doesn't quite matter how the state is established or appointed so long as it fulfils its function without being impeded by any antithetical political will. And a little further reflection reveals that Hayek uses *democracy*, as he had *freedom*, in a purely rhetorical fashion, which is unconnected to any understandable or accepted *political* view of democracy – Hayek's democracy is another way of affirming nothing more than atomised absolute individualism and the automatism of adaptive evolutionary processes. This is, in other words, a misappropriation of the term: 'democracy' can have little politically apprehensible meaning if the notion of the political will – a people's political will – is removed from it. The disabling of the political will that Hayek carries out fits in neatly with his sense of the unimportance of the state, the unimportance of the main organon for the exercise of political will. This coheres too with the sense of unimportance that the contemporary corporate capitalist state with the prevailing disablement of political will increasingly suffers from, so that it surrenders its state-identity and assumes a superficial corporate character (a mirroring and emulating character) while serving capitalist speculative interest in domestic and international spheres.

The various shortcomings and inadequacies of Hayek's social and political thinking percolate down to his other pragmatic recommendations – for example, his anti-egalitarian arguments, his ideas of education, his reservations about various facets of welfare economics – but I do not intend to take these up separately here. The examination of Hayek here was intended: (a) to give an account of the full-scale blossoming of anti-political philosophy in concert with the consolidation of advanced capitalism, and (b) to give a demonstration of the philosophical inadequacies and inconsistencies therein. These, I feel, have been sufficiently achieved in this chapter.

15   Nozick's Anti-Political Philosophy

Anti-political philosophy in the context of contemporary corporate capitalism continues to rest primarily on the theoretical construction offered by Hayek. It would be tedious to chart out the various instances in which the Hayekian position has arguably been reconfirmed and elaborated or modified.[1] A more fruitful path to follow in this study would be to focus on those anti-political philosophers who have either elaborated Hayek's position through arguments which are distinct from those given above, or been able to present an anti-political philosophical position that rests on substantially different arguments. It seems to me that Robert Nozick's work presents an appropriate and familiar example of the former, and Francis Fukuyama's ideas form a suitable and unusual instance of the latter. The rest of this study is devoted to observations on the works of these thinkers.

While Nozick broadly subscribes to Hayek-like first principles and espouses a political agenda which conforms to Hayek's, he is concerned with rendering this with more of a commitment to notions of philosophical rigour and adequacy. This means that Nozick is often careful to sidestep some of the more obvious inadequacies of Hayek's arguments, and makes significant adjustments and changes in these to retain roughly the same position. This does not however mean that Nozick manages to give greater philosophical validity to that anti-political position; Nozick's arguments, while more sound and persuasive than Hayek's in certain ways (from a philosophical perspective Nozick is inevitably sharper than the excessively assertive and rather diffuse polymath Hayek), are also subject to their own peculiar inadequacies. *Anarchy, State, and Utopia* (1974) is Nozick's most sustained exploration of the anti-political philosophical position that he espouses, and it is to this that I mainly address myself, with some necessary allusions to his more substantial later studies in philosophical analysis (which do not always have an explicit political orientation).

In *Anarchy, State, and Utopia* Nozick adheres to two more or less distinct conventions of philosophical reasoning to maintain philosophical rigour. The first (associated with analytical philosophy) has to do with *testing* such formulations as he encounters or comes up with by exposing them to plausible hypothetical situations. The idea is that a philosophical formulation can be accepted as such only if it is of general import (or at least of general import within the constraints it acknowledges), and it would therefore become unacceptable if any plausible situation can be conceived wherein the formulation is untenable. A situation used for testing formulations can be considered to be plausible insofar as no reason can be found that would render the arising of such a situation *impossible*: that such a situation might seem to be most unlikely or improbable or only a very remote possibility doesn't detract from its plausibility, for however unlikely a situation may be it can still come to pass. In analytical philosophy a formulation which can withstand such testing is considered to be acceptable. This is a convention of western philosophical rationality (used continuously from Plato onwards) which is not without its problems. It is, for instance, impossible to determine when any formulation can be considered to be adequately tested through such hypothetical situations since the most ingenious situations (which can be considered to be plausible in the above sense) can be produced almost indefinitely. In Nozick's work this mode of testing usually takes the form of raising specific questions about obvious-sounding or widely accepted philosophical formulations that he disagrees with, such that these questions cannot be answered if the formulation is accepted without qualification or modification.[2] Ironically, it can be demonstrated (and occasionally is below) that Nozick's own formulations can be questioned and treated with scepticism in a similar fashion.

The second convention of philosophical reasoning that Nozick uses has to do with presenting his formulations as being consistent with a logically necessary process that devolves inevitably from an acceptable original or simple condition – let's call this an *original condition onward* argument. This has been the mainstay of modern western political philosophy: so, if one assumes that there existed originally an anarchic state of nature wherein certain natural laws of selection and competition prevailed and certain innate human tendencies were available (as Hobbes or Locke did) then it can be demonstrated that from that condition through certain inevitable processes something like the complex present condition can come to exist, and along with that certain coherent commitments; or if one assumes that there existed an original condition whereby anarchy was overcome by social contract (as Grotius or Rousseau did) that can be used to similar effect; and so can the assumption that in an original condition only indistinguishable use-labour values existed with the possibility of division of labour (as Marx did); and so can the assumption that there originally existed a primitive state of unselfconsciousness with the potential for the rational growth of increasingly complex degrees of self-consciousness and collective consciousness and even transcendental consciousness (roughly the line taken by Kant and Hegel) ... and so on. Nozick depends on this form of argument, inspired mainly by Locke. Traditionally original condition onward arguments had assumed that the description of such processes could be considered historically valid, thus wedding teleology with historical documentation, perhaps most potently in Marxist historiography. Rawls's use of an original condition onward argument from social contract liberates it from the rather unnecessary connection with historical documentation and teleology[3] by suggesting that the conceptual coherence and elucidatory power of such arguments are sufficient to consider them adequate grounds for philosophical formulation and for the determination of commitments. Nozick uses his original condition onward argument from a Locke-inspired state of nature in the spirit of Rawls, that is without making it historically valid. Again, the philosophical convention of the original condition onward argument is not without its weaknesses: quite a large number of original conditions can be considered to be acceptable – all of which could lead to quite different inferences – and there is no conclusive reason why any particular one should be chosen over others. It is also often unclear whether commitments become available and are justified *through* such arguments, or whether the a priori assumption of certain commitments actually *leads* to the construction of such arguments.

It is not my intention to embark on a general examination of the weaknesses and strengths of these philosophical conventions (though that is well worth undertaking). What I do argue below is that Nozick's particular use of these conventions is fraught with peculiar problems. Before that though, some account of Nozick's first principles and consequent theoretical constructions is needed.

The content of Nozick's anti-political philosophy, which is presented in terms of the above philosophical conventions, develops from certain first-principle assertions (as it does for the philosophers examined already), though Nozick takes care not to draw attention to these as such. They are hidden away in the development of the original condition onward argument as incidental and self-evident truths; but they are easily identifiable as being formulations which Nozick doesn't attempt to prove or test, which are simply asserted, and which form the *raison d'être* of the original condition onward argument and consequent commitments. Unsurprisingly Nozick's first principles are very close to Hayek's first principles of absolute individualism and of the limits of conceptualisation combined with adaptive evolution. Parallel to Hayek's absolute individualism, in *Anarchy, State, and Utopia* we find the following pure assertion (and therefore with a first-principle character):

> Individually, we each sometimes choose to undergo some pain or sacrifice for a greater benefit or to avoid a greater harm: we go to the dentists to avoid worse suffering later; we do some unpleasant work for its results; some persons diet to improve their health or looks; some save money to support themselves when they are older. In each case, some cost is borne for the sake of the greater overall good. Why not, *similarly*, hold that some persons have to bear some costs that benefit other persons more, for the sake of the overall social good? But there is no *social entity* with a good that undergoes some sacrifice for its own good. *There are only individual people, different individual people, with their own individual lives* [my emphasis]. Using one of these people for the benefit of others, uses him and benefits the others. Nothing more. Talk of an overall social good covers this up.[4]

The form of a clinching argument that this statement presents – drawing on the comparison between balances of what is desirable and undesirable for individuals and collectives, and producing the idea of the 'entity' with a flourish to show there is no comparison – shouldn't be allowed to mislead. If Nozick hadn't predefined an 'entity' as being only 'individual entity' this argument wouldn't have worked. It is arguable that the concept of an 'entity' can be extended to different collectives too: 'collective entities' bound together by languages, rituals, laws, customs, hierarchies, mutually dependant working practices, are contained in the very core of what it is to be human (indeed 'collective entities' have a biological status which may well extend to human). In fact, clearly this is not an argument, this is simply a first-principle assertion: *there are only individual people*.

As a philosopher Nozick is, of course, aware that the assumption of absolute individualism is not without problems, if not immediately within the sphere of anti-political philosophy (though it seems to me obvious that this is problematic) then certainly in terms of its impact on basic ideas of analytical philosophy itself. This, it seems to me, is the thrust of the extended study *Philosophical Explanations* (1981). In this he carefully gives content to the notion of 'individual entity' by examining what it means to have an identity. Predictably, he predetermines this effort by more or less assuming that identity is a matter of essential self-recognition in the 'individual entity', and formulates his efforts as an answer to the problem of describing such an understanding of identity only under these conditions. It doesn't seem to occur to him that such a question wouldn't be at all problematic if he didn't presume that identity only has to attach to an essential individual self-identity. Perfectly predictably, given the circular logic involved here, both the answers he comes up with are tautological. His first description of an essential individual identity is framed as an answer to a question: roughly 'How do we know that an entity x at time t_1 is the same as what appears as that entity at time t_2?' – to which he answers with what he calls the theory of closest continuer:

> The closest continuer view presents a necessary condition for identity; something at t_2 is not the same entity as x at t_1 if it is not x's closest continuer. And 'closest' means closer than all others; if two things at t_2 tie in closeness to x at t_1, then neither is the same entity as x. However, something may be the closest continuer of x without being close enough to it to be x. How close something must be to x to be x, it appears, depends on the kind of entity x is, as do the dimensions along which closeness is measured.[5]

It seems that under far too many conditions the closest continuer theory may *fail* to establish identity, irrespective of whether identity is claimed by x or recognised in x. If this seems to be a non-answer, that is largely because it is with regard to a non-question. The question has to have already presumed that the identity of x at t_1 and t_2 is coherent to be framed at all. The question can only make sense if the identity of some other (not the self) which is x is at issue – but that is not the question Nozick addresses, because that would require some understanding of who the self is (let's say y) who asks this regarding the other who is x. This mode of describing the essential individual self's sense of identity is clearly a non-starter, though Nozick sticks with it. The second description of essential individual identity is given as 'reflexive self-reference': in brief, the very ability of an individual entity to refer to himself (to designate his self as 'I') and to *know* that this reference is self-reference, amounts to a description of identity.[6] This is straightforwardly tautological: the only reason we can hypothesise a notion of individual identity is because the individual entity refers to itself (says 'I'): to describe why it does so by simply saying *because* the individual entity says 'I' and means self is nonsensical (as nonsensical as my saying 'I am I' if someone asked me 'Who are you?'). But Nozick sticks with this too.

If Nozick fails to give content to his notion of absolute (or inviolable) individualism it is because it has no content beyond its assertion: it is an arbitrary first principle. Nozick probably undertook this doomed and futile effort not because these uninspired answers came to him, but because he had a philosopher's suspicion that it is difficult to sustain this first principle in philosophical analysis. It is difficult to understand what knowledge and scepticism are, what free will means, what ethics are if one consistently limits oneself to an absolute individualism – if one has to see these as *contained* in some sense *within* an essential 'individual entity'. By trying to give content to the essential 'individual entity' in the above fashion he hoped to be able to demonstrate how these concerns of analytical philosophy (knowledge, ethics) could be located within the essential 'individual entity' (to find a *within* there has to be *content*). All the questions he proceeds to ask and resolve after offering the above doubtful notions of identity are questions and answers that are designed to find ways of doing this. The questions and answers are indicative in themselves. Nozick asks himself how we are to answer philosophical sceptical arguments which undermine the possibility of knowledge,[7] and decides that this is best done by an account of knowledge as a *tracking* of beliefs which allows for a lack of closure in knowledge and which is based ultimately in the 'individual entity's' experiences of living:

> According to our account of knowledge as tracking, to know that one knows that *p* is to truly believe that one knows that *p*, and to have this belief track the fact that one knows. Spelling it out further, this belief that one knows tracks the fact of tracking that *p*; that is, the belief that one knows tracks the fact that one's belief

that *p* tracks the fact that *p*. Thus, with knowledge that one knows that *p*, there is tracking embedded in tracking – a particular tracking is tracked.[8]

Though Nozick seems to consider this an adequate accommodation of certain kinds of scepticism and a refutation of scepticism in general, it seems fairly self-evident that this collection of circularities and tautologies sets up a process of endless regression which actually leaves the possibility of a sceptical subversion of knowledge open.[9] In a similar mould Nozick also tries to resolve the problem of free will and values (and especially ethical values) as *problems* that devolve to and can be resolved at the level of the essential individual entity – and ends up with similarly self-defeating and circular formulations. I realise that this is a matter that needs to be fully demonstrated, and I regret that I cannot undertake this here for lack of space; at any rate, the general tenor of Nozick's difficulties with his understanding of absolute individualism are, I feel, sufficiently clear.

Instead of giving a detailed account of the deficiencies of Nozick's attempts at analytical philosophy here, the situation can be summed up from a different direction. If Nozick hadn't so single-mindedly stuck to a narrowly conceived absolute individualism (the idea that everything has to be resolved within the essential 'individual entity') then these theoretical contortions would become unnecessary. If Nozick, for instance, acknowledged that even the identity of the individual self is a matter to some extent of recognition by others (a far from unfamiliar idea in the realm of analytical philosophy),[10] then most of the questions he poses would become less problematic, and most of the theoretical contortions he goes through (usually in vain) would become redundant. When he later addresses himself to the analysis of principles and rationality in *The Nature of Rationality* (1993) he finds that he has to make a half-hearted acknowledgement of self with relation to others[11] – an earlier and firmer acknowledgement of this would have saved a lot of unnecessary agonising. At any rate, the peculiar problems of Nozick's account and fine-tuning of the first principle of absolute individualism (parallel to Hayek's), which plays such a prominent role in his anti-political philosophy (and such philosophy in general), are starkly revealed in his own later analytical philosophical reflections.

In *Anarchy, State, and Utopia* (coming back to this) also appears Nozick's second first principle – again parallel to Hayek, and consistent with Hayekian anti-political philosophy. This too is related to an assertion of the limitations of conceptualisation and the validity of politically disabling spontaneous processes (like adaptive evolution), but Nozick doesn't present this in Hayek's ham-handed fashion. It is more subtly given as an explanative method instead – the so called *invisible-hand explanation*; however, its purely assertive first-principle character (not simply with epistemological but also with empirical effect) is easily discerned:

> [Invisible-hand explanations] show some overall pattern or design, which one would have thought had to be produced by an individual's or group's successful attempt to realize a pattern, but which instead was produced and maintained by a process that in no way had the overall pattern or design 'in mind'. [...] Invisible-hand explanations minimize the use of notions constituting the phenomena to be explained; in contrast to the straightforward explanations, they don't explain complicated patterns by including the full-blown pattern-notions as objects of people's desires or beliefs. Invisible-hand explanations of phenomena thus yield greater understanding than do explanations of them as brought about by design as the object of people's intentions. It therefore is no surprise that they are more satisfying.[12]

The attempt here to prove that what Nozick calls 'invisible-hand explanations' are more privileged than 'straightforward explanations' is confusing at several levels. One way in which that argument could be read is as follows: all explanations of perceived designs and patterns are retrospective (that is, after the design or pattern has manifested itself); seen in retrospect, it is often the case that conceptualisations which could be thought of as being realised in the design or pattern in question were not available before that design or pattern is manifest, and conceptualisations which were available are often not seen to be realised as such in retrospect or are seen to be realised in ways which were in fact not conceptualised; consequently it is best not to try to explain retrospectively discerned designs and patterns as conceptualised in advance, but to see them as developing through processes which are indifferent to such conceptualisation (i.e., an invisible-hand explanation). In brief, there is a slippage between the designs and patterns that people may conceive and the designs and patterns that are manifest in retrospect. But, the fact that what people conceive may not be what is realised is no reason to assume that what is realised is *indifferent* to what is conceived. It is quite as possible that irrespective of the slippages between what is conceived and what is realised, there is a complex relation between them that needs to be worked out case by case (and this would still be other than an invisible-hand explanation, and closer to a straightforward explanation). Further, even if it is true that in some or even most instances a pattern or design that may be conceived is not the pattern or design that becomes manifest in retrospect, it is possible that in some – perhaps a few cases – it does. In such cases straightforward explanations have to be retained (at the very least, it must be acknowledged that invisible-hand explanations are not the only sort that should be presumed). Another argument in favour of invisible-hand explanations is: when the design or pattern manifest in a given field is examined with a view to explaining why it has come about it is better to have an extrinsic and therefore complete view of the field, rather than an intrinsic and therefore necessarily limited view of the field (if one stands inside a field one cannot see it as a whole, it is better if one tries to see that field from a distance to do this – from an aeroplane perhaps); straightforward explanations are attempts to explain the field from the inside and are less likely to discern the complete pattern or design manifest in it, while invisible-hand explanations are attempts to explain the field from outside with a full view of the manifest designs and patterns – consequently the latter are stronger. This too is not quite right: can one dispense with the inside view if one has an outside view of the field? why should one view be considered more complete than the other, rather than simply different? Further, the outside vantage point is not necessarily the best from which to explain how it came to be so (all its explanative offerings would be no more than after-the-fact and distant suppositions). Who is to say which explanation is better: those within or those outside the field? There seems to be no unambiguous answer to this. (This might be tantamount to asking with regard to a long straight line of people, whether the straightness of the line is because the people in it have chosen to make it straight, or because by a set of circumstances that none of them could fully control they have somehow come to stand unwittingly in a straight line? There is clearly no way of predetermining the mode of explaining this; closer investigation was first to be carried out of the circumstances under which and the reasons for which the straight line of people appears.) There seems to be no *reason* why invisible-hand explanations should be considered more privileged or more satisfying; Nozick simply decides that invisible-hand explanations are preferable as a matter of first principle.

There are further confusions attached to this. It is not quite clear whether Nozick considers a mode of *explaining* a perceived design or pattern as being the same as actually *apprehending* how that process or design came about. In the convention of unravelling an original condition onward argument that Nozick undertakes in *Anarchy, State, and Utopia*, he does seem to assume somewhere along the line (it is not quite clear precisely where) that being able to offer an invisible-hand explanation of how the state appears is in itself the same as having apprehended how the state must have appeared, and provides sufficient grounds for deriving commitments regarding how the state should continue to be acted on and towards. But what justifies the transition from a possible explanation to a certainty that that must have been the case and should be considered so? Scientists generally make a rigorous distinction between possible explanations and confirmed explanations (Popper understands this only too well); some understanding of this distinction should exercise the philosopher too, even if the methods of scientific confirmation cannot directly apply to philosophical concerns.

At any rate, the parallels between Nozick's second first principle of invisible-hand explanations and Hayek's second first principle of the limitations of conceptualisation combined with adaptive evolutionary mechanisms are, I feel, apparent. Nozick's principle has implicit in it the familiarly Hayekian certainty about the limitations of human conceptualisation in any holistic sense (here expressed as the inadequacy of straightforward explanations); the *modus operandi* of invisible-hand explanations (particularly since these are assumed to be the *only* way patterns and designs should be thought of as coming to be realised) with its indifference to conceptual efforts is very close indeed to Hayekian adaptive evolution; and the second first principles of both Hayek and Nozick are equally politically disabling. However, with the typical foreboding of a rigorous philosopher, Nozick in his later analytical philosophy makes some qualifications about invisible-hand explanation which sets it apart from Hayek's first principle – though without much changing its politically disabling effect. Unlike Hayek's conviction that adaptive evolution not only has been but must continue to be, one finds in Nozick's analytical philosophy some uncertainty as to whether invisible-hand explanations which apply in retrospect should continue to apply or must necessarily apply in prospect. Thus, in

Philosophical Explanations one finds Nozick wondering whether it isn't possible for invisible-hand processes themselves to be controlled (is it possible that someone may initiate an act whereby a predictable invisible-hand-like chain of events would follow?).[13] Nozick also asks straightforwardly and inconclusively whether the perception that invisible-hand processes have existed (such explanations are made) commits us to expecting that they should continue – and on the whole he seems inclined not to believe that to be the case:

> Mention of reflective thinking about ethics indicates a substantial stumbling block to carrying through an explanation of ethics in a thoroughgoing invisible hand fashion: consciousness, language, and self-consciousness. The question is not whether there will be evolutionary explanations of how consciousness, language, and self-consciousness arise and are selected for. The question is whether once these do arise by a blind process, they then operate and lead to some things unblindly. (Do precepts with concepts *stay* blind?) That there is an invisible hand explanation of our having our cognitive capacities does not mean that there is an invisible hand explanation of my writing the contents of this book.[14]

The questioning of adaptive evolution through a questioning of invisible hand processes (though Nozick doesn't consider these to be *necessarily* the same, he does understand evolutionary thinking as being the primary invisible hand explanation) continues in *The Nature of Rationality*. In an extended account of the relationship between evolutionary processes and rationality he presents two notions: one, that rationality itself 'may have the evolutionary function of enabling organisms to better cope with new and changing current situations or future ones that are presaged in some possibly complex, current indications'[15] (and that this is evidenced by the difficulty we have in rationally justifying some of the assumptions which underlie rationality); and two, 'to whatever extent some rational processes *are* a product of innately controlled developmental patterns, these processes are shaped and overlain by socially instilled processes, norms and procedures'.[16] These considerations move promisingly against the spirit of Hayek's *contained overdeterminism* – and give some evidence of Nozick's comparatively greater philosophical rigour – but they have no apparent impact on Nozick's anti-political philosophy, which more or less stays at the level of

Anarchy, State, and Utopia. Nozick's anti-political philosophy presents exactly the same kind of *contained overdeterminism* as Hayek's.

With this account of Nozick's use of philosophical conventions and understanding of first principles it becomes possible to run through the main contentions of the anti-political philosophy which is laid out in *Anarchy, State, and Utopia*. This develops in the following manner: Nozick believes that if he is able to chart out an original condition onwards argument, starting from a state of nature and ending with a conceptualisation of the minimal state, which is fully consistent with his first principles (that is, that maintains the inviolability of the individual and coheres with invisible-hand explanations), and if at the same time he can show that any other conceptualisation of the state and any other original condition onwards argument is unsustainable through the conventional method of testing by plausible hypothetical situations, then a sufficient case would be made for accepting the minimal state and the commitments which arise out of that. Nozick's understanding of the minimal state is basically the same as Hayek's – it consists in allocating to the political state no more than a policing and protective function, and disallows all other means of collective action and planning and redistribution to the state on the grounds that this would encourage violation of the position of absolute individualism – and in asserting this, like Hayek, Nozick strips the main organon of a political will and of any effective ability to exercise a political will. The first principle of privileging invisible-hand explanations doesn't leave any space for other agencies to exercise a political will either. Nozick, in short, joins Hayek in becoming one of the foremost anti-political philosophers of our time, who provide validation for the disabling of political will involved in contemporary corporate capitalism.

Nozick's charting of an original condition onwards argument proceeds along the following steps. I emphasise some of the ideas in the following summary because I return to these to show how inadequate Nozick's account of these is. For Nozick a plausible original condition is one such as Locke speculates on, one in which there is an anarchic collection of atomic individuals looking after their own interests and developing *original property claims*. A desirable understanding of the state, such that it coheres with the basic idea of ensuring the inviolability of individuals, is that it is an organisation which (following Weber with some irrelevant reservations) has a monopoly on force, and moreover a monopoly on force that can be used for no other purpose than to protect the inviolability of each and every individual under its jurisdiction (that is, it is a minimal state). If a series of invisible-hand-like steps can be shown to exist such that the proposed original condition moves naturally and inevitably towards the desirable conceptualisation of the minimal state without at any point violating the first principles, then *the desirable conceptualisation of the state should be considered acceptable and necessary*. The first step that Nozick sees as rising with invisible-hand naturalness from the original state of nature is the growth of protection associations in the wake of the formation of property claims, since individuals would pay such associations to protect their acquired properties and themselves. Such protective associations would only protect those whom they are contracted and paid to protect. What distinguishes such protective associations from the desirable political state is that the former only protects its clients, while the latter protects everyone under its jurisdiction (at least in principle). It seems difficult in the first instance, Nozick observes, to make a suitably invisible-hand step from the protective association to the desirable state because the latter's too-democratic dispensation of protection appears to be redistributive in character (protecting everyone though some pay more for such protection and some don't pay at all), which both flouts the first principle of absolute individualism and smells of planning and social contract. But Nozick overcomes this apparent difficulty by showing that, in fact, what is involved in the shift from protective association to desirable state is not redistributive justice, but a *principle of compensation* – which gets formalised in an invisible-hand fashion. With this principle of compensation in hand, and the natural and unplanned possibility that certain protective associations would gradually grow dominant and establish territorial agreements and privileges, the invisible-hand explanation of the emergence of the desirable political state is easily completed. Showing this makes Nozick's case, as far as he is concerned.

   The argument is weak in itself even if the shaky foundation of questionable philosophical conventions and tenuous first principles on which it rests is momentarily overlooked. Again, a detailed exposition of this would occupy more space than is feasible here, but a few observations about some of the points that I have emphasised in the above summary will serve to indicate the kind of weaknesses that are discernible. One of these points is Nozick's assumption that if a suitable invisible-hand process can be shown in the original condition onwards argument leading to the desirable minimal state, *the desirable state should be considered acceptable and necessary.* This is a curiously circular argument: nothing much is demonstrated in this other than the idea that if one assumes what a desirable state is it can be shown to emerge by invisible-hand processes from the given original condition. But does that mean that other conceptions of a desirable state can't appear with similar modes of explanation from similar beginning points? Does it mean that undesirable states can't be shown to appear by invisible-hand processes from a state of nature? If it is predecided that a minimal state is desirable why is it necessary to show that it arises from invisible-hand processes – isn't its desirability enough for it to be considered acceptable? What is there to show that a conjunction of the two first principles is necessary, if it can be demonstrated that they can also contradict each other? Why should such a conjunction be contemplated if it is considered that the two first principles are not first principles in the same way – absolute individualism is clearly for Nozick a value-determining principle, while an invisible-hand explanation is value-indifferent or value-blind? Unless such questions are resolved it is very doubtful whether Nozick's construction could be said to demonstrate anything of political (or anti-political) import.

Another of Nozick's principles that I have emphasised above is the *principle of compensation.* This is central, as is evident in the above summary, in that it averts the necessity for falling back on redistributive justice, and is used to show how a natural invisible-hand process of justice in compensatory terms can lead to regularised and acceptable property holdings and exchanges. In the original condition onwards argument this takes some such form: at some point all individuals could be thought of as holding legitimately acquired property, and from that point all future developments through the phase of protective associations to the minimal state could be seen to be coincidental with balanced (and therefore fair) transfers and exchanges of such legitimately held property. Imbalances that occur can be corrected by redressing them, not by attempting any wholesale redistribution. The idea of compensation can, of course, be extended to spheres of state activity other than the protection of property rights – say, the operation of criminal laws and punishments. However, Nozick's assertion that redistribution and compensation are radically different can be questioned: it can be argued that every redistributive theory (even those that Nozick singles out, Marx's and Rawls's) have clear-cut compensatory principles worked into them, and political (as opposed to anti-political) philosophers have always depended on these.[17] Besides, Nozick's basic statement of the principle of compensation is ill-formulated:

> Something fully compensates a person for a loss if and only if it makes him no worse off than he otherwise would have been; it compensates person X for person Y's action A if X is no worse off receiving it, Y having done A, than X would have been without receiving it if Y had not done A.[18]

This is meaningful only if suitable scales of loss and compensation are set out (say, the measure is in financial terms as loss of earnings perhaps), and it is meaningless in any general sense (if for example every *effect* of the action A on X has to be erased). Nozick does seem to imply that the principle of compensation can be applied in a general sense, especially when he goes on to consider compensation of psychological effects (causing fear).[19] In that sense compensation cannot really occur, for arguably the effects of an action A on X cannot really be erased entirely if A has taken place – at the least A can always be remembered as having taken place. In other words, the principle of compensation can only be thought of as a case-specific or context-specific matter, limited in application, arbitrary in its choice of measures, and no more (perhaps less) perfect than a rational idea of redistribution.

Finally, I have also emphasised in the above summary Nozick's dependence on some notion of *original property claim* or original acquisition as giving the benchmark for the operation of fair transfers and acquisitions following a principle of compensation thereafter. This involves some notion of an original claim of property that was previously unowned. Effectively, for fairness to prevail through the invisible-hand process that Nozick lays out it must be assumed that the original claim itself was fair – that somehow, spontaneously, the manner in which unowned property was declared owned was fair. Nozick discusses one of the serious problems that comes with this assumption in the form of a discussion of Locke's proviso: 'A process normally giving rise to a permanent bequeathable property right in a previously unowned thing will not do so if the position of others no longer at liberty to use the thing is thereby worsened.'[20] The self-evident problems that Locke's proviso calls attention to are *not* resolved by Nozick – simply because they cannot be – and he merely ends this discussion by asserting : 'I believe that the free operation of a market system will not actually run afoul of the Lockean proviso.'[21] That any original claim to unowned property must have been fair is so obviously untenable that the best Nozick can do with this idea is evade a discussion of it:

> [The topic of *original acquisition of holdings*] includes the issues of how unheld things may come to be held, the process, or processes, by which unheld things may come to be held, the things that may come to be held by these processes, the extent of what comes to be held by a particular process, and so on. We shall refer to the complicated truth about this topic, which we shall not formulate here, as the principle of justice in acquisition.[22]

What does justice mean here? What is the complicated truth? Whose notion of property is just? Is ownership of property a universal concept, and if it is thought so is it universal in the same way? What is the status of common property? Is common property property at all in Nozick's terms? The problems are so numerous that they are hardly worth enumerating here.

It seems to me that the above presents both a sufficient account of Nozick's particular take on a Hayekian anti-political philosophy, and gives a sense of the many weaknesses and inadequacies in this. Before concluding these reflections on Nozick's anti-political philosophy it might be useful to consider the ways in which it particularly supports contemporary corporate capitalist organisation. This obviously occurs both in the explicit disabling of political will that is contained in the idea of the minimal state, and in the implicit recommendation that free-market situations be nurtured and left to their own devices that an equation with spontaneous or 'natural' invisible-hand explanation provides. Though it doesn't ostensibly give way to the superficial rhetorical subterfuges found in Hayek's understanding of freedom, and it is also careful to avoid the transposition from economic methodology that Hayek performs (it does have the appearance of being more philosophically rigorous, and more rigorously grounded in political philosophical convention), essentially Nozick's thinking is devoted to doing little more than elaborating anti-political positions which Hayek had already enunciated. Nozick too is anxious to maintain the atomisation of individuals, to discourage holistic or comprehensive conceptualisations, to ensure that thinking of political or social matters doesn't centre on notions of collectivity (thus undercutting those terms themselves), to leave no space for the exercise of a political will. In fact, there is one respect in which Nozick goes even further than Hayek in being congenial to contemporary corporate capitalism: unlike Popper or Hayek, he doesn't condemn utopian thinking to oblivion altogether – his discussion of utopian thinking and his presentation of a 'framework for utopia' cleverly appropriates utopianism into the service of corporate capitalism.

Actually Nozick is fully in sympathy with Popper's and Hayek's rejections of utopian thinking insofar as that is associated with comprehensive conceptualisation and concordant social and political planning. Having rather arbitrarily decided that a utopia is best defined as the place where everyone would most want to live, he goes on to argue that since everyone is different from everyone else it is impossible that there can be any one place where everyone would most want to live:

> The idea that there is one best composite answer to all of these questions, one best society for *everyone* to live in, seems to me to be an incredible one. (And the idea that, if there is one, we now know enough to describe it is even more incredible.)[23]

That familiarly Hayekian sentiment sounds persuasive here only because there is a clever play on singulars and plurals. What does 'one best society' mean? Why must it be assumed that a utopian idea is restrictive to the extent of making a naturally heterogeneous humanity conform to an artificially homogeneous environment? If utopian ideas have tended to do so in the past that is a sufficient case for saying that utopian ideas need to be reconsidered, but not for saying that utopian ideas (as thinking of an ideal social and political condition which can accommodate a heterogeneous humanity) have to be disregarded. Does the fact that everyone is different from everyone else mean that there is no common ground to be found amongst them? What would humanity or society mean if such common ground cannot be conceived? The full absurdity of the statement quoted above is revealed if we considered its opposite (if that statement is incredible then its opposite might well be considered credible): that since everyone is different from everyone else the most satisfactory condition would be for everyone to have their own completely independent and self-sufficient and self-governing environments (their own oxymoronic societies of one) – perhaps the state of nature that Nozick started with was a utopia of sorts from his perspective. This does seem to me to be entirely incredible.

Nozick, despite that, doesn't fall into the trap of expressing conclusive sentiments; he leaves a hypothetical space for the possibility of utopia, he even provides a 'framework' through which utopia may arise. This is a matter of particular interest here. The argument goes that since singular conceptualisations of utopia are impossible, or at any rate impossible given the current state of knowledge, if a utopia is at all possible it is most likely to emerge by an invisible-hand process too – or what Nozick calls a 'design process' in this context. If all sorts of different utopian concepts are allowed some realisation in small communities which coexist, Nozick suggests, then through a process of *filtering*, through a process of interaction and modification and trying new ideas and giving up unsuccessful ones, something like a utopia might eventually emerge. Different small communities can try out their different utopian concepts in a more or less experimental fashion and the rest can be left to posterity and invisible hands – this, in brief, constitutes Nozick's framework for a utopia:

> The filtering process, the process of eliminating communities, that our framework involves is very simple: people try out living in various communities, and they leave or slightly modify the ones they don't like (find defective). Some communities will be abandoned, others will struggle along, others will split, others will flourish, gain members, and be duplicated elsewhere. Each community must win and hold the voluntary adherence of its members. No pattern is *imposed* on everyone, and the result will be one pattern if and only if everyone voluntarily chooses to live in accordance with that pattern of community.[24]

Nozick doesn't flesh out the mode of coexistence of these communities. Perhaps, one presumes, they would be independent units that would be autonomous while broadly under one or some minimal state. Perhaps this is a vision of a decentred world in which states are replaced by small communities. Most significantly, Nozick doesn't try to flesh out the economics of such an order of experimental communities. Are all of them going to attempt to be independent productive communities? Are they going to be necessarily interdependent and competitive productive communities? In trying to answer these questions one is inevitably struck by the thought that this description of would-be utopian communities is actually very close to the manner in which capitalist corporations now wishfully conceive of and present themselves under current corporate capitalist organisation. The contemporary capitalist corporation, we have seen, obscures the speculative interests which govern it and its disabling of the political will (its continuous attempt to evade state control) by presenting itself as a complete community, the product of utopian managerial visions – with its own hierarchy, its own state-like apparatus, its own intentional system, sometimes its own culture, its own way of life, its self-containedness, etc. – and ultimately with its expansive, space-occupying (in various senses) zeal, or its determination to win out in some sort of filtering process against other such communities. The step from Nozick's reflections on a framework for utopia to the ostensible self-image that capitalist corporations in contemporary corporate capitalism ceaselessly promote is very small indeed; small enough for us to think of Nozick as an up-to-date anti-political philosopher of contemporary corporate capitalism.

The *identification* of corporate capitalist formations with a framework for utopia is an interesting *volte-face* in the anti-political philosophical process from Popper to Hayek to Nozick, and finds much firmer expression from a rather different direction in the work of Fukuyama – to whom I now turn.

16 Fukuyama's Anti-Political Philosophy

Francis Fukuyama's two major works, *The End of History and the Last Man* (1992) and *Trust: The Social Virtues and the Creation of Prosperity* (1995), present an anti-political philosophy which validates the disabling of political will in the context of contemporary corporate capitalism from a perspective that seems to be almost diametrically opposed to the ones developed by Popper, Hayek and Nozick. Where the latter dwell on the connotations and implications of individualism – preferably absolute individualism – Fukuyama is concerned with the necessary role of collectivities (or the culture thereof) in the development of corporate capitalism. Where the Popper–Hayek–Nozick line of thinking is assertively anti-historicist in character, Fukuyama is assertively historicist. Where Popper–Hayek–Nozick are dismissive of any motivation which doesn't cohere with individual self-interest, Fukuyama feels that a drive for recognition and a culturally installed capacity for trust do often and unavoidably supersede individual self-interest. Where Popper–Hayek–Nozick discount the possibility of comprehensive utopian conceptualisations, Fukuyama believes that a comprehensive utopian conceptualisation has emerged already and its universal realisation is possible, and that this is that of corporate capitalist liberal democracy.

Interestingly, Fukuyama doesn't try to validate his theses by resorting to the analytical processes which the philosophers discussed above rely on. By and large he presents his hypotheses as ready-made theses which don't need analytical philosophical backing, don't depend on an apparatus of first principles and rigorously employed analytical rationalisations. Fukuyama's theses are simply presented as such: he devotes space to working out their connotations fully once they are assumed, he draws on authoritative philosophical arguments (usually within the domain of political philosophy) which seem to endorse these theses, he draws links between these theses and other existing political philosophical positions. He doesn't try to work out a conceptual process by which such theses are arrived at; at best he refers to those who have arrived at similar theses through their own conceptual processes, and leaves it at that. Instead, he then proceeds to demonstrate the validity of the pronounced theses by showing that they apply to the *real* world, by fitting them to a wide range of empirical and well-documented data. There is an interesting double validation involved in this argumentative process: one, the theses seem to be prevalidated by fitting in with existing ranges of data (as philosopher Fukuyama assumes the persona of the scientific observer who carefully notes and categorises existing data to verify his suspicions); and two, theses which seem to fit a field of real-world applications so neatly could be thought of as purposively oriented towards valid application in the future. This is a methodology that deserves further attention, and indeed most of the following observations revolve around this.

The comparative lack of an analytical philosophical apparatus in the enunciation of his philosophical position means that Fukuyama's basic arguments are easily summarised. In *The End of History* Fukuyama decides that the teleological conceptualisation of universal history which is associated with both the German idealist and the Marxist philosophies of history – but which has increasingly come to be seen as irrelevant and indeed untenable in the practice of history – should not be discounted, because there are in fact certain mechanisms which are universally valid and which give world history a more or less progressive direction. There are two such mechanisms which Fukuyama discerns: one, the development of natural science and technological ability, which may have appeared in different contexts at differing levels and paces, but which have gradually spread and been transmitted, with the effect of directing quite different social formations in a similar direction and towards a more homogeneous world order; two, the human need for recognition which has been and continues to be evidenced in all the different social and political conflicts that mark different contextual histories of different periods. The idea of recognition is one that Fukuyama picks up primarily from Plato's concept of *thymos*, Kojève's interpretation of Hegel, and Locke's understanding of the paucity of master–slave relations. Some idea of this is best conveyed in Fukuyama's own words:

> The desire for recognition arising out of *thymos* is a deeply paradoxical phenomenon because the latter is the psychological seat of justice and selflessness while at the same time being closely

related to selfishness. The thymotic self demands recognition for its *own* sense of the worthiness of things, both itself and of other people. The desire for recognition remains a form of self-assertion, a projection of one's own values on the outside world, and gives rise to feelings of anger when those values are not recognized by other people.[1]

Clearly, what Fukuyama's understanding of recognition as a universal motive force does achieve is a synthesis of individual aspiration (which wishes to be recognised) and collective placement (which recognises). The argument continues that these two universal mechanisms lead naturally toward capitalist liberal democracies. Capitalism provides the ideal environment for the maximisation of developments in natural science and technological innovations. A liberal democracy ensures that universal recognition (in the form of citizen's rights) is given to all individuals who claim collective allegiance to it. Consequently the direction that is given to world history by these two mechanisms ensures a gradual convergence from different points towards capitalist liberal democracy, which could be considered the end of history – a utopia if it should become universally realised. The main problem that Fukuyama envisages in this convergence is that the universal recognition that liberal democracies give would not be sufficient, that space would always have to be left for greater individual bids for recognition (*megalothymia*) which is also a natural aspect of the desire for recognition, and that this itself could subvert the liberal democratic universalisation of recognition:

> Liberal democracy could, in the long run, be subverted internally either by an excess of *megalothymia*, or by an excess of *isothymia* – that is, the fanatical desire for equal recognition. It is my intuition that it is the former that will constitute the greater threat to democracy in the end. A civilization that indulges in unbridled *isothymia*, that fanatically seeks to eliminate every manifestation of unequal recognition, will quickly run into limits imposed by nature itself. [...] If liberal democracy is ever subverted by *megalothymia*, it will be because liberal democracy needs *megalothymia* and will never survive on the basis of universal and equal recognition alone.[2]

This problem is also solved, as Fukuyama understands it, by the wedding of corporate capitalism with liberal democracy, because capitalist processes can allow for an adequate flowering of *mega-lothymia* while coexisting with liberal democracy.

The basic argument of *Trust*, which is coextensive with that of *The End of History* as Fukuyama is at pains to show in the last chapter,[3] is summarised with equal ease. Here Fukuyama asserts that what economic theorists and others who have tried to understand corporate capitalist processes have consistently overlooked, and have even diverted attention away from by an overdetermination of the role of individual self-interest and rationalism, is the determinative influence of culture. The success of corporate capitalism in specific contexts – or the smooth and profitable functioning and coexistence of capitalist corporations with political states and other social formations – depends on the extent to which certain collective ethical norms, particularly trust, prevail within those contexts. The prevalence of such ethical norms in turn derives from the manner in which social organisation has developed historically (what Fukuyama loosely thinks of as culture), that is, from the manner in which familial or communal or statist affiliations and associations have operated and been formalised over the course of time. Fukuyama calls this 'social capital':

> Social capital is a capability that arises from the prevalence of trust in a society or in certain parts of it. It can be embodied in the smallest and most basic social group, the family, as well as the largest of all groups, the nation, and in all the other groups in between. Social capital differs from other forms of human capital insofar as it is usually created and transmitted through cultural mechanisms like religion, tradition or historical habit.[4]

Thus the cultural history of each context more or less determines the kind of ethical principles which prevail therein, the conditions of trust which pertain therein, and these determine the character of corporate capitalist development, and also the degree of facility with which such development occurs. So, depending on whether in a particular context there is a prevailing culture of trust primarily with regard to kinship associations, or with regard to religious or other communities, or with regard to strong state-like organisations, corporate capitalism will develop accordingly by exploiting these pre-existing networks of trust and will assume a distinctive character; and depending on the degree of trust that exists in each context (in some cases high, in others low) the development of corporate capitalism will be facilitated. Apropos the latter, Fukuyama is convinced that high-trust conditions are optimal for the success of corporate capitalism, and that the future success of corporate capitalism will depend to some measure on the ability to nurture congenial cultural conditions and on not being misled by any notion of absolute individual self-interest. Despite the prescriptive appearance of that, however, Fukuyama sees the determinative influence of culture as largely an uncontrollable and inevitable matter which could be seen to work in a corporate capitalist context through *spontaneous sociability*, 'the capacity to form new associations and to cooperate within the terms of reference they establish', which are distinct from such given formations as the family or those under the aegis of government.[5] Since these cultural determinations (often from non-liberal origins) have such a significant and increasingly self-aware role to play in that great universal convergence towards corporate capitalist liberal democracy, it is the case, according to Fukuyama, that the most successful modern societies (the sort that may prevail at the end of history) are not really modern in the rationalistic and individualistic manner in which we are accustomed to think of modernism:

> If democracy and capitalism work best when they are leavened with cultural traditions that arise from nonliberal sources, then it should be clear that modernity and tradition can coexist in a stable equilibrium for extended periods of time. The process of economic rationalization and development is an extremely powerful social force that compels societies to modernize along certain uniform lines. [...] But since there are limits to the effectiveness of contract and economic rationality, the character of modernity will never be completely uniform. [...] The most successful forms of modernity, in other words, are not completely modern; that is, they are not based on the universal proliferation of liberal economic principles throughout the society.[6]

These arguments undoubtedly possess the allure of neatness: insofar as they are stated and elaborated by Fukuyama, familiar but not directly or necessarily related ideas seem to slot together and settle into a coherent and comprehensive picture, much like small pieces of a jigsaw puzzle coming together to form a whole. It seems to be pointless to try to examine *each* of these ideas separately with the techniques of analytical philosophy because this has been done all too often, and the possible pro and contra arguments are all well known. What gives these separate ideas (the mechanism of scientific and technological development, the drive for recognition, the direction of history, the characteristics of liberal democracy, the concept of trust, the idea of spontaneous sociability, the determinacy of culture, etc.) a particular efficacy in Fukuyama's work is the manner in which they are drawn together, the manner in which they fit together to give the larger picture. For Fukuyama these ideas don't fit together for any necessary reason; ultimately what holds these ideas together persuasively is the fact that the picture that emerges is shown to be true to life, as it were, after the fact; Fukuyama evokes a range of empirical information and observations to demonstrate that the picture that has emerged is consistent with these. However, if we do make (against the grain of his reasoning) a cursory examination from an analytical philosophical perspective of the ideas Fukuyama draws on and the interrelations between them that he establishes, at least a few points can be pertinently made.

The looseness with which Fukuyama uses his terms allows him to give them a range of connotations and applications which appear to be superficially plausible; naturally from an analytical philosophical perspective one may wonder whether this superficial plausibility can be sustained in a more rigorous examination of these terms. Consider the key terms of Fukuyama's two arguments – *recognition* and *trust*. Fukuyama uses recognition in at least the following senses: as an acknowledgement of the humanness of individuals (to recognise a person A as being human), as the identification of specific individuals as individuals (to recognise that A is A), in the desire for individuals to be part of some collective (to recognise that A is, for instance, the citizen of a certain country), in the desire for a collective to which one belongs to be at least equal and perhaps greater than other comparable collectives (to recognise that A's country is no worse and possibly better than other countries), in the desire that a specific individual has to be considered more memorable than others or to be famous (to recognise that A is more worthy of respect, for instance, than most other individuals). Though it is clearly possible to use the word *recognition* to cover these quite different senses, it doesn't mean that these quite different senses can be theorised in a monological fashion: arguably to say that people desire recognition cannot really mean anything sensible unless the word is qualified by the sense in which it should be understood. It is quite possible that if the different connotations are rigorously differentiated it would be found that Fukuyama's superficially plausible formulation becomes less tenable, that the things Fukuyama brings together by the use of the word 'recognition' actually cannot usefully be brought together in that way. Further, it is also worth pondering whether it is sensible to speak of a desire for recognition as within individual people and collectives without giving adequate consideration to the conditions under which recognition (in whatever sense) is given. If we limit ourselves to some understanding of recognition as fame, is it possible to understand the desire for fame without understanding the sociological, ethical, political, etc. conditions under which fame becomes conceivable and thereafter perhaps desirable? Is it possible that if these conditions are examined it might be so contrived that fame is *not* sought (just as, for example, the monastic scribe may labour selflessly on an illuminated manuscript without stamping his name on it)? Similar questions can be raised with regard to the term *trust*. Fukuyama seems to see trust in any kind of action based on mutual dependence, the success of which cannot be ensured by contractual obligation. But are all such cases comparable as manifestations of one thing (trust)? Is the trust that applies to love or friendship comparable to the trust that may apply between strangers who belong to some cultural collective (a religious or linguistic or national collective), comparable to the trust that one may simply have in any human being, comparable to the trust that one may have in the justice of God? Are these all 'trust' in the same way? Fukuyama more or less assumes that they are – that trust in the family, the organisation, the community, the state are somehow comparable – but this clearly can bear further analytical interrogation, which may well not support Fukuyama's use of that term. More importantly, is it possible to average these different kinds of trust into one abstract quantity of social trust, so that a hierarchy of high-trust, moderate-trust, and low-trust societies can be comparatively placed? Under rigorous examination the latter could well prove to be a most tenuous comparative cultural inference.

I am more concerned here with charting out possible ways of questioning Fukuyama's premises from an analytical philosophical perspective than with launching upon a full exploration of these. After all, such an examination would be a bit excessive since, as I have observed before, analytical philosophical rigour is not what Fukuyama seeks or depends on. In the spirit of marking out possible modes of analytical questioning I could go a step further: the use of these terms in this loose fashion to explain such a wide range of phenomena does seem indicative of what I called *contained overdeterminism* in Chapter 11. The kind of privileging of certain factors that Fukuyama assumes in his argument – recognition and technological development, trust and spontaneous sociability – is not wholly explained. Why should the ethical principle of trust supersede other ethical principles such as fairness, or justness? If the latter are considered to be unimportant or somehow secondary to trust then an argument needs to be adduced to explain that. If the importance of trust is only with regard to success in corporate capitalism, then his choice of ethical qualities is ideologically predetermined. Similarly, why should the drive for recognition be considered to supersede the drive for pleasure, or the drive for perfection (in whatever terms)? Perhaps Fukuyama privileges recognition because it fits in with his predecided ideological leaning towards liberal democracy. On the whole, I feel that the only sound reason why Fukuyama privileges certain factors is because he is ideologically predetermined – because it is convenient to do so given his ideological proclivities. But then the impression that he manages to convey that these ideological positions are necessary *because* of the supersedent importance of the chosen factors is erroneous; he privileges these factors because they fit in with his ideological position, and then proceeds to sell his ideological position by carrying out a contained overdetermination of these factors within his argument. There is a careful circularity involved here. There is, in fact, in Fukuyama's work not much more than an assertion of an ideological position and its associated terms. Such an assertion cannot be taken seriously unless given in the context of an examination of other ideologies – which Fukuyama doesn't undertake. But, as I have said already, this sort of analytical critique is slightly beside the point for Fukuyama: ultimately his assertion of an ideological position doesn't rest on the analytical validity of that position, but on its empirical validity. What Fukuyama would undoubtedly say if faced with such arguments is that they don't matter: it is not he who asserts such a position, it is empirically evident as a supersedent position (it is the case that capitalist liberal democracy is simply triumphing over contending ideologies). But the analytical critique is not invalidated by that response. Does the fact that a particular ideological position happens to be popular form a sufficient reason for dismissing contending ideological positions without adequate examination?

Moving on, what is of immediate interest in the context of this study is the fact that Fukuyama's arguments are designed to disable the political will in a manner that validates contemporary corporate capitalist organisation. I think this is self-evident in the above summaries, but it is worth underlining in case this has somehow not come across. In brief, both the universal historical process which is directed by the mechanism of the development of natural science and technology and by the mechanism of the drive for recognition toward corporate capitalist liberal democracy, and the process of the development of corporate capitalism in economic terms which is directed toward greater or lesser degrees of success by the cultural preconditions which exist (in the forms of trust and the potential for spontaneous sociability), are conceived by Fukuyama as being essentially automatic processes. While certain microelements in these processes could be seen to be consciously instituted and coor- dinated, in the broadest sense these processes unravel irrespective of any political will or contemplation of outcome. The motive forces which drive these processes toward their more or less inevitable final state are such as are outside the control of the human psyche (collective or individual) – they are the a priori cultural and psycho- logical conditions, which simply are effective whether there is any conscious desire to make them effective or otherwise. Thus the desire for rationalisation, the longing for recognition, the dependence on certain kinds of trust and possible spontaneous socialisations are actually given as ahistorical factors which seem to manifest themselves inevitably in all historical contexts, which display a kind of uncontrollable stickiness. Under these circumstances the emergence of corporate capitalist liberal democracy in any context is simply to be taken as *fait accompli*, primarily a matter of time – and the question really is how quickly this emergence takes place and is accepted as being the desirable final state. The only space that is left for a political will is that which may expedite the rate of change toward that final state – and these are the only prescriptive moments in Fukuyama's argument (that the drive for recognition should be nurtured, that *megalothymia* should be contained within corporate capitalist processes, that traditions of trust should not be destroyed by excessive individualism, etc.). But even these prescrip- tive moments, which seem to invite some sort of exercise of a political will with certain means and ends in mind, are not actually invitations for such an exercise of political will in any dynamic sense. At best, this is a recommendation of quietism – the only dynamic here is in not being dynamic, in *withdrawing* all initiatives that obstruct the automatic initiatives which spontaneously lead to a desirable final condition of corporate capitalist liberal democracy. From an apparently different direction Fukuyama effectively disables the political will and declares the *naturalness* of corporate capitalist liberal democracy in much the same way as Popper–Hayek–Nozick did. Fukuyama's end of history is not an impossibility of history, it is in reality more a recommendation that no conceptualisation beyond corporate capitalist liberal democracy as he understands this need be attempted. Don't try to conceive beyond what has been conceived already, is the disabling message – reminiscent of Hayek – that Fukuyama conveys.

That Fukuyama tries to convey this politically disabling message in terms of empirical accounting rather than of analytical philo-sophical conceptualisation is consistent with the nature of that message. If these processes are seen as conceptual processes, that would defeat their automatic character: necessarily he has to (and does) make out that what he asserts simply has happened, rather than that it has to be, or has been, conceived as happening. Fukuyama's empirical accounting is fairly impressive: different ranges of historical data are synthesised and juxtaposed in *The End of History* to show that there is a growing consensus regarding liberal democracy in the world, that the mechanism of natural science and technology and that of the drive of recognition can be used to understand the historical movements of a variety of contexts; and a suitably wide range of cultural characteristics and observations regarding different contexts are linked in *Trust* (sometimes inge-niously) to the development of capitalist corporate structures in those contexts. Inevitably this effort at empirical accounting can both be admired for its intellectual scope, and if necessary be dissected and questioned in detail. But such a protracted effort is unnecessary here – as a methodology this is by itself unequal to validating his essential arguments. That really is all that needs to be grasped to understand the weakness of Fukuyama's anti-political philosophy. *No amount of empirical accounting in retrospect can validate a general observation with prospective effect.* This is something that Popper had correctly realised, as I have observed above. *No retro-spective discernment of a pattern can be understood to be necessarily contingent on prospective eventualities.* This is a fallacy in Hayek's understanding of adaptive evolution and the need to nurture it – I have given my arguments about this already. Fukuyama does mistakenly assume that empirical accounting can validate his essential argument, and he does erroneously feel that what is retrospectively discernible can give rise to formulations that are prospectively applicable. Fukuyama's observation that there is evidence of a great convergence toward corporate capitalist liberal democracy in our world does not justify the feeling that this is therefore a position that has to be accepted and reached. Arguably other convergences of similar magnitude have manifested themselves at different historical moments – consensus about the need for religious social organisation, about the inevitability of monarchical politics and feudal social orders, and so on. Universal human history, if attempted, can throw up remarkably homogeneous phenomena in the midst of diversities (indeed that is why universal history was conceived in the first instance), but that is no reason for inferring that these apparent consensuses are unnegotiable or unquestionable. Even less do they justify the supposition that these provide sufficient basis for positing final ends. Hegel had famously drawn on his universal history based on an encyclopaedic empirical accounting to assert that the Germany of his time gave some inkling of a final end,[7] and it didn't take long for Hegel's Germany to be relegated to history itself. There is no reason to believe that Fukuyama's corporate capitalist liberal democracy will fare any better.

17   The Need for Rational Utopian Thinking

An apparently formidable but structurally flawed edifice of anti-political philosophy lends support to the disabling of political will, the promotion of limited speculative interests behind the assertion of automatic processes, the obfuscations and subterfuges, the blatant injustices and inequities of contemporary corporate capitalism. I suspect that a philosophy that actively disables the political will is probably, by dint of that fact, self-contradictory. I believe philosophy is by definition a creation of concepts,[1] and that it is a constant assertion of the human urge to plan and regulate the world (especially when the aspect of the world under inspection is the social and political world) – a dynamic process that rebels against being subjugated to automatic processes. To use philosophy for the self-defeating purpose of recommending quietism and acceptance of disabling spontaneous processes, for *not* conceiving beyond a certain point, is self-defeating. This is obviously a grand assertion itself – one that I do not undertake to elaborate and validate here – but it is one that instinctively strikes me as being true.

The outline given above of corporate capitalist organisation that disables the political will, and of the anti-political philosophy that lends support to it, cannot be circumscribed or put into relief without trying to elucidate the possibilities open to *political* (as opposed to *anti-political*) philosophy in our time. This study in fact cannot be complete without such an effort – and, I fear, in that sense this study will have to remain incomplete. It is necessary that in the context of contemporary corporate capitalism more conceptual effort be made to revitalise an effective political will. Such effort is not entirely lacking: there are political philosophers and political philosophies – usually either liberal democratic and communitarian (but not in the Fukuyama mould and certainly clearly distanced from the Popper–Hayek–Nozick line) or market socialist[2] – which do discuss possible ways in which a political will can be exercised. However, it seems to me that such studies do not have a sufficiently lucid apprehension of what they are up against, of the extent to which the political will is systematically disabled in the context of contemporary corporate capitalism and with the aid of anti-political philosophy. To that extent such political philosophies are promising efforts which are unlikely to make any effective intervention in social and political matters; to do so they would have to clearly contextualise themselves in terms of a sound understanding of how a disabling of political will works at both pragmatic and conceptual levels.

Though this study must regretfully remain incomplete (not for long, I am convinced), as an immediate conclusion I briefly attempt the following: I outline one of the possibilities for *political* philosophy that could be seen to arise from the preceding discussion.

One of the characteristic features of the anti-political philosophy that I have discussed above has been its anti-utopian attitude – where *utopia* is understood primarily in the common usage as the 'good place', and always secondarily but ironically carries its root meaning of being 'no place'. The political philosophy of Mannheim which self-defeatingly revealed certain anti-political directions had placed utopian thinking as the irrational overdetermination of hostility to a given state of affairs, the contrary of ideology which was understood as an irrational overdetermination of dominant interests. The anti-political tendency of Popper was vehemently anti-utopian: Popper associated utopian thinking with holistic, historicist and totalitarian conceptualisation that could lead dangerously astray. Hayek's full-blown anti-political philosophy fully endorsed Popper's anti-utopianism: in utopian thinking Hayek saw not only everything Popper had associated with it, but also a determination actually to distort the truth of adaptive evolution and lead away from the need to nurture it. Nozick also expresses his incredulity at the notion that utopian thinking as he understood it (the conceptualisation of a place where everyone would wish to live) could be taken seriously: his framework for utopia is really a prescription for neutralising utopian conceptualisations, and insidiously suggests that corporatism already has a utopian direction. Fukuyama's feeling that corporate capitalist liberal democracy is as close as we are likely to get to utopia, and that the growing universal convergence towards such a formation indicates the imminence of a final condition which all could consider to be desirable, is also a mode of neutralising utopian conceptualisation.

The distrust of utopian thinking is a significant consensus in anti-political thinking. It isn't a distrust that can be dismissed easily, because the association between utopian thinking and the experience of totalitarianism in recent history is not wholly misplaced. Yet the association is not written in stone either. It is generally assumed, for instance, that experiences of totalitarianism arising out of different kinds of fascism (especially German) must be related to some utopian conception. Different fascist regimes and alignments have tried to sell their twisted perspectives in terms of pseudo-utopian visions – visions of perfectly homogeneous and therefore harmonious societies (where homogeneity is asserted as a matter of racial identity or national affiliation or religious conviction or some other communal identifier). But these are pseudo-utopias because they are poorly conceptualised, if conceptualised at all; they have little rational content. The static vision of a final state is given in an iconic fashion – images hold sway – and there is no rational process of conceptualisation *leading* to a utopian outcome, no conceptual existence of utopia beyond the blind assertion of a vision that demands something like religious faith. Fascism doesn't arise out of a conceptual effort but out of the lack of one, out of faith rather than reasoning, or out of hatred rather than reasoning.

Communist governments in different contexts have also strengthened the association between utopian thinking and a destructive and ultimately doomed totalitarianism. Here there clearly is a conceptual basis to the ideological effort, but I doubt whether it is the utopian element in the conceptual basis that is to be held responsible for the emergence of totalitarianism and the disastrous effects thereof. It is more or less well understood now that the utopian element in the different forms of Marxism that have guided different communist governments was insufficiently developed before being acted upon.[3] There is actually no clearly realised utopia in Marxist thinking: no rationalised and lucidly envisioned economic and legislative and judicial arrangement of a communist state. There is almost everything else: a critique of a given social arrangement which makes a utopian conceptualisation necessary, the steps whereby the utopian conceptualisation may be discussed and enunciated, the agenda of those who may subscribe to such a utopian conceptualisation. But the utopian conceptualisation itself is drastically weak – indeed seldom rising above the visionary – and incomplete in terms of most rationalistic and pragmatic considerations. That these enormous gaps in utopian conceptualisation, that an incomplete utopian conceptualisation, can only lead to failure in a too precipitate field of practice and action is inevitable. But it isn't just that which needs to be noted: the transition from a would-be-utopian programme to totalitarian misadventure, which has been evidenced in most attempts at communist governance in recent history, is not because such utopian rational conceptualisation in a Marxist mould as exists has been adhered to, but because it hasn't. It is irrationality which is at odds with most forms of rational Marxist conceptualisation, or irrationalities within elaborations of Marxist precepts, which have allowed the rise of demagogues, the routinisation of unfreedom, the oppressive economic experimentations, etc., that have marked the experience of communist countries. Such experiences do not form grounds for associating utopian thinking with totalitarianism and dictatorships; such experiences are warnings against acting upon imperfectly conceived utopian ideas, for guarding against irrationality within utopian conceptualisations, for guarding against visionary pseudo-utopias which are unsupported by rational conceptualisation. Such experiences do not prove the impossibility of rational utopian thinking, or any necessary relationship between utopian thinking and totalitarianism.

I am aware that in that last paragraph I have made a series of observations that can only be substantiated by a voluminous study of the subject. This is evidently not my present purpose. My point is not to substantiate these observations, but to posit them, with a view to showing that they are familiar too and can be tested by drawing on the same historical experience that anti-political philosophers repeatedly refer to, and that these observations are not easily dismissed either. And I have made these observations to avoid any misconception about my main contention here: *that in a contemporary corporate capitalist context wherein there occurs a disabling of political will, one way of revitalising the political will may be through the encouragement – indeed the active pursuit – of rational utopian thinking, and moreover rational utopian thinking that is necessarily fully cognisant of the dangers of irrationality and visionary ideas and repressive demagogy or totalitarianism, and that possesses a complete awareness of the implications of pertinent historical experience.*

The pursuit of rational utopian conceptualisation with a view to revitalising the political will might appear to be a rather pat oppositionist position to assume apropos the kind of anti-political philosophical arguments I have discussed above. This is true to some extent: I do feel that the distrust of utopian thinking which characterises much anti-political philosophy is to some extent the result of a desire to check political philosophy, to disable the political will and to fall in more or less unresistingly with contemporary corporate capitalist organisation. But it isn't simply opposition to anti-political philosophy that motivates my perception of a need for rational utopian thinking; it seems to me to be the case that rational utopian thinking *is* a significant means of realising the potential of the political will. *As I understand it, utopianism is in the first instance a recognition that the condition of the world, whether in terms of an immediate context or as a whole, is not ideal (i.e. that there is cause for dissatisfaction which can be identified) – usually in terms of some notion of social and political justice. Utopian thinking thereafter progresses on the conviction that the identifiable causes for dissatisfaction can be removed through means which are under human control; that if certain voluntary measures (whether incremental or revolutionary in character) are adopted, identified causes for dissatisfaction can be overcome. And finally utopian thinking tries to imagine, in a concrete and comprehensive fashion, the world from which the causes of dissatisfaction have been removed; this allows for some apprehension of the effects the assumed voluntary measures may have in unpredictable areas of social and political existence: in brief, the final test of utopian thinking rests on the imagining of a plausible utopian condition.* If this account of rational utopianism seems acceptable, it should be clear why it could be a significant counterforce against anti-political philosophy. The recognition of the condition of living in a social and political organisation that disables the political will, and the desire to rectify this situation, is a recognition that the given predominantly corporate capitalist social order is not satisfactory. The belief that this can be rectified by voluntary (as opposed to automatic or spontaneous) means is both a reassertion and an exercise of the political will – a freeing of the political will from its shackles. The imagining of a concrete world wherein the political will can be plausibly and realistically enabled (in economic and legislative and judicial terms) would maintain a check which would ensure that the processes of reassertion and exercise of the self-freeing political will remain rational – carefulness in this regard would deter the enabling conceptualisation from going astray, from lapsing into dogmatic visionary inflections, or from falling into irrationality.

Without actually attempting any such political philosophical conceptualisation here, the considerations which would have to underlie and guide such an effort can be elucidated further. The following points are, I think, relevant – and when they are done this study will be complete.

(a) The dynamics of the political will rests first in the interpreting–acting agency of the political state in respect of the intentional system of the people–land–resources it is with regard to and of nothing else, and second in the oppositional expression or (if necessary) action that any alignment or collective or individual within or outside that intentional system may rationally and justifiably take against the political state's interpretations–actions. A utopian conceptualisation which hopes to regenerate the political will would have to ensure that both these are equally enabled and encouraged and protected. To a large extent this would be ensured if the utopian conceptualisation contemplates a series of checks and balances whereby the state would be under the control of the people–land–resources to a necessary degree just as the state would control the people–land–resources to a necessary degree. This paradox is a commonplace of most modern political philosophy, and it is widely accepted that the institution and retention of democratic processes is the most effective way of responding to it. Unless other ways to do this effectively are discovered – I can't think of any – this would mean that all utopian conceptualisation would be concerned with democratic governance in a true sense (such that both the above are enabled, and do not simply *seem* to be enabled).

(b) The recognition of a condition which is unsatisfactory (which necessitates the contemplation of remedial measures and the imagining of a world in which such measures have been taken) – this is the root of utopian thinking – is always necessarily a contextual matter. The conceived remedial measures and the imagined world that follows ultimately reflect no more than dissatisfactions, which are expressed in the context where such a conceptualisation is attempted. In rational utopian conceptualisation therefore there should be no misapprehension about the imagined rectified world: *an imagined rectified world, the utopia, is never a final condition – it is always conditional on the context in which it is conceived, and has to be left open to change and modification as other contexts (in terms of both time and place) are brought to bear upon it and other dissatisfactions are identified – utopian conceptualisations are, in other words, inevitably transitory conceptualisations which enable no more than a careful understanding of what is lacking in the given world and a careful consideration of the measures which may be taken to make the world otherwise.* It follows from this that the rejuvenation and exercise of political will doesn't simply rest in the process of trying to reach any particular final utopia, but in the process of utopian conceptualisations which always seek to extirpate what is unsatisfactory, are always aware that such attempts have wider repercussions than may be evident at first, and always look for other causes of dissatisfaction. *It would be fair to say that the enablement of the political will is not an end which coincides with a final utopia, but is implicit and coeval and coincident with a continuous process of utopian conceptualisation, a constant search for and belief in perfectibility but without ever declaring any condition to be achieved perfection.*

(c) The fact that utopian conceptualisations are conditional on the contexts within which they occur inevitably means that in any particular period there is likely to be a range of utopian conceptualisations, some of which may even be contradictory. It seems to me that in whatever context a utopian conceptualisation may be undertaken, the process of that conceptualisation would – in being utopian – attempt to reach a universal level of applicability. Insofar as different utopian conceptualisations from different contexts arise through the identification of different causes of dissatisfaction, the rational way to strive toward a greater degree of universality would rest in finding common ground, in considering the interplay of the different causes which impelled the utopian conceptual process. Insofar as contradictory utopian conceptualisations may arise even from the identification of the same causes of dissatisfaction, a rational process of universalisation would consist in either locating the reasons for the contradictions and negotiating among them, or in an attempt to discover grounds for choosing one over the others.

(d) The final step of the process of utopian conceptualisation, the imagining of a rectified world, which has so often in the past been mistaken for a final condition, serves no other purpose than to test the plausibility of the conceived remedial measures and to check in a concrete fashion the possible unexpected repercussions these may have. This should never be lost sight of. In fact the reason why this final step is undertaken is not to celebrate the utopian conceptualisation itself – to give it a mystical aura, to render it a paradise-like vision of perfection – but to consider the dystopic possibilities that may shadow any utopian conceptualisation. To some extent utopian thinking has always shouldered its dark underside, the dystopic aspect that arises from it: this has been observed before – recently, for example, by Krishan Kumar:

Like the religious and the secular, utopia and anti-utopia are anti-thetical yet interdependent. They are 'contrast concepts', getting their meaning and significance from their mutual differences. But the relationship is not symmetrical or equal. The anti-utopia is formed by utopia, and feeds parasitically on it. It depends for its survival on the persistence of utopia. Utopia is the original, anti-utopia the copy – only, as it were, coloured black.[4]

Arguably, it seems to me that those who have engaged in rational utopian conceptualisations in the past have often retained a sense of this irony which leaves them unconvinced of that conceptualisation – so that utopia has come to signify not only the good place which is no place, but also the impossible place that would never be. This is probably not because the utopian thinkers have been sceptical of the possibilities of the political will, but they have been sceptical of the perfection of their utopias. In the future, rational utopian conceptualisation did imagine the rectified condition, the transient rational utopia, only to reveal the dystopic possibilities – to keep the *process* of utopian conceptualisation alive.

(e) The political will can be rejuvenated in the process of utopian conceptualisation itself, and the effects of the political will can become manifest not in the striving after a final condition but in the implementation of those measures which have withstood *all* the steps of utopian conceptualisation to a satisfactory extent. This is likely to happen rarely – but it can certainly happen; it may necessitate the implementation of measures which may be small or radical; and such action could be considered justified if it is in the hope of realising a better world, but not if it seeks a final world or an end of history.

(f) It is quite possible that in the foreseeable future the rejuvenation of the political will through utopian conceptualisation will seek and find ways of coexisting with and supporting what continues to be the most productive and effective economic process yet conceived – the market-based capitalist process. The capitalist organisation which may sustain itself with and be sustained by the enabled political will (a utopian concept without flesh yet) will undoubtedly be quite different from the contemporary corporate capitalist organisation which consolidates itself through the disabled political will.

Notes

PART I

Chapter 1

1. Translations of Marx's early 'Critique of Hegel's Doctrine of State' (1843), pp.57–198, and 'Economic and Philosophical Manuscripts' (1844), pp.279–400, are available in *Marx: Early Writings*, intro. Lucio Colletti, trans. Rodney Livingstone and Gregor Benton (Harmondsworth: Penguin, 1975).

2. Though Marx had given a reasonably clear materialistic description of the proletariat class in 'The Contribution to the Critique of Hegel's Philosophy of Right, Introduction' (1843–1844), pp.243–258, and in his 'Excerpts from James Mill's *Elements of Political Economy*' (1844), pp.259–278, the consideration of labour in the 'Economic and Philosophical Manuscripts' (1844) is primarily in the more or less metaphysical alienation of the worker in Hegelian terms (*Marx: Early Writings*, 1975). Marx and Engels's *The German Ideology* (1845–1846) (Moscow: Progress Publishers, 1976) places the proletariat class within a complete apprehension of class society and class conflict, and this enables the political programme which is famously enunciated in Marx and Engels's *The Communist Manifesto* (1848) – the Harmondsworth: Penguin, 1967, edition has a useful contextualising introduction by A.J.P. Taylor.

3. In the last few decades, the work of Raymond Williams, Fredric Jameson, Terry Eagleton, Stuart Hall, Lucien Goldmann, Cliff Slaughter, Henri Lefebvre, Ernesto Laclau in the broad field of cultural studies; of Ngugi wa Thiong'o, Gayatri Spivak, Partho Chatterji, Aijaz Ahmad with regard to post-colonial studies; Joan Kelly, Juliet Mitchell, Catherine McKinnon, Michelle Barrett, Heidi Hertmann, Lise Vogel in gender studies, come to mind readily (to name just a few). See also note 10.

4. The approach to knowledge, associated with certain disciplinary perspectives, in terms of basic quanta of knowledge is an idea I have examined in *Two Texts and I: Disciplines of Knowledge and the Literary Subject* (Madison NJ: Fairleigh Dickinson University Press/London: Associated University Presses, 1999), pp.66–69.

5. The former especially in Jürgen Habermas's *Legitimation Crisis*, trans. Thomas McCarthy (London: Heinemann, 1976), and to some extent in *Toward A Rational Society*, trans. Jeremy J. Shapiro (London: Heinemann, 1971) – mainly in essays addressing the relationship of science/technology to politics/ideology. These are developed further in his concept of communicative action, which finds full expression in *The Theory of Communicative Action*, trans. Thomas McCarthy (Boston: Beacon, 1984 [vol.1] and 1987 [vol.2]).

6. A simplistic overview of Habermas's project might see it as an attempt to synthesise idealistic philosophy with positivistic thinking to derive a universal theory of effective social – for Habermas communicative – action. This necessarily begins in some sense with German idealistic philosophy, the universalistic ambition of which lingers in his understanding of later theoretical ventures – most explicitly in *Knowledge and Human Interests*, trans. Jeremy J. Shapiro (Cambridge: Polity, 1968/1987), and *The Philosophical Discourse of Modernity*, trans. Fredrick Lawrence (Cambridge: Polity, 1985/1987), in both of which Kant and Hegel are seen as initiators of *modern* epistemology.

7. See, for example, Neil J. Smelser, 'Social Sciences and Social Problems', *International Sociology*, 11: 3, 1996, pp.275–290.

8. This is an assertion which I have elaborated on in *Marxism, History, and Intellectuals: Toward A Reconceptualized Transformative Socialism* (Madison NJ: Fairleigh Dickinson University Press/London: Associated University Presses, 2000), pp.223–235.

9. From his somewhat esoteric view of 'life politics' in *Modernity and Self-Identity* (Cambridge: Polity, 1991), Anthony Giddens has turned to more pragmatic political and economic policy in such books as *Beyond Left and Right* (Cambridge: Polity, 1994) and *The Third Way* (Cambridge: Polity, 1998). British Prime Minister Tony Blair's political writings (e.g. *The Third Way: New Politics for A New Society* (London: Fabian Society, 1999)) draw on Giddens-like terminology, and Blair-led New Labour policy statements on 'public–private partnerships' and the need to 'restructure' the welfare state, for instance, are consonant with Giddens's ideas.

10. The main recent arguments for and against class analysis are to be found in such overviews of the matter as R. Breen and D. Rothman, *Class Stratification* (London: Harvester, 1995), and particularly against in J. Pakulski and M. Waters, *The Death of Class* (London: Sage, 1996). The latter should be read in conjunction with the report on the 'Symposium of Class' in the journal *Theory and Society*, 25:5, 1996, which carries a statement by Pakulski and Waters and responses to them. See also R. Breen and D. Rothman, 'Class Analysis and Class Theory', *Sociology*, 29:3, 1995, pp.453–474; and J.H. Goldthorpe and G. Marshall, 'The Promising Future of Class Analysis', *Sociology*, 26:3, 1992, pp.453–474. In general, the following grey areas of class analysis have attracted attention in sociological journals in the nineteen-nineties: the problems of negotiating between the analysis of gender positions/roles/perceptions and class perception; the ambiguities of the shifts from class location/status/identity to individualised location/status/identity; and the difficulties of using class analysis to explain social mobility. It would be tedious to list all the available articles relevant to these.

11. Floya Anthias, 'Rethinking Social Divisions: Some Notes Towards A Theoretical Framework', *The Sociological Review*, 46:3, August 1998, pp.508–509.

12. Ibid., p.531.

Chapter 2

1. See, for example, Philippe Schmitter, 'Neo-Corporation and the State', *The Political Economy of the State*, ed. Wyn Grant (London: Macmillan, 1985), pp.32–62.
2. Robert Nisbet, *The Social Philosophers: Community and Conflict in Western Thought* (London: Heinemann, 1973), pp.432–442.
3. R.M. MacIver, *The Modern State* (London: Oxford University Press, 1926), pp.5–6.
4. Max Weber, *The Theory of Social and Economic Organization*, ed. intro. Talcott Parsons (New York: Free Press/ London: Collier-Macmillan, 1947), p.155.
5. Ibid., p.156.
6. Ibid., p.155.
7. Emile Durkheim, 'The Concept of the State', *Durkheim on Politics and the State*, ed. Anthony Giddens (Cambridge: Polity, 1986), p.40.
8. Max Weber, *Economy and Society, Vol. 2*, ed. Guenther Roth and Claus Wittich (Berkeley: University of California Press, 1978), p.922.
9. In recent years the hazy ground of the nation, as some sort of conception *within* a collective, has been influentially examined (and with different emphases) by the following: Elie Kedourie, *Nationalism* (London: Hutchinson, 1960); Hugh Seton-Watson, *Nations and States* (London: Methuen, 1977); John Breuilly, *Nationalism and the State* (Manchester: Manchester University Press, 1982); Ernest Gellner, *Nations and Nationalism* (Oxford: Blackwell, 1983) and *Nationalism* (London: Weidenfeld and Nicolson, 1997); Homi K. Bhabha ed., *Nation and Narration* (London: Routledge, 1990); Benedict Anderson, *Imagined Communities* (London: Verso, 1991); Partho Chatterji, *The Nation and its Fragments* (Princeton: Princeton University Press, 1993).
10. Nicos Poulantzas, *Political Power and Social Classes*, trans. Timothy O'Hagan (London: NLB, 1968/1975), p.44.
11. Apart from Poulantzas's work, illuminating recent elaborations of the Marxist understanding of the state appear in the following: J.B. Sanderson, *An Interpretation of the Political Ideas of Marx and Engels* (London: Longmans, 1969), chapter 4; Bob Jessop, 'Marx and Engels on the State', *Politics, Ideology and the State*, ed. Sally Hibbin (London: Lawrence and Wishart, 1978); David McLellan, 'Marx, Engels and Lenin on the State', *The Withering Away of the State?* ed. Leslie Holmes (London: Sage, 1981); Bob Jessop, *Nicos Poulantzas: Marxist Theory and Political Strategy* (London: Macmillan, 1985).
12. Friedrich Engels, *Anti-Dühring* (London: Lawrence and Wishart, 1975), p.333. On this see pp.73–5 in Chapter 6 of the present volume.
13. V.I. Lenin, *The State and Revolution*, trans. Robert Service (Harmondsworth: Penguin, 1992), chapter 1.

Chapter 3

1. Karl Marx, *Capital: A Critical Analysis of Capitalist Production, Vol.1*, ed. F. Engels, trans. Samuel Moore and Edward Aveling (London: Lawrence and Wishart, 1954), pp.150–151.

2. Ibid., p.293.
3. Ibid., p.588.
4. John Kenneth Galbraith, *The New Industrial State* (2nd ed.), (Harmondsworth: Penguin, 1967/1972), p.87.
5. Ibid., p.88.
6. Details of *Legitimation Crisis* and *The New Industrial State* have been given already (n.5 and n.29). Raymond Aron, *Eighteen Lectures on Industrial Society*, trans. M.K. Bottomore (London: Weidenfeld and Nicolson, 1961/1967). Ernest Mandel, *Late Capitalism*, trans. Joris De Bres (London: Verso, 1972/1975).
7. Essentially the theme of both Herbert Marcuse's *One-Dimensional Man* (London: Sphere, 1964) and *An Essay on Liberation* (Boston: Beacon, 1969). Marcuse himself reflects on this paradox in *One-Dimensional Man*, p.13.
8. Henri Lefebvre, *The Survival of Capitalism: Reproduction of the Relations of Production*, trans. Frank Bryant (London: Allison and Busby, 1973/1976), p.21.

Chapter 4

1. *Capital, Vol.1*, p.173.
2. Mandel, *Late Capitalism*, pp.25–28.
3. Marx, *Capital, Vol.1*, p.505.
4. Karl Marx, *Capital: A Critique of Political Economy, Vol.3 (The Process of Capitalist Production as a Whole)*, ed. F. Engels (London: Lawrence and Wishart, 1959), chapters 2 and 3.
5. Marx, *Capital, Vol.1*, p.163.
6. Karl Marx, *Capital: A Critique of Political Economy, Vol.2 (The Process of Circulation of Capital)*, ed. F. Engels, trans. I. Lasker (London: Lawrence and Wishart, 1956), p.103.
7. Ibid., p.399.
8. Ibid., p.407–415.
9. Marx, *Capital, Vol.3*, chapters 2 and 3.
10. Ibid., p.212.
11. Ibid., chapter 14.
12. Ibid., p.213.
13. Ibid., p.242.
14. Marx, *Capital, Vol.1*, p.542.
15. Especially ibid., p.505.
16. Division of labour and the phase of manufacture are described in ibid., chapter 14.
17. Ibid., p.547.
18. Mandel, *Late Capitalism*, chapter 6, especially pp.192–193.
19. In this context see Mandel, *Late Capitalism*, chapter 16; Joseph Schumpeter, *Capitalism, Socialism, and Democracy* (London: George Allen and Unwin, 1943/1976), chapter 13, section 2; Immanuel Wallerstein, *Historical Capitalism* (London: Verso, 1983), pp.83–85.
20. See, for example, Gugluielmo Carchedi, *Frontiers of Political Economy* (London: Verso, 1991), pp.126–127.
21. Mandel, *Late Capitalism*, p.207.

22. Gupta, *Marxism, History, and Intellectuals*.

23. Marcuse, *One-Dimensional Man*, pp.34–42.

24. See, for example, Clifford Geertz, 'The Way We Think Now: Toward an Ethnography of Modern Thought', *Local Knowledge* (New York: Basic, 1983); Régis Debray, *Teachers, Writers, Celebrities*, trans. David Macey (London: Verso, 1979); Tony Becher, *Academic Tribes and Territories* (Buckingham and Bristol: Open University Press and SRHE, 1989); Ronald Barnett ed., *Academic Community: Discourse or Discord?* (London: Jessica Kingsley, 1994).

25. Often those who are best able to recognise the allure of the modes of knowledge-organisation presented by these 'movements' are also those who perceive their self-defeat. See, for example, Fredric Jameson, *Postmodernism or the Cultural Logic of Late Capitalism* (London: Verso, 1991); Christopher Norris, *What's Wrong With Postmodernism* (Brighton: Harvester, 1990); Terry Eagleton, *The Illusions of Postmodernism* (Oxford: Blackwell, 1996); Aijaz Ahmad, *In Theory* (London: Verso, 1992).

26. On this see pp.84–91 in Chapter 6 of the present volume.

27. Schumpeter, *Capitalism, Socialism and Democracy*, p.134.

28. Ibid., chapter 13.

29. These views are not dissimilar to those found in Mandel, *Late Capitalism*, chapter 16, or in Alvin W. Gouldner, *The Future of Intellectuals and the Rise of the New Class* (London: Macmillan, 1979).

30. Schumpeter, *Capitalism, Socialism and Democracy*, pp.145–155.

31. Mandel, *Late Capitalism*, pp.197–198.

32. See Chapter 3, note 7.

33. Habermas, *Legitimation Crisis*, part II.

34. Lefebuve, *Survival of Capitalism*, p.21.

35. For example, all four parts of Samir Amin, Giovanni Arrighi, Andre Gunder Frank, Immanuel Wallerstein, *Dynamics of Global Crisis* (London: Macmillan, 1982) are written with the prospect of capitalism's imminent demise in mind.

Chapter 5

1. John R. Searle, *Intentionality: An Essay in the Philosophy of Mind* (Cambridge: Cambridge University Press, 1983).

2. Daniel C. Dennett, *The Intentional Stance* (Cambridge Mass.: MIT Press, 1987):

   [F]olk psychology might best be viewed as a rationalistic calculus of interpretation and prediction – an idealizing, abstract, instrumentalistic interpretation method that has evolved because it works and works because we have evolved. We approach each other as *intentional systems*, that is, as entities whose behaviour can be predicted by the method of attributing beliefs, desires, and rational acumen [...]. (pp.48–49)

3. As in John Searle's *The Construction of Social Reality* (Harmondsworth: Penguin, 1995), or Daniel C. Dennett's *Elbow Room: The Varieties of Free*

Will Worth Wanting (Oxford: Clarendon, 1984), or Paul Grice's *The Conception of Value* (Oxford: Clarendon, 1991).

4. Daniel C. Dennett, *Brainstorms: Philosophical Essays on Mind and Psychology* (Hassocks, Sussex: Harvester, 1978), p.3.
5. Ibid., p.7.
6. Ibid., p.16.
7. Given in all the three principles for attributing beliefs, desires, and rational acumen to intentional systems in Dennett, *The Intentional Stance*, pp.48–49.
8. The manner in which concepts of organic nationhood defined by a political state almost inevitably lead to racial alignments (even if not originally intended to) is demonstrated repeatedly in the useful collection of Italian, German and other European and non-European documents available in Roger Griffin ed., *Fascism* (Oxford: Oxford University Press, 1995).

PART II

Chapter 6

1. This can be inferred, for instance, from the 'Critique of Feuerbach' in Karl Marx and Friedrich Engels, *The German Ideology* (Moscow: Progress, 1976), especially in the account of primary 'historical' (since Marx rejected the term 'prehistorical') facts laid out in pp.47–51, and in the differentiation between 'Natural instruments of production and those created by civilisation', pp.71–72. This is not 'idealised' in the sense of being a desirable end, but in so far as it marks an initial point from which degrees of dissociation in division of labour can be conceived. It is the ideal that can only exist for Marx when animality and humanity, nature and consciousness, are inseparable – a primitive state.
2. Ibid., pp.72–74.
3. Ibid., pp.75–82 discusses division of labour in the phase of manufacture, and thereafter in large-scale industry. These are, of course, discussed in detail in Karl Marx, *Capital, Vol. 1* (Moscow: Progress, 1954), chapters 14 and 15.
4. Sidney Pollard, *The Genesis of Modern Management* (London: Edward Arnold, 1965); Graeme Salaman, *Class and the Corporation* (Glasgow: Fontana, 1981).
5. Karl Marx, *Capital, Vol. 2* (London: Lawrence and Wishart, 1956), p.126.
6. Ibid., p.152.
7. Ibid., p.134.
8. Friedrich Engels, *Anti-Dühring* (London: Lawrence and Wishart, 1975), pp.330–331.
9. Ibid., p.333.
10. To some extent a comparative approach, such as in Anthony Giddens, *Capitalism and Modern Social Theory: An Analysis of the Writings of Marx,*

Durkheim and Weber (Cambridge: Cambridge University Press, 1971), throws light upon this.

11. Emile Durkheim, *The Division of Labour in Society*, trans. George Simpson (New York: The Free Press/ London: Collier-Macmillan, 1933), p.130.
12. Ibid., p.131.
13. Ibid., p.234.
14. Marco Orrù, *Anomie: History and Meanings* (Boston: Allen & Unwin, 1987), p.95.
15. Durkheim, *The Division of Labour in Society*, pp.353–354.
16. Ibid., pp.366–367.
17. Ibid., pp.358–361.
18. Ibid., p.360.
19. Ibid., p.389.
20. See, for for example, such popular textbooks as G.A. Cole, *Management: Theory and Practice* (4th ed.) (London: DP, 1993), pp.21–24, and Derek S. Pugh and David J. Hickson, *Writers on Organization* (5th edn) (Harmondsworth: Penguin, 1996).
21. Max Weber, *Economy and Society, Vol. 1*, ed. Guenther Roth and Claus Wittich (Berkeley: University of California Press, 1978), p.215.
22. Max Weber, *Economy and Society, Vol. 2*, ed. Guenther Roth and Claus Wittich (Berkeley: University of California Press, 1978), pp.956–958.
23. Ibid., p.956.
24. Weber, *Economy and Society, Vol.1*, p.85.
25. Ibid., pp.85–86.
26. Ibid., p.91.
27. Ibid., p.92.
28. Max Weber, *The Protestant Ethic and the Spirit of Capitalism*, trans. Talcott Parsons (London: Unwin, 1985).
29. Weber, *Economy and Society, Vol.1*, p.93.
30. Ibid., p.98.
31. Ibid., p.108.
32. Ibid., p.114.
33. Ibid., pp.136–137.
34. Ibid., p.138.
35. Ibid., pp.139–140.

Chapter 7

1. John Kaler, 'Positioning Business Ethics in Relation to Management and Political Philosophy', *Journal of Business Ethics*, 24, 2000, pp.259–260.
2. Ibid., pp.261–262.
3. 'Bidding War', *Newsweek*, 24 July 2000, p.5.
4. Fredrick Winslow Taylor. *The Principles of Scientific Management* (New York: Harper & Row, 1911), pp.25–26.
5. Ibid., p.36.
6. Ibid., p.24.
7. Ibid., pp.13–14. And at greater length in Fredrick Winslow Taylor, *Shop Management* (New York: Harper and Brothers, 1903), pp.34–39.
8. Taylor, *The Principles of Scientific Management*, p.36.

9. Henri Fayol, *General and Industrial Management*, trans. Constance Storrs (London: Sir Isaac Pitman and Sons, 1916/1949), pp.5–6. These are elaborated on in chapter 5.
10. Ibid., p.6.
11. Ibid., p.8.
12. Ibid., p.6.
13. Peter F. Drucker, *The Practice of Management* (London: Pan, 1955), p.13.
14. Ibid., p.14.
15. Ibid., p.18.
16. See, for example, the reasons given to encourage managers to make a minimal theoretical effort – only a minimum though, for the author had already given his permission to his readers to skip the theoretical chapters if they so wish – in Tom Peters, *Thriving on Chaos* (London: Pan, 1987), p.39.
17. Tom Peters and Robert H. Waterman Jr, *In Search of Excellence: Lessons from America's Best-Run Companies* (London: HarperCollins, 1982), p.53.
18. Fayol, *General and Industrial Management*, chapter 4.
19. For a clear and brief statement of the matter from an anti-Fayolian position, see Henry Mintzberg, 'The Manager's Job: Folklore and Fact', *Harvard Business Review*, March–April 1992, pp.163–176.
20. Peters and Waterman, *In Search of Excellence*, p.114.
21. Ibid., p.116.
22. For systems theory and evolution see: Bela H. Banathy, 'Evolution Guided by Design: A Systems Perspective', *Systems Research and Behavioral Science*, 15:3, May–June 1998, pp.161–172; C. Wailand, 'Evolutionary Systems Management of Organizations', *World Futures*, 36: 2–4, pp.141–154.

    For complexity theory and coevolution see: Larry E. Geiner, 'Evolution and Revolution as Organizations Grow', *Harvard Business Review*, 1998, pp.55–68; Kathleen M. Eisenhardt and Venkatram Ramaswamy, 'Coevolving: At Last, a Way to Make Synergies Work', *Harvard Business Review*, January–February 2000, pp.91–102; Suzanne Kelly, 'What Business Can Learn from the Simple Science of Complexity', *Journal for Quality and Participation*, 22:5, September–October 1999, pp.44–46; Fiorenza Bellusi, 'Towards the Post-Fordist Economy: Emerging Organizational Models', *International Journal of Technology Management*, 20: 1/2, 2000, pp.20–43.
23. Tom Peters and Nancy Austin, *A Passion for Excellence: The Leadership Difference* (Glasgow: Fontana Collins, 1985), p.116.
24. Peters, *Thriving on Chaos*, p.36.
25. Peters and Austin, *A Passion for Excellence*, p.271.
26. Ibid., p.277.
27. Deborah Cameron, *It's Good to Talk* (London: Sage, 2000).
28. Peters and Austin, *A Passion for Excellence*, p.286.
29. Ibid., p.289.
30. Suman Gupta, *Marxism, History and Intellectuals: Toward a Reconceptualized Transformative Socialism* (Madison, NJ: Fairleigh Dickinson University Press, 2000).
31. P.D. Anthony, *The Ideology of Work* (London: Tavistock, 1977), p.294.

Chapter 8

1. Thomas Frank, *The Conquest of Cool: Business Culture, Counterculture, and the Rise of Hip Consciousness* (Chicago: University of Chicago Press, 1997); Thomas Frank and Matt Weiland, *Commodify Your Dissent: Salvos from the Baffler* (New York: W.W. Norton, 1997). For a critique of Frank's position from a managerial perspective see Mary Britton King, 'Make Love, Not Work: New Management Theory and the Social Self', *Radical History Review*, 76, Winter 2000, pp.15–24.
2. Peter F. Drucker, 'Overpaid Executives: The Greed Effect', *The Frontiers of Management* (London: Heinemann, 1986), pp.138–143.
3. John Kaler, 'Positioning Business Ethics in Relation to Management and Political Philosophy', p.261.
4. Haim Levy and Marshall Sarnat, *Portfolio and Investment Selection: Theory and Practice* (Englewood Cliffs NJ: Prentice-Hall International, 1984), p.563.
5. Ibid., p.569.
6. Michael Armstrong and Helen Murlis, *Reward Management: A Handbook of Remuneration Strategy and Practice* (3rd edn) (London: Institute of Personnel and Development/Kogan Page, 1988/1994), p.310.
7. R. Greenbury, *Director's Remuneration* (London: Gee, 1995).
8. 'The Forbes Super 100' list from which this is taken was that available in October 1999 on the Forbes internet site www.forbes.com
9. A useful overview of the field is available in Luis R. Gomes-Mejia, George Paulin, and Arden Grabke, 'Executive Compensation: Research and Practical Implications', Gerald R. Ferris, Sherman D. Rosen and Donald T. Barnum eds, *Handbook of Human Resource Management* (Cambridge MA and Oxford: Blackwell, 1995), pp.548–569. This presents a range of different theories that guide different views of executive remuneration, and effectively demonstrates the ambiguity of the area.
10. See, for example, the studies cited and figures given about this in Michael Armstrong, *Managing Reward Systems* (Buckingham: Open University Press, 1993), p.76.
11. The legal allocation of overall fiduciary responsibility to directors and senior managers of a corporation, while usually offering effective protection only for shareholders against infringement of trust, seems to me to be a recognition of the symbolic value of upper level managerial roles. Section 309 of the Companies Act 1985, for instance, recognises fiduciary responsibilities of management towards employees, but notoriously little provision is made against infringement of such responsibility in British Company Law (see R. Lewis ed., *Labour Law in Britain* (Oxford: Basil Blackwell, 1986)). On the issue of fiduciary obligations generally, see: P.D. Finn, *Fiduciary Obligations* (Sydney: Law Book Company, 1977); Susan P. Shapiro, *Conflicting Responsibilities: Maneuvering Through The Minefield of Fiduciary Obligations* (Chicago: American Bar Foundation, 1995); Richard A. Booth, 'Stockholders, Stakeholders, and Bagholders (or How Investor Diversification Affects Fiduciary Duty)', *The Business Lawyer*, 53:2, February 1988, pp.429–478; Bruce Langtry, 'Stakeholders and the Moral Responsibilities of Business', *Business Ethics Quarterly*, 4:4, October

1994, pp.431–443; Thomas Lee Hazen, 'Management Buyouts and Corporate Governance Paradigms', *Wake Forest Law Review*, 25:1, 1990, pp.1–13.

For management theory perspectives linking executive pay to symbolic roles, see: Gomes-Mejia *et al.*, 'Executive Compensation', pp.553–554; R.M. Steers and G.R. Ungson, 'Strategic Issues in Executive Compensation Decisions', in D.B. Balkin and Luis R. Gomes-Mejia eds, *New Perspectives on Compensation* (Englewood Cliffs NJ: Prentice-Hall, 1987), pp.294–308.

12. A common enough observation. See, for example, Alfred Rappaport, 'New Thinking on How to Link Executive Pay with Performance', *Harvard Business Review*, March–April 1999, p.92.

13. Precisely the point that is picked up in the analysis of the 1999 British CEO compensation and company performance figures in Anthony Hilton, 'Weighing Up the Fat Cats', *Management Today*, July 1999, pp.47–51.

14. See, for example, G. Colvin, 'How to Pay the CEO Right', *Fortune*, 16 April 1992, pp.60–72; Bruce Walters, Tim Hardin, James Schick, 'Top Executive Compensation: Equity or Excess? Implications for Regaining American Competitiveness', *Journal of Business Ethics*, 14, 1995, pp.230–231.

15. Many empirical studies of the issue have expressed doubts about the relationship between compensation and performance. See, for example, M. Firth, M. Tam, M. Tang, 'The Determinants of Top Management Pay', *Omega*, 27:6, December 1999, pp.617–635; M.C. Attaway, 'A Study of the Relationship between Company Performance and CEO Compensation', *American Business Review*, 18:1, January 2000, pp.77–85; W.G. Sanders, A. Davis-Blake, J.W. Fredrickson, 'Prizes With Strings Attached: Determinants of the Structures of CEO Compensation', *Academy of Management Journal*, 1995, pp.266–270. It is often noted that there is more of a relation between company size and compensation rather than between performance and compensation: in this context see P.F. Kostiuk, 'Firm Size and Executive Performance', *Journal of Human Resources*, 25:1, Winter 1989, pp.90–105. An interesting paper providing evidence of scepticism among upper-level managers themselves about the relationship between performance and compensation is: Timothy J. Morris and Mark Fenton O'Creevy, 'Opening Up the Black Box: A UK Case Study of Top Managers' Attitudes to their Performance Related Pay', *The International Journal of Human Resource Management*, 7:3, September 1996, pp.708–720.

16. For an interesting feature on this from a managerial point of view see Joel Stern, 'Executive Pay Plans Make Companies Perform Badly', *The Sunday Times* (Business Section), 17 October 1999, p.4. For the effects of short-term managerial target-setting on employees and the health of the corporation generally, see Jeffrey S. Harrison and James O. Fiet, 'New CEOs Pursue Their Own Self-Interest by Sacrificing Stakeholder Value', *Journal of Business Ethics*, 19:3, April 1999, pp.301–308.

17. Graef Crystal, *In Search of Excess: The Overcompensation of the American Executives* (New York: Norton, 1992).

18. The following are a few examples of discussions of the conflict between ownership and control and the nuances of agency theory in the context of executive compensation: E.F. Fama and M.C. Jensen, 'Separation of Ownership and Control', *Journal of Law and Economics*, 26, 1983; E. F.Fama, 'Agency Problems and the Theory of the Firm', *Journal of Political Economy*, 88:2, April 1980, pp.288–307; E.A. Dyl, 'Corporate Control and Management Compensation: Evidence of the Agency Problem', *Managerial and Decision Economics*, 9:1, March 1988, pp.21–25; H. Mehran, 'Executive Compensation Structure, Ownership and Firm Performance', *Journal of Financial Economics*, 38:2, 1995, pp.163–184; M. Firth, 'Corporate Takeovers, Stockholder Returns and Executive Rewards', *Managerial and Decision Economics*, 12:6, December 1991, pp.421–428; L.G. Goldberg and T.L. Idson, 'Executive Compensation and Agency Effects', *Financial Review*, 30:2, May 1995, pp.313–336; L.R. Gomez-Mejia, H. Tosi, T. Hinkin, 'Management Control, Performance and Executive Compensation', *Academy of Management Journal*, 30:1, March 1987, pp.51–70; Gary Young, Yvonne Stedham, and Rafik Beekum, 'Boards of Directors and the Adoption of a CEO Performance Evaluation Process: Agency- and Institutional-Theory Perspectives', *Journal of Management Studies*, 27:2, March 2000, pp.277–295; Neil A. Shankman, 'Reframing the Debate Between Agency and Stakeholder Theories of the Firm', *Journal of Business Ethics*, 19:4 (Part 1), 1999, pp.319–334; Richard H. Fosberg, 'Leadership Structure and CEO Compensation', *American Business Review*, 17:1, January 1999, pp.50–56; John Byrd, Robert Parrino, Gunnar Pritsch, 'Stockholder–Manager Conflicts and Firm Value', *Financial Analysts Journal*, 54:3, May–June 1998, pp.14–30; Andrei Shleifer and Robert W. Vishny, 'A Survey of Corporate Governance', *Journal of Finance*, 52:2, June 1997, pp.737–783; Robert Mangel and Harbin Singh, 'Ownership Structure, Board Relations and CEO Compensation in Large US Corporations', *Accounting and Business Research*, 23:91, 1993, pp.339–350; C. Prendergast, 'What Trade-off of Risk and Incentives?' *American Economic Review*, 90:2, May 2000, pp.421–425; Jason D. Shaw, Nina Gupta, and John E. Delery, 'Empirical Organizational-Level Examinations of Agency and Collaborative Predictions of Performance Contingent Compensation', *Strategic Management Journal*, 21:5, May 2000, pp.611–623; James S. Ang, 'Agency Costs and Ownership Structure', *Journal of Finance*, 55:1, February 2000, pp.81–106; Norman E. Bowie and R. Edward Freeman eds, *Ethics and Agency Theory: An Introduction* (New York: Oxford University Press, 1992).

19. A popular exposition on the paucity of conventional predictive economic modelling is available in Paul Ormerod, *Butterfly Economics: A New General Theory of Social and Economic Behaviour* (London: Faber and Faber, 1998). This has of course been asserted often in the past by some of the so-called Austrian School of economists, especially Hayek, whose ideas are discussed in Chapter 14.

20. See note 18.

21. On the relative positions of big shareholders and small shareholders, and the alignment of the former with upper-level managers, see the following: Ernst Maug, 'Large Shareholders as Monitors: Is There a Trade-off Between

Liquidity and Control?' *Journal of Finance*, 53:1, February 1998, pp.65–98; Chris W. Roth, 'Concentration of Ownership and the Composition of the Board: An Examination of Canadian Publicly-Listed Corporations', *Canadian Business Law Journal*, 26:2, 1996, pp.226–243; Randall K. Morck, 'On the Economics of Concentrated Ownership', *Canadian Business Law Journal*, 26:1, 1996, pp.63–85; 'Why Lose Tiny Shareholders?' *Management Today*, June 1995, pp.13–16; Graef Crystal, 'Big Shareholders Wimp Out on Executive Pay Issue', *Pensions and Investment Age*, 21:26, 27 December 1993, p.11; M. Dewatripont, 'The "Leading Shareholder" Strategy, Takeover Contests and Stock Price Dynamics', *European Economic Review*, 37:5, June 1993, pp.983–1004; Fredrick P. Zampa and Albert E. McCormick Jr, '"Proxy Power" and Corporate Democracy: The Characteristics and Efficacy of Stockholder-Initiated Proxy Issues', *American Journal of Economics and Sociology*, 50:1, January 1991, pp.1–15; Richard E. Caves, 'Lessons from Privatization in Britain: State Enterprise Behavior, Public Choice, and Corporate Governance', *Journal of Economic Behavior and Governance*, 13:2, March 1990, pp.145–169.
22.   Marx, *Capital, Vol.3*, chapter 2.
23.   The most famous exposition of the liberal arguments regarding distributive justice appears in John Rawls, *A Theory of Justice* (Oxford: Oxford University Press, 1971). Useful elaborations of this variety of liberalism are found in David Miller, *Social Justice* (Oxford: Clarendon, 1976); Amy Gutmann, *Liberal Equality* (Cambridge: Cambridge University Press, 1980); Thomas Nagel, *Equality and Partiality* (New York: Oxford University Press, 1991); and John Rawls, *Political Liberalism* (New York: Columbia University Press, 1993).
24.   For formulations and arguments regarding complex egalitarianism, see: Michael Walzer, *Spheres of Justice* (New York: Basic, 1983); David Miller and Michael Walzer eds, *Pluralism, Justice and Equality* (Oxford: Oxford University Press, 1995).
25.   The distinction between Company Law and Labour Law in Britain has notoriously been the reason for her distance from other EU nations apropos certain nuances of the obligation of companies towards workers, and the homogenisation of working conditions under EC law.
26.   In Company Law members (shareholders) are defined in Companies Act 1985, sec.22; directors in Partnership Act 1890, sec.5, and Companies Act 1947, sec.26(1); shadow directors in Companies Act 1985, sec.741(2); and all officers (which lumps together directors, managers and secretaries) in Companies Act 1985, sec. 744.
27.   Thus in Britain prior to 1984 executive share options were taxed as income. The 1984 Finance Act removed the income tax liability and made options gains subject to capital gains tax. From 1984 to 1989 options gains were taxed at 30 per cent while upper level income tax was 60 per cent – one of the reasons for the immense growth of options schemes. The 1989 Finance Act raised capital gains tax to 40 per cent and brought upper level income tax to 40 per cent thus erasing the tax advantages of options schemes, but such schemes continued to be popular. Perhaps the reason is to be found in Clare Gascoigne, 'Weigh Up Your Share Options', *Financial Times*, 13 October 1999, which gives

some cogent advice on how not to pay much tax on options gains, and observes: 'It is easier to plan to minimise capital gains tax or avoid it altogether.'

Chapter 9

1. Some of the works of 'corporatist' theory starting from Offé and Schmitter: Claus Offé, 'Advanced Capitalism and the Welfare State', *Politics and Society*, 1, 1972, pp.479–488; Philippe C. Schmitter, 'Still the Century of Corporatism?' *Review of Politics*, 36, January 1974, pp.93–98; Philippe Schmitter and Gerhard Lehmbruch ed. *Trends Toward Corporatist Intermediation* (Beverly Hills: Sage, 1979); Alan Cawson, *Political Structure and Social Policy* (London: Heinemann, 1982); Alan Cawson, *Corporatism and Political Theory* (London: Basil Blackwell, 1986); Peter Williamson, *Varieties of Corporatism* (Cambridge: Cambridge University Press, 1985); Harold Wilensky and Lowell Turner, *Democratic Corporatism and Policy Linkages* (Berkeley CA: Institute of International Studies, 1987); M. Harrison ed., *Corporatism and the Welfare State* (London: Gower, 1984).
2. Alan Cawson and Peter Saunders, 'Corporatism, Competitive Politics and Class Struggle', Roger King ed., *Capital and Politics* (London: Routledge and Kegan Paul, 1983), pp.16–17.
3. For example, Leo Panitch, 'Recent Theorizations of Corporatism', *British Journal of Sociology*, 31, June 1980, pp.217–239.
4. Mark James Gobeyn, *Corporatist Decline in Advanced Capitalism* (Westport CT: Greenwood, 1993), p.11.
5. Ibid., p.92.
6. The existentialist connotations of bad faith are explored in Jean-Paul Sartre, *Being and Nothingness*, trans. Hazel E. Barnes (New York: Washington Square Press, 1956), Part 2, chapter 2: 'bad faith is not restricted to denying the qualities which I possess, to not seeing the being which I am. It attempts also to constitute myself as being what I am not' (p.111). On a more political note the concept of bad faith is used trenchantly (and for us relevantly) in Sartre's analysis of the inevitable bad faith of the bourgeois intellectual who conforms to capitalist society (becomes a technician of practical knowledge without going outside his specialism, refusing to universalise his insights and thinking) in 'A Plea for Intellectuals', in *Between Existentialism and Marxism*, trans. John Matthews (London: NLB, 1974).
7. The need to reduce state control, to give the private sector free play, to increase the transparency of the state was the constant theme of Margaret Thatcher's speeches prior to the 1979 elections: see, in this context, Margaret Thatcher, *Let Our Children Grow Tall: Selected Speeches, 1975–1977* (London: Centre for Policy Studies, 1977), especially the speech entitled 'Let Me Give You My Vision' at the Conservative Party Conference in Blackpool, 1975. The symbolic nature of such announcements, as the harbinger of a new epoch in corporate capitalism, is rather beautifully presented in the BBC television documentary '1997-Fast Forward' (24 February 1997) in the *People's Century* series, which quotes Ronald Reagan's announcement of the Republican state's intention to become

more transparent after the election victory of 1980: 'In the present crisis government is not the solution to our problem, government is the problem.'

8. The libertarian or neo-liberal understanding of the neutral state is to be found in such works as Robert Nozick, *Anarchy, State and Utopia* (Oxford: Basil Blackwell, 1974), and Bruce Ackerman, *Social Justice in the Liberal State* (New Haven: Yale University Press, 1980).

9. See Engels, *Anti-Dühring*, pp.330–331, 333.

10. See Gupta, *Marxism, History, and Intellectuals*, pp.198–201.

11. Ibid., Part III ('A Modest Proposal', pp.186–221).

Chapter 10

1. Overviews of theoretical developments in international relations, such as are to be found in Brian C. Schmidt, *The Political Discourse of Anarchy* (Albany: State University of New York, 1998), or Barry Buzan, Charles Jones and Richard Little, *The Logic of Anarchy* (New York: Columbia University Press, 1993), or Robert O. Keohane ed., *Neorealism and Its Critics* (New York: Columbia University Press, 1986), testify to this.

2. Kenneth N. Waltz, *Theory of International Politics* (New York: McGraw Hill, 1979), p.40. A useful philosophical examination of systems in international politics is available in Martin Hollis and Steve Smith, *Explaining and Understanding International Relations* (Oxford: Clarendon, 1990).

3. Waltz, *Theory of International Politics*, p.104.

4. Ibid., pp.93–94.

5. See, for example, Alexander Wendt, 'The Agent-Structure Problem in International Relations Theory', *International Organization*, 41:3, pp.335–370; John G. Ruggie, 'Continuity and Transformation in the World Polity: Towards a Neorealist Synthesis', in Robert O. Keohane ed., *Neorealism and Its Critics*, pp.141–148; Richard Ashley, 'Untying the Sovereign State: A Double Reading of the Anarchy Problematique', *Millennium*, 17: 2, pp.227–262.

6. On the fallacy of this expectation in the context of Hobbes's philosophy, see Friedrich V. Kratochwil, *Rules, Norms and Decisions: On the Conditions of Practical and Legal Reasoning in International Relations and Domestic Affairs* (Cambridge: Cambridge University Press, 1989), pp.3–4.

7. On the historical location of the idea of *realpolitik* in mid-nineteenth-century Europe, see Alan Cassels, *Ideology and International Relations in the Modern World* (London: Routledge, 1996), p.70.

8. A matter which Waltz didn't explore sufficiently, and which is explored with some sense of correcting or opposing Waltz in such works as Friedrich V. Kratochwil, *Rules, Norms and Decisions*; James C. Hsiung, *Anarchy and Order: The Interplay of Politics and Law in International Relations* (Boulder, Col.: Lynne Reinner, 1997); Terry Nardin, *Law, Morality and the Relations of States* (Princeton: Princeton University Press, 1983).

9. Nardin, *Law, Morality*, p.9.

10. Ibid., p.23.

11. Ibid., p.24.

12. Best exemplified undoubtedly in the debates underlying European integration: see such historical accounts as Richard McAllister, *From EC to EU* (London: Routledge, 1997) or Martin J. Dedman, *The Origins and Development of the European Union, 1945–1995: A History of European Integration* (London: Routledge, 1996).

13. In this context it is worth examining American foreign policy towards western European and other capitalist countries after the war: see, for example, William C. Cromwell, *The United States and the European Pillar: The Strained Alliance* (Basingstoke: Macmillan, 1992), and especially Richard J. Barnet, *Allies: America, Europe, and Japan since the War* (London: Jonathan Cape, 1983).

14. The most substantial commentary on the coerciveness of the extension of capitalist interests made through the machinations of corporate capitalist states in international politics is undoubtedly that provided by Noam Chomsky in his many books on American foreign policy in different contexts. Chomsky gives a relevant overview of his perspective on this in *World Orders, Old and New* (London: Pluto Press, 1994).

15. A useful account of the manner in which such economic organisations (IMF, World Bank, WTO) contribute to global governance in terms of case studies is available in Robert O'Brien, Anne Marie Goetz, Jan Aart Scholte, Marc Williams, *Contesting Global Governance: Multilateral Economic Institutions and Global Social Movements* (Cambridge: Cambridge University Press, 2000). Analyses of, and scepticism regarding, the capitalist ideology and capitalist expansionism that is promoted by such organisations are legion: see, for example, John Cavanagh, Daphne Wysham, Marcos Arruda eds., *Beyond Bretton Woods: Alternatives to the Global Economic Order* (London: Pluto Press, 1994); Susan George and Fabrizio Sabelli, *Faith and Credit: The World Bank's Secular Empire* (Harmondsworth: Penguin, 1994).

16. J.A. Hobson, *Imperialism: A Study* (London: Allen & Unwin, 1902/1938); V.I. Lenin, *Imperialism: The Highest Stage of Capitalism* in his *Collected Works, Vol. 38* (Moscow: Progress, 1958).

17. Kenneth N. Waltz, *Theory of International Politics*, chapter 2.

PART III

Chapter 11

1. Jonathan Friedman's *Cultural Identity and the Global Process* (London: Sage, 1994) is an eloquent exposition of the disintegrative tendencies of identity politics in the context of globalisation.

2. That, for instance, ethnicism and racialism have been and are rooted in capitalist processes is persuasively argued by Immanuel Wallerstein, *Historical Capitalism* (London: Verso, 1983). On this point also see Immanuel Wallerstein, *The Capitalist World-Economy* (Cambridge: Cambridge University Press/Paris: Editions de la Maison des Sciences de l'Homme, 1979), part II. The connection between corporate capitalism

and racism is examined in concrete terms in such books as Melvin M. Leiman's *The Political Economy of Racism* (London: Pluto Press, 1993).

3. Gupta, *Marxism, History and Intellectuals*, pp.224–235.

4. Systems theory as developed for the purposes of sociological description by theorists such as Talcott Parsons, Niklas Luhmann, Jurgen Habermas, Anthony Giddens, despite their differences, ultimately fall back on the autoconstruction or autoperpetuation of systems, and of the inevitability of systems. The literature relevant to this is voluminous, and too familiar to require bibliographical references. The equation of systems-oriented thinking with the disabling of political will is rarely made. A useful exception is Ulrich Beck in *Risk Society: Towards A New Modernity*, trans. Mark Ritter (London: Sage, 1992), whose views on this are succinctly given especially on p.33. In general Beck's book is most effective as a musing on the disabled political will from his particular perspective of the status of risks in modern industrial society.

5. Karl R. Popper, *The Poverty of Historicism* (London: Routledge & Kegan Paul, 1957), pp.136–139, is devoted to finding common ground with Hayek.

6. In *The Poverty of Historicism*, p.67, Popper presents the notion of holistic utopian social engineering, which he argues most vociferously against, through quotations from Karl Mannheim's *Man and Society in an Age of Reconstruction* (London: Routledge & Kegan Paul, 1940). Mannheim's (amongst others) 'sociology of knowledge' is also singled out for criticism in Popper's *The Open Society and Its Enemies, Vol.2: Hegel and Marx* (London: Routledge & Kegan Paul, 1945), chapter 23. Mannheim was clearly sensitive to the kind of criticism about his concepts of a sociology of knowledge and planning offered by Popper – on this see Chapter 12, note 18.

Chapter 12

1. Karl Mannheim, 'On the Logic of Philosophical Systematization', chapter 1, section 1, *Essays on Sociology and Social Psychology* (London: Routledge & Kegan Paul, 1953), pp.307–310.

2. Karl Mannheim, 'Historicism', chapter 3, *Essays on the Sociology of Knowledge* (London: Routledge & Kegan Paul, 1952), p.86.

3. See Karl Mannheim, 'On the Interpretation of *Weltanschauung*', chapter 2, *Sociology of Knowledge*, pp.37–42; and *Man and Society*, pp.51–57.

4. Karl Mannheim, *Ideology and Utopia: An Introduction to the Sociology of Knowledge* (London: Routledge & Kegan Paul, 1936), p.3.

5. Mannheim, 'The Problem of A Sociology of Knowledge', chapter 4, *Sociology of Knowledge*, p.53: 'we may assert that the vital and practical as well as the theoretical and intellectual currents of our time seem to point toward a temporary fading out of epistemological problems, and toward the emergence of the *sociology of knowledge* as the focal discipline [...]'.

6. Mannheim, *Man and Society*, p.53.

7. Thus, Mannheim applauds the anti-rationalist movement for revealing the dynamism of *Weltanschauung* in 'On the Interpretation of *Weltanschauung*', *Sociology of Knowledge*, pp.37–39.

8. Mannheim, *Ideology and Utopia*, p.36.
9. Mannheim, *Man and Society*, pp.41–44.
10. Mannheim, *Ideology and Utopia*, p.83.
11. Ibid, p.87.
12. Ibid., pp.94–95.
13. Ibid., p.264.
14. Ibid., p.266.
15. Mannheim, *Man and Society*, pp.173–178.
16. Ibid., 149.
17. Ibid., p.154.
18. This is marked in Mannheim's increasing concessions to notions of freedom and spontaneous development, which are close to Popper's thinking in his later writings on democratic planning. In this context see his formulae for a new sort of democratic planning in 'Planned Society and the Problem of Human Personality', part 4, *Sociology and Social Psychology*, p.307. Similarly, Mannheim's account of democratic power in *Freedom, Power and Democratic Planning* (London: Routledge & Kegan Paul, 1950), especially on p.47, has more of a sense of being a self-regulating system, without however abandoning social controls.
19. Mannheim, *Freedom, Power and Democratic Planning*, pp.288–289.

Chapter 13

1. Karl R. Popper, *The Open Society and Its Enemies, Vol.1: Plato* (London: Routledge & Kegan Paul, 1945), p.89.
2. The quotation is from ibid., p.94; the elaboration occurs over pp.95–106.
3. Ibid., pp.100–102. Here Popper questions the equation Plato had allegedly made between individualism and egoism as opposed to collectivism and altruism by observing that:

> Collectivism is not opposed to egoism, nor is it identical with altruism or unselfishness. Collective or group egoism, for instance class egoism, is a very common thing [...] and this shows clearly enough that collectivism as such is not opposed to selfishness. On the other hand, an anti-collectivist, i.e. an individualist, can, at the same time, be an altruist; he can be ready to make sacrifices in order to help individuals. (p.100)

A little later Popper concludes that: 'This individualism, united with altruism, has become the basis of our western civilization' (p.102).
4. Karl R. Popper and John C. Eccles, *The Self and Its Brain: An Argument for Interactionism* (Heidelberg: Springer International, 1977), p.122 (the first five chapters are by Popper).
5. Ibid., p.144.
6. Ibid., pp. 145–146.
7. Karl R. Popper, *The Logic of Scientific Discovery* (London: Hutchinson, 1959): the modes of testing are briefly stated on pp.32–33, and the conditions for satisfying experience on p.39.

8. Ibid., p.48. Of interest apropos this point is Popper's rather fine distinction: 'I do not demand that every scientific statement *must in fact have been tested* before it is accepted. I only demand that every such statement must be *capable* of being tested.'

9. Ibid., p.33.

10. Thomas Kuhn, *The Structure of Scientific Revolutions* (enlarged 2nd edition) (Chicago: University of Chicago Press, 1970), thinks of a scientific paradigm as 'like an accepted judicial decision in the common law, it is an object for further articulation and specification under new or more stringent conditions' (p.23).

11. Popper, *The Logic of Scientific Discovery*, p.111.

12. See Karl R. Popper, *Objective Knowledge* (Oxford: Clarendon, 1972), especially p.7.

13. For useful discussions by critics of Popper's views on induction (and other analytical matters) and Popper's response to them see P.A. Schilpp ed., *The Philosophy of Karl Popper* (La Salle, Ill.: Open Court, 1974). An extended discussion of the strengths of Popper's views on induction is available in Anthony O'Hear, *Karl Popper* (London: Routledge & Kegan Paul, 1980), chapters 2, 3, and 4.

14. Popper, *The Open Society, Vol.2*, p.217.

15. Ibid., p.222.

16. This is something that, as a scientist, Steven Weinberg forcefully argues in *Dreams of a Final Theory* (London: Vintage, 1993), p.133; and which underlies Louis Althusser's examination of the relation between the philosophical attitudes of scientists and philosophers in *Philosophy and the Spontaneous Philosophy of Scientists* (London: Verso, 1990).

17. Popper, *The Open Society, Vol.1*, p.125.

18. Ibid., p.127.

19. Popper, *The Poverty of Historicism*, pp.66–67.

20. Popper, *The Open Society, Vol.1*, p.158.

21. Popper, *The Poverty of Historicism*, p.50.

22. Popper, *The Logic of Scientific Discovery*, p.280.

Chapter 14

1. It might seem to be inappropriate to begin with a comparison of Hayek and Popper rather than with the influence of the Austrian school of economics (from Carl Menger and Eugen Böhm-Bawerk) on Hayek's thinking. Unquestionably, the work of Ludwig von Mises, as an anti-political philosopher proper, is worthy of analysis along with Hayek's in this context: much of it appeared after the war (*Omnipotent Government*, 1944; *Planned Chaos*, 1947; *Planning for Freedom*, 1952; *The Anti-Capitalist Mentality*, 1956; *The Epistemological Problems of Economics*, 1960), was closely parallel to Hayek's, and some of Hayek's formulations were clearly drawn from Mises. In fact the closeness between Hayek and Mises is such that that itself dissuades me from undertaking such a comparative analysis – it would be a repetitive enterprise. Besides, it seems to me that Hayek's anti-political philosophical position is more clearly enunciated than Mises's (Mises was more emphatically an economist who spoke with the

authority of economic knowledge) – Hayek provides, it seems to me, an anti-political philosophical crystallisation of the Austrian school that cannot really be attributed to any of its other members. And not least significantly, Hayek is the more popular figure in philosophical terms, who is constantly and directly evoked and drawn upon where a disablement of political will prevails.

2. F.A. Hayek, *The Constitution of Liberty* (London: Routledge & Kegan Paul, 1960), p.29.

3. F.A. Hayek, *The Road to Serfdom* (London: Routledge & Kegan Paul, 1944), p.44.

4. Ibid.

5. Ludwig Wittgenstein, *Philosophical Investigations*, trans. G.E.M. Anscombe (Oxford: Basil Blackwell, 1953), particularly passages 243–344.

6. Hayek, *The Constitution of Liberty*, pp.32–35.

7. Ibid., pp.56–62.

8. As in F.A. Hayek, *The Fatal Conceit: The Errors of Socialism* (London: Routledge, 1988), and in papers in F.A. Hayek, *Knowledge, Evolution and Society* (London: Adam Smith Institute, 1983) and F.A. Hayek, *New Studies in Philosophy, Politics, Economics and The History of Ideas* (London: Routledge & Kegan Paul, 1978).

9. The first line of *The Constituton of Liberty*, p.11, reads: 'We are concerned in this book with that condition of men in which coercion of some by others is reduced as much as possible in society. This state we shall describe throughout as a state of liberty or freedom.' A definition of coercion appears a bit later as: 'By "coercion" we mean such control of the environment or circumstances of a person by another that, in order to avoid greater evil, he is forced to act not according to a coherent plan of his own but to serve the ends of another' (pp.20–21). I do not think this an appropriate place to undertake a full analysis of the connotations of that definition of coercion. Interesting elaborations of the concept of coercion are available in Robert Nozick, 'Coercion', S. Morgenbesser, P. Suppes, and M. White eds, *Philosophy, Science and Method: Essays in Honor of Ernest Nagel* (New York: St. Martin's Press, 1969); and Harry G. Frankfurt, 'Coercion and Moral Responsibility', Ted Honderich ed., *Essays on Freedom of Action* (London: Routledge & Kegan Paul,1973). For an account of the deficiencies of Hayek's notion of coercion, see C. Kukathas, *Hayek and Modern Liberalism* (Oxford: Clarendon, 1989), chapter 4; and David Miller, *Market, State and Community: Theoretical Foundations of Market Socialism* (Oxford: Clarendon, 1989), pp.26–30.

10. Thus the first chapter of *The Constitution of Liberty* is devoted to arguing against concepts such as 'political freedom' and 'metaphysical freedom'.

11. Ibid., p.61.

12. F.A. Hayek, *The Pure Theory of Capital* (London: Routledge & Kegan Paul, 1941), p.247.

13. Hayek, *The Constitution of Liberty*; the whole of part II is devoted to this.

14. This is neatly summarised in F.A. Hayek, 'Economic Freedom and Representative Government' (1973) in his *Economic Freedom* (Oxford: Basil Blackwell, 1991), p.389, where he delineates constraints under

which government services which are necessary to social needs can be rendered.

15. Hayek, *The Constitution of Liberty*, chapter 7.
16. The main argument of the essay 'Economic Freedom and Representative Government' in *Economic Freedom*.

Chapter 15

1. Among the many texts apart from Nozick's which have elaborated on Hayekian arguments are: Milton Friedman, *Capitalism and Freedom* (Chicago: University of Chicago Press, 1962); Milton and Rose Friedman, *Free to Choose* (London: Secker & Warburg, 1980); Michael Oakeshott, *Rationalism in Politics and Other Essays* (Indianapolis: Libertyfund, 1962) – especially the essay 'The Political Economy of Freedom'; Michael Oakeshott, *On Human Conduct* (Oxford: Clarendon, 1975); M. Rothbard, *The Ethics of Liberty* (Atlantic Highlands, NJ: Humanities Press, 1982); Peter L. Berger, *The Capitalist Revolution* (Aldershot: Gower, 1987); Arthur Seldon, *Capitalism* (Oxford: Basil Blackwell, 1990).
2. A suggestive example of this is Nozick's speculations on the possibility of an 'experience machine' in Robert Nozick, *Anarchy, State, and Utopia* (Oxford: Basil Blackwell, 1974), pp.42–45.
3. In presenting his two principles of justice as an original position, John Rawls in *A Theory of Justice* (Oxford: Oxford University Press, 1971), p.120, makes it clear that this is only to give form to the instinctive notion of 'justice as fairness' and has no real basis.
4. Nozick, *Anarchy, State, and Utopia*, pp.32–33.
5. Robert Nozick, *Philosophical Explanations* (Oxford: Clarendon, 1981), p.34.
6. Ibid., pp.71–78.
7. Ibid., chapter 3.
8. Ibid., p.208.
9. Nozick's argument here deserves closer analysis, and my simplistic assertion doesn't do justice to its details. But it is not so much my intention to disprove Nozick on this point as to show the general tendency of his thinking.
10. Without giving this systematic consideration, it seems to me that Saul Kripke's 'Naming and Necessity' in D. Davidson and G. Horman eds, *Semantics of Natural Language* (Dodrecht: D. Reidel, 1972), as indeed Noam Chomsky's reservations about this in his *Reflections on Language* (London: Temple Smith, 1975), may be of interest here.
11. Robert Nozick, *The Nature of Rationality* (Princeton: Princeton University Press, 1993), pp.9–12.
12. Nozick, *Anarchy, State, and Utopia*, pp.18–19.
13. Nozick, *Philosophical Explanations*, footnote on p.343.
14. Ibid., p.347.
15. Nozick, *The Nature of Rationality*, p.120.
16. Ibid., p.125.
17. Nozick also uses Amartya Sen's argument of the non-linearity of social choice here (from Amartya Sen, *Collective Choice and Social Welfare* (San

Francisco: Holden-Day, 1970)) to undermine redistributive concepts and strengthen his understanding of individual rights in *Anarchy, State, and Utopia*, pp.164–166. Sen's own championing of economic planning is opposed to Nozick's position – his criticism of Nozick's understanding of individual rights is given briefly in *On Ethics and Economics* (Oxford: Basil Blackwell, 1987), p.56.

18. Nozick, *Anarchy, State, and Utopia*, p.57.
19. Ibid., pp.65–71.
20. Ibid., p.178.
21. Ibid., p.182.
22. Ibid., p.150. On the lack of content and the shortcomings in Nozick's principles in this regard, see David Miller, *Market, State and Community* (Oxford: Clarendon, 1989), pp.48–49 particularly; and G.A. Cohen, *Self-Ownership, Freedom and Equality* (Cambridge: Cambridge University Press and Paris: Maison des sciences de l'Homme, 1995), chapters 1 and 2.
23. Nozick, *Anarchy, State, and Utopia*, p.311.
24. Ibid., p.316.

Chapter 16

1. Francis Fukuyama, *The End of History and the Last Man* (Harmondsworth: Penguin, 1992), p.172.
2. Ibid., p.314.
3. Francis Fukuyama, *Trust: The Social Virtues and the Creation of Prosperity* (New York: The Free Press, 1995), chapter 31.
4. Ibid., p.26.
5. Ibid., p.27.
6. Ibid., pp.351–352.
7. So in G.W.F. Hegel's *The Philosophy of History*, trans. J. Sibree (New York: Dover, 1956) he takes his Universal History to the finality of a grand intellectual synthesis in the 'modern' German world – at '*the last stage in History, our world, our own time*' (p.442).

Chapter 17

1. This coincides with the view of philosophy offered in Gilles Deleuze and Felix Guattari, *What Is Philosophy?*, trans. Hugh Tomlinson and Graham Burchill (London: Verso, 1994). Philosophy, they maintain, is 'the discipline that involves *creating* concepts' (p.5).
2. I have in mind the works of political philosophers such as John Rawls, Thomas Nagel, Amartya Sen, Noam Chomsky, Pierre Bordieu, David Miller, Michael Walzer, Ulrich Beck, G.A. Cohen, David Coates, Leo Panitch, among, of course, many others.
3. This is due, no doubt, to Marx's own eagerness to take his *scientific* socialism beyond the phase he thought of as *utopian* socialist (associated with Saint-Simon, Fourier, Owen).
4. Krishan Kumar, *Utopia and Anti-Utopia in Modern Times* (Oxford: Basil Blackwell, 1987), p.100.

Index

Titles of books are indexed only if they are directly mentioned within the text. Many books which I have quoted but not named by title within the text are not so indexed – details about these discussions are found under the name of the author.

Where especially broad terms are indexed – such as sociology – only those pages are referred where the discussion alludes to the broadest sense of these terms. More detailed studies which might come under these broad terms – such as Weber's or Durkheim's *within* sociology – are indexed separately under appropriately narrower terms.